Reusable Software Components

Object-Oriented Embedded Systems Programming in C

Ted Van Sickle

To join a Prentice Hall PTR internet mailing list point to http://www.prenhall.com/register

Prentice Hall PTR
Upper Saddle River, New Jersey 07458
http://www.prenhall.com

Library of Congress Cataloging-in-Publication Data

Van Sickle, Ted
Reusable software components : object-oriented embedded systems programming in C / Ted Van Sickle.
p. cm.
Includes bibliographical references and index.
ISBN 0-13-613688-5
1. Object-oriented programming (Computer science) I. C Computer programming language) 3. Embedded computer systems—Programming 4. Computer software—Reusability. I. Title.
QA76..64.V365 1977
629.8′9–dc20 96-29412
CIP

Editorial/production supervision: *Nicholas Radhuber*
Manufacturing manager: *Alexis Heydt*
Acquisitions editor: *Paul Becker*
Editorial assistant: *Maureen Diana*
Cover design: *Design Source*
Cover design director: *Jerry Votta*

Published by Prentice Hall PTR
Prentice-Hall, Inc.
A Simon & Schuster Company
Upper Saddle River, New Jersey 07458

The publisher offers discounts on this book when ordered in bulk quantities.
For more information, contact:
Corporate Sales Department
PTR Prentice Hall
One Lake Street
Upper Saddle River, NJ 07458
Phone: 800-382-3419, Fax: 201-236-7141
E-mail: dan_rush@prenhall.com

Printed in the United States of America
10 9 8 7 6 5 4 3 2 1
ISBN 0-13-613688-5
Prentice-Hall International (UK) Limited, *London*
Prentice-Hall of Australia Pty. Limited, *Sydney*
Prentice-Hall Canada, Inc., *Toronto*
Prentice-Hall Hispanoamericana, S.A., *Mexico*
Prentice-Hall of India Private Limited, *New Delhi*
Prentice-Hall of Japan, Inc., *Tokyo*
Simon & Schuster Asia Pte. Ltd., *Singapore*
Editora Prentice-Hall do Brasil, Ltda., *Rio de Janeiro*

Prentice Hall Series on Programming Tools and Methodologies

P.J. Plauger — *Series Advisor*

Lipkin	*String Processing and Text Manipulation In C Selected Data Structures and Techniques*
Plauger	*Standard C: A Reference*
	The Standard C Library
	Programming on Purpose I: Essays on Programming Design
	Programming on Purpose II: Essays on Software People
	Programming on Purpose III: Essays on Software Technology
	The Standard C++ Library
Jongerius	*Writing Bug-Free C Code for Windows*
Van Sickle	*Reusable Software Components: Object-Oriented Embedded Systems Programming in C*

CONTENTS

PREFACE

This book introduces you to new and useful techniques of programming microcontrollers with the high-level language C. The concept of reusable components evolved from research aimed at object-oriented programming for microcontrollers in C. It was found that classes written in C can be packaged as components for easy reuse and modification needed to extend their capability.

In this book you will learn how to create classes in C. Instances of these classes are objects, and within the limits of the microcontroller and other peripherals, as many instances of these objects as are needed can be created. We call these classes components. Such software components have advantages over the corresponding hardware components. In the construction of components, we can apply the concepts of inheritance and polymorphism. Inheritance allows extension of the basic component to meet new requirements without modification of the basic class code. Polymorphism, or late binding, permits the program to select one of several alternative functions or methods. The choice of which to execute cannot be determined until run time. It will be found that careful application of polymorphism can allow a saving of program code.

One of the features of any high-level language is to implement an abstraction in which the underlying computer seemingly disappears. The total programmer interface with the computer is through the language. Often, the basic nature of the computer being programmed is of little concern to the programmer. True for the computer, but untrue for the peripherals. Most of the skill needed to program microcontrollers with a high-level language involves the efficient coding of the interface between the main computer and its program with the peripherals of the system. The code in this book is for an M68HC16 family part. This code is also usable on the

M68300 series of components. The main difference will be that the initialization of the core computers is slightly different, and since most peripherals are common between the chips, the only header file change needed will be the basic core part header. The microcontroller code contained in this book, where possible, has been compiled and tested on an M68300 component.

Chapter 1 contains a very brief summary of object-oriented programming (OOP). The main purpose of the chapter is to introduce some of the language of OOP, how classes and objects are used, what to expect from inheritance and virtual functions, and the many limitations of C as OOP language.

Objects written in C are explored in Chapter 2. Here we start with the simplest concept of an object and develop it into a class. We make a class that can support multiple instantiations of itself in the form of different objects. Inheritance is examined and implemented. We then see how virtual functions can be implemented and used. Finally, several mechanisms to improve the appearance, maintainability, and size of the code written with these techniques are shown. All the code in Chapter 2 is written for a DOS-based machine. The code in the remainder of the book is written for the MC68HC16Y1 microcontroller.

The contents of Chapter 3 show the development of several useful objects for microcontroller programs. Here the classes cover some typical data structure classes that can be used in your programs. These data structures have been developed to meet a programming need for some embedded system.

In Chapter 4 we develop a class that creates instances of an asynchronous serial port. This serial port driver is interrupt-controlled and block-oriented. Its implementation is object-oriented. Instances of serial port objects can be created, and with proper care by the basic program, these instances can be run simultaneously. The microcontroller programmed here contains a dual-channel asynchronous serial port that is comprised of two distinct universal asynchronous receiver–transmitters (UARTs). Although this application might seem to be a perfect example where it is possible to merge the software drivers for these two on-board devices into a single class, it is a case where the merging of the two programs will essentially double the total code, and it will increase the complexity of the software driver considerably. It was decided that the natural integration of multiple devices into a single object-oriented interface would best be demonstrated with the on-board general-purpose timer described in Chapters 5 and 6.

Several timer functions are developed in Chapters 5 and 6. These timers are based on the timers in the general-purpose timer (GPT). The GPT contains both output compare operations and input capture functions. You will find development of components to make use of the output compare systems in Chapter 5. There are four output compare systems on board the chip. Object-oriented interfaces to these output compare systems are created in a single class. Mechanizations are provided to attach a delay object to any timer. When needed, multiple operations can be controlled by each timer through the use of a linked list of object-oriented drivers that are executed with each output compare interrupt. Input capture operations are used to measure time between events. An object-oriented interface to the several on-board input capture systems is completed, and applications to make precision time measurements are shown in Chapter 6.

Chapter 7 is a data manual. The test is on components, and most components that we encounter in hardware have an associated data sheet. Data sheets for all the components derived in this book have been collected together and placed in Chapter 7. Here you can find how to use each software component, its parameters, and the essential items needed to use the class as a super class for the derivation of another class. I suspect that this chapter will be a well-used chapter of the book.

In Appendix A you will find a very brief description of the Cosmic C compiler used to develop code for the M68HC16 series of components. Appendix B includes several important header files needed to compile code for this chip family.

A CD-ROM is included with this book for your convenience. The contents of the CD-ROM should be installed on your hard drive. A command like:

x: > install y:

where x: is the volume of your CD-ROM drive and y: is the volume of the destination drive. This install command will create three directories on your hard drive: programs, html, and Cosmic.

The directory Programs contains all the executable code contained in the book. It is organized by chapter to help you find what you need. The directory Cosmic contains a demonstration C compiler from Cosmic software. This fine product will compile all the code contained in this book. The directory HTML contains a complete copy of the book. You are about to use one of the fine developments that has come from the World Wide Web. The language used to generate Web pages is called html for Hypertext Markup Language. This language allows you to create data pages that are formatted by the language rather than by the author. Look into any of the *.htm files in this directory to see what HTML files look like.

To access an HTML file you must use a Web Browser such as Netscape or any of the other popular programs. Once you get the program running, you can bring up the text with a command like:

file://localhost/c:/<path>/contents.htm

where <path> is the path of your html files. From that point on, it is merely point and click to move through the book.

I would like to take this opportunity to extend my thanks to the Semiconductor Products Sector of Motorola, Inc. for their support in the production of this book. Neil Krohn, my manager, is always there with encouragement to try new business ideas. This, my second book, has been written with his support and blessing. I could not have completed it without his help. My associates Lou Pagnuccon and A. J. Pohlmeyer have provided me with many interesting discussions that have shaped the contents of this book. Finally, I would also like to thank Brian Wilkie, Corporate Vice President and General Manager of the Advanced Microcontroller Division.

Ted Van Sickle
1995

1

OBJECTS AND COMPONENTS

Object-oriented programming offers significant advantages when building large programs. Unfortunately, object-oriented compilers are large and complicated, and the language generated is also usually quite large and complicated. Worse yet, object-oriented programs are often large and complicated compared to an equivalent program written in a procedural language. It is not expected that we will see a true object-oriented compiler that will work for a small microcontroller until there is serious improvement in both microcontroller and compiler technology. These small machines are held back by limited memory space for both program and data as well as limited on-chip resources that make them unsatisfactory destinations for code created by a full-scale object-oriented compiler.

The embedded systems community is experiencing an expansion of program size and requirements. There has been some attempt to address these growing needs with the construction of larger and more powerful microcontrollers. Motorola, for example, has developed the M68HC16 and the M68300 families of microcontrollers to address the needs of the community for larger machines. Even with the large memory spaces and the vast on-chip resources of these machines, there is still the practical need to minimize the system requirement for additional memory. Therefore, code created by an object-oriented compiler would work on a system based on these chips, but the total system would be more complicated and more expensive than an equivalent system prepared with a procedural language.

Nevertheless, there are still serious advantages that can be obtained through the use of an object-oriented approach to programming any large project. In the course of this book it is intended to show an object-oriented approach that can be used with C. Many of the advantages of object-oriented programming can be had, but there are also several important capabilities found with any object-oriented language that cannot be obtained directly from C. Let us, therefore, talk of the code that we generated as being object-oriented-like rather than object oriented.

The ideal code language for many embedded systems is C. C produces tight code and is really RAM efficient. It can also produce quite fast code. However, C does not have many of the features to produce true object-oriented code. Most ideas associated with an object can be obtained in C. Those important features that are lost cause the object-oriented code and the objects created in C to deviate from the ideals that we all have for an object-oriented program. I am going to call these objects written in C either components or objects, interchangeably.

Object-oriented programming is semantic in nature. Therefore, a reasonable approach to examine our object-oriented-like programming technique is to look at the semantics of true object-oriented programming and determine the differences between what we propose here and an object-oriented program. The following few pages are a simple dictionary that describes important concepts of an object-oriented programming style as well as our ability to implement these ideas using the C programming language.

Most dictionaries order their contents in some sense. Usually, the ordering is alphabetical. The ordering here is structural rather than alphabetical. It is probably a good idea to read through and understand the word definitions that follow because these words are used throughout the book. The meanings given here are the meanings associated with these words.

Class A class is a template for an object. Classes are constructed of structures and are therefore types. These structures will be given type names with the typedef keyword, and they are treated within a program the same way as any of the usual language-defined types.

Members The elements that make up a structure are called the structures or class members.

Attribute An attribute is a class member that is a variable. Class attributes are usually hidden from the remainder of the program. Since C has no hiding provision, the class attributes in a C program cannot be truly hidden from the remainder of the program. It is extremely important, however, that a class attribute be untouched directly by the remainder of the program. Therefore, programmers using a class must agree to access any class attributes through the class methods only.

Method A method is a member function associated with a class. Methods are generally used to access class attributes, but they are also used to accomplish any functional operations related to their class. Since these functions are members of the class, they will usually appear as pointers to functions of the class rather than as function names.

Member Function *See* Methods.

Constructor A constructor is a function associated with a class that is executed automatically when a class comes into scope in an object-oriented language. This code creates and initializes an instance of the class type. In C, however, there is no provision for this automatic execution. Therefore, it is necessary for the program to execute the class constructor every time a class is created. The constructor in C returns a pointer to an object that is an instance of the class, and class members can be accessed through this pointer.

Destructor A destructor is a function associated with a class. In an object-oriented language, a destructor is executed whenever an object goes out of scope. The destructor deletes the object and frees memory in which the object is stored. C does not provide for automatic execution of the destructor; therefore, the program must execute the destructor of an object whenever an object is no longer needed.

ENCAPSULATION Encapsulation is a concept that describes the enclosing of a member function and attributes into a single unit that is a type. With the protection afforded by private and protected modes within the class formed by an object-oriented language, the only access to the attributes of the class is through the class members. Since C does not provide the protection of an object-oriented language, encapsulation must be enforced by an agreement between programmers to access class attributes only through class methods.

Private Private is a protection mode provided by an object-oriented language such as C++. Class members that are private can be accessed only through class methods.

Protected Protected is another protection mode provided by an object-oriented language such as C++. Class members that are protected can be accessed through class methods and through class methods of an **inherited** class.

Public Public is a protection mode in which any public attribute or method can be accessed from anywhere in the program. All attributes and methods in a C program are public automatically, and it is up to programmers to agree to treat any variables that should not be public as having a higher level of protection.

Friend A friend function is a function that can access any attribute or method, protected or public, in a class.

Function Overload Function overload is an object-oriented concept that permits several functions to have the same name. The correct choice for the function to be executed at any point in the program is made by the compiler. Each function must have a unique argument signature. The argument signature is the pattern of argument types, and the compiler will choose the correct version of the function to execute even though there are several versions of functions with the same name. C has no provision for function overload.

Operator Overload The programmer is able to create new types at will in an object-oriented program. It is desirable that the programmer be able to perform operations on the new types with the usual language operators. An object-oriented language provides for operator overload to implement this feature. With operator overload, the programmer can specify the operation to be executed on the new types. The compiler will use the type information inherent in the program to determine which operator code to use when it encounters an overloaded operator. Operator overload is not available in C.

INHERITANCE Inheritance is an object-oriented language concept that allows a new class to be created that will have access to some of the attributes and methods of an existing class. This new class can implement additional features that were not present in the older class. Usually, inheritance can be implemented at link time and as such does not require access to the source code of class being inherited from. Inheritance is an object-oriented feature that can be implemented completely in the C language.

Base Class, Super Class, Parent Class These names are assigned synonymously to a class from which another class will be derived. In this book, the term *base class* is generally used.

Derived Class, Child Class These classes are those created by inheritance from a base class.

Abstract Class An abstract class is a class that is a base class only. No instance of an abstract class will ever be created; however, an abstract class will be a base class from which other derived classes will be inherited.

Instantiation Instantiation is the code operation required to create an instance of a new object. The class is a template of an object, and an object is an instance of a class. Therefore, execution of the constructor will create an instance of the object.

Object An object is an instance of a type defined by a class.

Component A component is an object.

POLYMORPHISM *Polymorphism* means many forms. Different methods with a common name and similar operations in several inherited classes can exist. Under normal circumstances, use of such a set of functions is impossible because at link time, a class method normally must be linked to any function that calls it. Here the particular method executed depends on the object being accessed by the program. This choice is not known at link time. Polymorphism is the mechanism that allows the correct function to be chosen at run time. Polymorphism can be implemented in C.

Virtual Function A virtual function is a function that is linked at run time rather than at link time. Virtual functions are implemented in C.

Header, Definition File A header or definition file usually contains the class definition, all of the function prototypes required for the class, any macro definitions needed to implement the class, and linkage, if any, to base classes from which the class is inherited. Header files usually contain no executable code beyond macro definitions. The header file must be included in any program that will use the class.

Implementation File An implementation file contains the code needed for all class methods, constructor, destructor, and hidden functions associated with a class. The implementation file is usually compiled separately and linked with the program.

In the glossary above, you will find three especially important concepts that form the basis for all object-oriented programming. These three, encapsulation, inheritance, and polymorphism, are identified by all-capital letters. Object-oriented programming is based on these three important concepts. You will note that both inheritance and polymorphism can be implemented in C, and encapsulation is not enforced by the C language. It is possible to hide functions that should be private and prevent their use from outside the class methods.

Let us look at what a class and objects instantiated from this class are. When we talk of objects in real life, we generally refer to things that exist in our daily experience. A laptop computer, a dog, an automobile, a light switch, and a washing machine might be cited as examples of objects we see daily. An object is generally defined as a thing that can be seen or touched or a thing that occupies space. We are going to extend these ideas a bit. The idea of an **object** indeed encompasses the above, but it also includes programming things that will exist in a program but never in the real world. Examples include such things as semaphores, linked lists, stacks, and other software entities that can be thought of as things or objects.

Most objects encountered in real life have **attributes.** The attributes of an object are those things that distinguish an object from a similar object, they might describe the state of the object, identify details of the object such as its color, or describe an internal setup of the object such as the program that controls temperature vs. time found in a sophisticated thermostat. Attributes are characteristics or qualities of a thing. Some attributes, such as the color of an automobile, can be changed with great effort. Others can be changed, but access to make the changes is usually through a special route contained within the object. A perfect example here is that the engine of an automobile can be started with a key and then only when the transmission is in *park* or *drive*. Of course, the states *park* or *drive* are other attributes of an automobile, so you can see that attributes can interact with each other. However, attributes cannot be changed helter-skelter from outside the object. It is inconceivable that an outside action should change the transmission state from *drive* to *park.* This action can be accomplished only by the shift of a lever that is a part of the automobile. In a sense, attributes are hidden from the outside and can be accessed only through designated actions contained within the object itself.

The discussion above is about an object. An object usually can be thought of being a specific instance of a **class.** To continue the idea of an automobile, we might have a class that includes all automobiles. Drawn from this class is any individual automobile: for example, Mary's Ford. This particular automobile is red, has four doors, is air conditioned, has cruise control, has a special sound system for entertainment, and has a V6 engine. This car is unique. There are probably other automobiles with exactly the same attributes, but they are not Mary's car. Mary's car is an instance of the class *automobile*, and no other instance of this class can be Mary's car.

We have seen two important components of a class. The first is the **attribute** and the second is the **method.** Classes have attributes that provide the uniqueness of different objects based on the class. These attributes can be given values at the time the object is created or at various times during the life of the class. For example, the automobile is painted red during its manufacture, and it is difficult to change its color. On the other hand, the state of the engine—*on* or *off*—is changed during operation of the automobile. Attributes are internal to the object and cannot be altered from the outside of the object without either some major effort or through routes from the object surface to the attribute's domain within the object. The class is the repository of the attributes: Each class will contain a list of attributes that each object derived from the class can have. Each object will have its own set of unique attributes drawn from those available to the class. The object's attributes are limited to those of the class from which it is derived.

It is undesirable for an attribute to be changed from outside the object. Essentially, all attributes, even though they are variable, are hidden from the outside world. They are private to the class or object. If an attribute is a variable, it is usually accessible for change or other access through special functions. The engine is turned on and off with the key, the radio is controlled by the operator, the gear shift is controlled by the driver, and so on. Access to these things is through a set of controls designed specifically to deal with the various attributes. In the software world, these access mechanisms are called methods.

Leaving the real-world analogy, we can look into objects and classes as software entities. The methods of a class are a set of functions that allow access into the private recesses of an object. Methods are a part of the class. Attributes are usually **private** and the only way that you may deal with these attributes is through a series of methods that are necessarily **public.** Here *public* means that these methods can be seen and used by anybody. The radio controls in your car, its gear shift, and the horn button are public methods that control attributes of the automobile. Methods usually cause something to happen. As operators we usually do not care how the method works, only that when used, the object behaves in an expected manner.

A class is a type. This type has the same status as any other type in the language. An instance of such a type is an object. Therefore, the class is found only once in a program, and as many instances of the class, or objects, as needed can be created through the use of define statements in the program.

Usually, attributes are private and methods are public. Of course, we can have public attributes and private methods. The private method is a function accessed only by the public methods and a public attribute can be seen and accessed from anywhere in a program. The public attribute is not often used. The block diagram shown in Figure 1.1 shows the layout of a class. Note that there is a heavy line around the innermost part of the class. A program using objects of this class should not be able to penetrate this heavy line except through the methods that are shown entering the private portion of the class. Any box that penetrates the private portion of the class has full access to all private data. The public methods are shown as method 1, method 2, and method 3. There are several special methods that can be associated with a class. Two, the constructor and destructor, are needed to create an object and to destroy an instance of an object when needed. In an object-oriented programming language such as C++, the **constructor** will be executed automatically whenever a define statement causes the creation of a new instance of an object. The **destructor** is executed when the object goes out of scope. We will be using C only, so execution of both constructor and destructor to create and destroy an object, when needed, will be the responsibility of the program. Usually, objects are created and destroyed when needed. Such an approach implies dynamic allocation of any needed memory to the objects during execution of the constructor. In a system where memory is limited, it will be necessary to allocate memory and free it when the object is no longer needed, to avoid overuse of the available system memory.

Another special type of method, called a **virtual** method, is used to implement polymorphism and is shown in detail in Chapter 2. Finally, a **friend** function is a function that has access to the private parts of an object but is not a method of

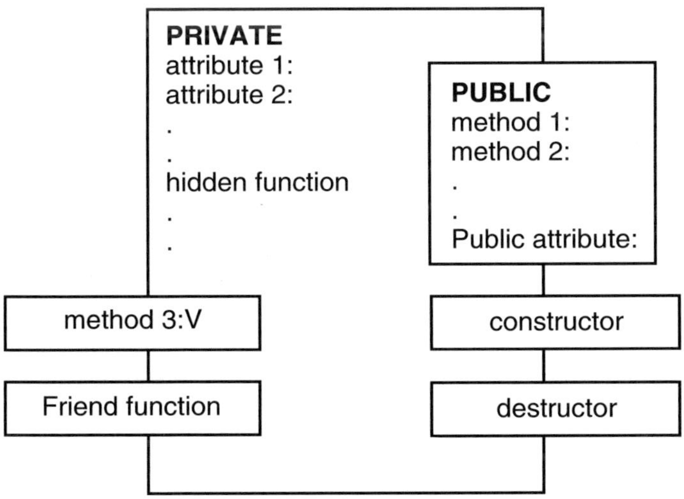

Figure 1.1 Block Diagram of a Class

the class. As such, a friend is a function that, by design, can get around the restrictions implied by the private access label attached to the attributes.

Another characteristic of an object/class system is that of inheritance. The idea of inheritance is simple. Any class can use another class in its own creation. When one class, the derived class, inherits the properties of another class, the base class, the derived class will have access to all the base class attributes and methods that have **protected** access rather than being private.

Why should we be so concerned about the access privileges of the members of a class? In looking at the class automobile above, we have seen that there are attributes that should be set by the operator and that these attributes should not be accessible to outside entities. The transmission setting, PRNDL, must be available to the driver only. If an outside force could alter the transmission setting while the automobile is being driven, there is no end to the mischief that could be played on unsuspecting drivers. It is the same problem in programming. Attributes are the things that make an object unique. Uncontrolled access to these attributes will open the program using the object to the same types of problems that drivers might have when they do not have complete control over their vehicles. Methods are created to perform all access needed on the attributes, and the design of the methods should be concerned with all aspects of the attribute. It makes sense to reject attributes that are not in a correct range, those that are of the wrong type, attributes that should not be changed at all. It is the methods' responsibility to filter these types of errors and keep the attributes of the object proper. If the attributes could be accessed from any part of the program without the help of the methods, a situation will arise where a part of the program will alter an attribute value and it will be wrong. By locking the attributes inside the object and not allowing access except through method calls, we avoid problems that can occur through unintended modifications of the attributes.

The class, which defines a type, has the representative components shown in Figure 1.1. We will see classes that contain no attributes, or no methods, and some that contain no constructor or destructor. A class is the code that pulls together all the components of an object and holds them together in a form that can be used easily by a program. In our code, a class will consist of two parts. The header file contains needed definitions, the structure that will be turned into a type usable throughout the program with a typedef keyword, function prototypes of methods needed by objects of the class, function prototypes of the constructor and destructor, and any macro-defined functions needed by the class. The structure at this point in the program is a declaration statement that identifies the nature of the structure to the compiler, but no instance of the structure yet exists. Header files do not contain executable code. This header file must be included with any code that is to make use of objects of this class.

Associated with the header file is a definition or implementation file. This file contains all the code for the various functions and methods needed to implement the class. Almost always there will be a constructor and a destructor. The constructor is a function that creates an instance of the class which is called an object. To create this instance, the constructor allocates memory to hold a copy of the object and then

copies its own arguments into the variable members of the structure. A pointer to this structure is returned to the calling program. Access to the particular object is through the pointer returned by the constructor. Most of the time, the destructor simply executes the free() function to return the memory used by an object to the free memory pool.

Member functions, or methods, show up in several different ways. The easiest way to handle member functions is to treat them as any other functions found in the program. Their code will be contained in the implementation file, and this file will be compiled and linked into the program. These functions will then be available to the entire program. In other instances it will be desirable to provide access to the methods through pointers to these functions that are placed in the structure that defines the class. This approach requires a single level of indirection to access the class methods. Other instances in which these pointers will be collected into a separate structure will be seen. Access to these methods will require two levels of indirection. There are other reasons that function pointer tables will be created to aid in run-time binding.

Many simple examples of the creation of classes and objects are shown in Chapter 2. These examples demonstrate implementation of inheritance, polymorphism, and other important coding techniques needed for object-oriented programming in C.

A class is a most reusable piece of code. A properly written and debugged hierarchy of classes can form the basis onto which any modifications of the existing classes can be easily made. These modifications are safe and effective if the code is written in a language that embodies all three primary concepts of object-oriented programming. Modifications to existing classes are made through **inheritance.** An inherited class has access to attributes and methods of the base class. Therefore, those things about a class that are unmodified by inheritance will continue to function as expected. Of course, newly added features will suffer all the problems of any new code, but the old code will remain unchanged.

The problem of attribute hiding cannot be avoided when writing object-oriented code in C. This unfortunate circumstance does open object-oriented code written in C to problems that would not exist if the attributes could be properly hidden. Therefore, it must be stated, and stated, and restated, that all program accesses to any object attribute must be only through class methods. Any programmer who violates this rule exposes the entire concept to trouble. In fact, one of the reasons it was decided to concentrate on the idea of reusable components rather than object-oriented programming is this inability of C to hide attributes within a structure.

The idea of a component is easy to understand now. Most programs we write for embedded systems consists of typical procedural programs. The goal here is to alter the program design approach. Like a circuit, a program will be treated as a collection of components that are connected by a program. Each component can be created by the programmer or by other programmers in the programming team, or can be purchased from an outside vendor. The components will be standard program items such as semaphores, lists in their many forms, or other data structure items. A major new addition to the list of components will be added here, the computer peripheral. All of these items could well be created as classes in an object-oriented language, but here we will create them in C and treat them as components with which we can build a program.

The abstraction of any high-level language hides the computer from the programmer. Usually, such things as registers and control bits in the registers are hidden from the programmer. This abstraction makes it easier for the language standard to define a language and avoid any worry about the computer being programmed. This abstraction works for essentially all mainline programs. This abstraction fails us terribly when we must work with peripherals that usually contain memory-mapped registers and input/output devices that must be accessed by the computer. The concept of a component supports our programming needs very well here. C provides the means to access and deal with the memory-mapped items found with the peripherals. If the peripheral is pulled into a component, it will be possible to contain all accesses to the peripheral control logic within the component, and the program will be able to treat the peripheral as it would any other logical device in the system. The peripheral devices can be controlled from a program using components without our breaking the abstraction of the high-level language because the component will hide from the main program, all the details of peripheral interface with the program.

2

OBJECT-ORIENTED PROGRAMMING IN C

Why would we want to do object-oriented programming (OOP) in C? There is one overwhelming reason that we cannot overlook. Today, there are no C++ compilers for our microcontrollers! The only approach to the use of C++ is by compiling the C++ program with a cfront. A cfront is a compiler that compiles C++ code into C code. The resultant code can then be compiled with a C compiler. A cfront will produce code aimed to be used on a large computer, and it is not too forgiving of the many tricks that are usually employed in C to permit the code to run on a microcontroller. Therefore, a clear alternative to writing code in C++ is to write object-oriented code in C. In many cases, C can do the same job as C++. There are clearly some features of C++ that must be lost when C is used to code OOP. Recall that the three key words of OOP are encapsulation, inheritance, and polymorphysm. With only a few compromises, OOP code in C retains most of these capabilities. The features that are lost are operator and function overloading and the protection modes of C++. We will see several examples of object-oriented programming in C and will examine the costs of doing our business in this language. Some features are completely lost, some are impaired, but many are still available and can be used to great advantage without the need for a C++ compiler.

CLASSES, OBJECTS, AND ENCAPSULATION

An object is usually considered to be a memory storage location. This is still true in OOP written in C. In Chapter 1 we saw a class that was described as an object template. Here we use the structure to create our object template. To begin, we use a structure that contains all the necessary data for the object. Associated with the object are the several functions needed to manipulate the attributes of the object. Let us choose a very simple object that we can explore easily. The object in this case is going to be a counter. The counter has only one attribute: the number of the count. This counter will work like a hand-held counter used by a theater usher who counts the number of people entering a theater. The counter content can be incremented and may be read. The attribute is the count, and there are two methods associated with the counter: increment and query.

Shown below is a header file named defines.h. This file is short and requires little explanation here. Several of the important defined constants needed in our programs are identified here, and the defines.h header can be included at the beginning of each file to create these definitions for each program module.

```
#ifndef DEFINES_H
#define DEFINES_H

#ifndef NULL
      #define NULL (void *)0
#endif
#define EOM 0
#define FOREVER while(TRUE)

typedef int Boolean;
typedef unsigned int WORD;
typedef unsigned char BYTE;

enum {FALSE,TRUE};
enum {OFF,ON};
enum {NO,YES};
enum {FAST,SLOW};

enum errors
{
      SEMAPHORE,
      SERIAL,
      TIMER,
      DELAY,
      PWM
};

enum edges
{
      DISABLE,
      RISING,
      FALLING,
      ANY
};
```

```
enum outputs
{
      DISCONNECT,
      TOGGLE,
      CLEAR,
      SET
};

#endif
```

Note that the header starts with two lines:

```
#ifndef DEFINES_H
#define DEFINES_H
```

Also note that the last line of the file is

```
#endif
```

These simple commands will cause any multiple inclusion of this file to be ignored. Therefore, there will be no multiple definitions of symbols found in the file regardless of the number of times that the file is included in different modules when the program is compiled. All header files should be protected from multiple inclusion by this simple mechanism. Most of the remainder of the defines.h header file contents is self-explanatory. The parameter NULL is not defined by the language. We define it here as a pointer to a type void, and the pointer has a zero value. This definition is protected by an #ifndef test to assure that there is no more than one inclusion of the definition for a NULL in a program. The macro FOREVER is very useful in most main programs for embedded systems. There are several enumerations that are convenient to define, which assign values to constant names needed through the book. The various items enumerated and macros defined are needed in typical programs. The enumeration that defines SERIAL, TIMER, and so on, is needed for the system error handler discussed in Chapter 4. The enumerations edges and outputs contain values helpful in writing code for the input capture system and the output compare system.

Shown below is the header file for our simple counter. This header file contains the protection from multiple inclusions and an include command to include the defines.h header in the program. Next, the header contains a typedef command for a structure type. The structure type has no tag name, but the structure is given a type name Counter. This structure contains only one member, called count, which is of the type WORD, identified by a typedef command in defines.h as an unsigned int.

```
#ifndef COUNTER_H
#define COUNTER_H
```

```
#include "defines.h"

struct
{
    WORD count;
}Counter;

void increment(void);
int query(void);

#endif
```

Also in the header file are two function prototypes. You will note that there is no function code for these functions in the header file. In OOP talk, this file is called the **class header** file. Such files should never contain executable code. All executable code associated with a class is included in the class implementation file. The class **implementation** file for our counter class is shown below. The header file that contains the header here is called counter0.h.

```
#include "counter0.h"

void increment(void)
{
    Counter.count++;
}

int query(void)
{
    return Counter.count;
}
```

The implementation file first includes the appropriate header file. The remainder of the code found in this file is executable code. The two functions here are increment() and query(). Recall that these function prototypes are included in the header file. This particular program structure follows C++ closely. If the programmer wishes to build a library of objects, it is possible to deliver to a customer a readable version of the header files and a compiled version of the implementation files. The way the objects can be used can be seen from the contents of the header file, and the details of how the objects work are hidden in the implementation file. Therefore, the programmer can sell the product with assurance that the program details are hidden from the user.

The two functions in this case perform simple actions. increment() causes the member count in the object Counter to be incremented, and query() returns the value of the member count to the calling program. A program that will test the performance of this object is shown below.

```
#include "counter0.h"
#include <stdio.h>

main()
{
    int i;

    for(i=0;i<12;i++)
        increment();
    printf("a=%d \n",query());
}
```

In this program it is assumed that counter0.c has been compiled and the compiled version is linked with the program above when it is compiled. The result of execution of this program is

```
a=12
```

as expected.

Let us examine this program in a little more detail to determine what we have and have not accomplished. First, Counter is an object. From an encapsulation standpoint, Counter does not meet the test. The attribute count is accessed by class methods. There is, however, no mechanism that prevents any portion of the program from accessing count once the object has been created. This portion of encapsulation, attribute hiding, is not a part of and cannot be easily implemented by C. All programmers must agree to access object attributes through the methods provided with the class only.

There is another difficulty. One would expect that the programmer should be able to create several instances of the object Counter. On the contrary, Counter in this case is itself an instance of a structure, and no mechanism is available for creating additional instances. You will observe that increment() and query() both operate on the member count in the structure Counter. If other versions of Counter were available, increment() and query() would have no means for accessing these other instances. To be practical, it is necessary that our class approach allow instantiation of several different instances of Counter, and the methods must access the individual instance that the programmer needs.

These problems are easily addressed. The methods will each have an argument that is a pointer to the object being accessed. A header file for the class Counter that implements this approach is shown below. Note here that a typedef construct is used to create the type Counter. This type contains only one WORD member. The function prototypes for increment() and query() now contain arguments that are pointers to the type Counter. When using this approach, we need a means to create an instance of Counter, or a pointer to the type Counter, and delete a specified instance. The function count_()—single underscore—is the constructor for the object Counter. This function will create an instance of Counter and return a pointer to that specific instance to the calling program. The destructor is count__(), double underscore. This function is executed with an argument that is a pointer returned from count_(). The destructor will destroy the specific instance of Count. We append a single underscore to the name of a constructor and a double underscore to the name of a destructor throughout the book.

```
#ifndef COUNTER_H
#define COUNTER_H

#include "defines.h"

typedef struct
{
    WORD count;
}Counter;

void increment(Counter *);
int query(Counter *);

Counter *counter_(void);
void counter__(Counter *);

#endif
```

Both of these functions exist in C++. Either can be defined as we do here, or the language provides a default version of both the destructor and the constructor. C requires that the program provide a constructor and a destructor. It is important that the program create each object when it is needed, and it is equally important that the object be destroyed when it is no longer needed. When an object disappears from a program, it is said to go out of scope. Whenever an object goes out of scope in a C program, the program must execute its destructor. Otherwise, the **heap**—the memory area from which the space needed to hold additional objects—will become fully used and the program cannot continue without error.

The implementation file is shown below. The functions increment() and query() are similar to those in the version above. In this case these functions have pointer arguments, and instead of merely incrementing or returning count, the value of count associated with the pointer on which this is operated prior to the functions' return.

```
#include "counter1.h"
#include <stdlib.h>    /* for the memory operations */

void increment(Counter *this)
{
    this->count++;
}
```

```
int query(Counter *this)
{
    return this->count;
}
Counter *counter_(void)
{
    Counter *this;

    if(this=(Counter *)(malloc(sizeof(Counter))==NULL))
        error_handler()
    this->count=0;
    return this;
}

void counter__(Counter *this)
{
    free(this);
}
```

The constructor takes no argument and returns pointer to a type Counter. Inside the constructor, a temporary pointer to a type Counter is created by the line of code

```
Counter *this;
```

The system call malloc() is used to get a memory block the size of Counter. malloc() returns a pointer to the type void, so the return can be cast onto a type Counter* which is stored in this. The pointer form for member access is used to initialize count, and this, the pointer, is returned to the calling program. The pointer returned from malloc() is tested to make certain that the operating system found enough memory to allocate another block to the program. If not enough memory were available, the malloc() function would return a NULL, which cannot be a valid pointer in C. The return value is tested to determine if it is a NULL. In the event that it is, a function error_handler() is executed. For the programs in this chapter, the error_handler() will be a stub routine that does nothing. This important function will be revisited in Chapter 4, where an error_handler() approach is developed. The routine counter creates a dynamic memory location which contains Count, initializes the value of count in that memory area, and returns a pointer to this location to the calling program. The variable *this* must always be defined in the constructor. In C++ there is a variable *this* that need not be defined in any method. This variable is always a pointer to the current object. We will use this as the same thing as you will find in C++. Anytime that this is used as a variable, it will be a pointer to the appropriate object.

The destructor, counter__(), uses the standard memory release call free() to return to the operating system the memory space occupied by the specific instance of Counter.

```
#include "counter1.h"
#include <stdio.h>

main()
{
    Counter *a=counter_();
    Counter *b=counter_();
    int i;

    for(i=0;i<12;i++)
    {
        increment(a);
        increment(b);
    }
    for(i=0;i<6;i++)
        increment(a);
    printf("a=%d and b=%d\n",query(a),query(b));
    counter__(a);
    counter__(b);
}
```

The performance of this version of Counter is demonstrated by the program above. Two instances of a counter are created by the two lines of code

```
Counter *a=counter_();
Counter *b=counter_();
```

Each line of code says: "Create an instance of a pointer to the type Counter. Initialize the pointer with the return from the constructor function counter_()." These lines of code are definition statements as well as initialization statements.

For demonstration purposes, the program increments both a and b 12 times and then increments a an additional six times. The output from this program is

```
a=18 and b=12
```

We have succeeded in modifying our approach to the creation of objects in C to allow multiple instances of a single object. Notice that the destructor was used at the end of the program to delete the instances of a and b that were created with the constructor.

The approach outlined above handily eliminates the problem of multiple instantiations. The program can now have as many instances of any given class as are needed to meet the program needs. So far, the cost to achieve these ends has been minimal. There is one copy of each method, the constructor and destructor associated with each program. In this case, each object will be two bytes long, and the constructor will allocate exactly two bytes for each instance of the object. The object-oriented approach has cost nothing, with the exception of the additional function calls in the main program needed to set up the objects and access the object attributes. We have gained the ability to deal with Counters as objects. The method function calls above are really mechanisms to send and receive messages to and from the object. Such accesses are uniform across the entire program, and the code created to access the Counters is very simple and to the point. This particular program is so simple that many would say that it is easier to write the code to do the job in other ways. True perhaps, but in no case would the straight procedural approach be so obvious as to what the program is doing.

If our program approach is to allow multiple instances of any object, it is necessary to have arguments for all object methods. The problem here is that the program has no means of determining which object is sending a message to any specific method. Therefore, the object identification must be included as a part of the message that is passed to the method. We will see later that when more complicated functions such as virtual functions and inheritance are employed, even a single additional argument is not sufficient to identify the program destination accurately when a message is sent to an object.

INHERITANCE

The current approach outlined above does not allow either inheritance or polymorphism as it stands. These features are so important that they must be considered when creating an object-oriented method of programming. Inheritance allows a new class to access all the attributes and methods of another class as if they were its own. The new class can extend the capability of the class being inherited from. Semantic problems creep into our list of difficulties with OOP now. Inheritance is a poor description of what we are doing at this point. Inheritance usually implies the passage of characteristics and traits from parent to child. Often, the classes are given the name **parent** or **child class.** As it turns out, this nomenclature is not truly descriptive of what happens in OOP inheritance. The parent class gives all its attributes and methods to the child class. The parent class can operate on its own, but the child class is forever dependent on the presence of the parent—an unlikely parent–child arrangement if ever there was one. Sometimes the parent class is called the **base class** or **super class.** In such cases the child class is usually called the **derived class.** These descriptions probably convey the actual happenings in inheritance better than the parent–child concept. We will continue to use inheritance here to describe what occurs when a new class takes all the characteristics of another class, but recognize that such an action is not inheritance in any real sense.

Let us examine what we can do to implement OOP inheritance in the C language without the OOP extensions found in C++. To create inheritance, we really need a mechanism to alter the structure that defines a class in another part of the program. True inheritance will allow the characteristics of the base structure to be incorporated into a new structure in the process of derivation of the new structure.

Once a structure has been defined by a program, it is not possible to change it. When inheriting, it is possible to include another class structure as a member of a new class structure. Such an approach will lead to extremely convoluted programs, and one of the purposes of OOP is to create smooth, uniform interfaces between portions of a program. The idea of using one class structure as a member of another class structure will lead to at least multiple indirection on accesses to the object attributes and methods. Some accesses would require one level of indirection, and others would require more. What a nightmare!

An approach will be developed that does require some indirection, but the indirection levels needed by the programmer will be uniform. Therefore, the demands on the programmer are somewhat more complicated than usual, but the benefits gained by having the OOP significantly outweigh the need for additional programmer involvement. In the following header file, observe that the #define statement that defines COUNT contains items that are attributes as well as function prototypes for the class typedefed as Count. The method prototypes use pointers to functions rather than the normal function name, and the arguments to these functions are pointers to the type struct cnt. It is not possible to use a pointer to the type Count, because Count is an undefined type at this point in the program. The class declaration is the structure cnt, and this structure is typedefed as a type Count when it is created. The members of struct cnt are simply those items defined as COUNT. As was done earlier, the constructor and destructor are prototyped in the header file named counter2.h.

```
#ifndef COUNT_H
#define COUNT_H

#include "defines.h"

#define COUNT \
    WORD count; \
    void (*increment)(struct cnt *);\
    WORD (*query)(struct cnt *);

typedef struct cnt
{
    COUNT
}Count;

Count *count_(void);
void count__(Count *);

#endif
```

The main difference between this header and the preceding one is that the member attributes and methods that are a part of the class are each defined in the

#define statement. The reason for this approach is not evident right now, but we will see the importance of making these several members of the structure a separately accessible entity and not keeping their definitions locked inside the structure that defines the class.

The implementation file is shown below. One of the first items that you will observe is that the method function implementations are declared to be static. A static declaration for a function causes the function to have file scope. Therefore, if another portion of the program needs an increment, there will be no name conflicts if the various files are each compiled separately. Otherwise, the functions increment() and query() are the same as those shown in the earlier counter1 version of the class.

```
#include "counter2.h"
#include <stdlib.h> /* needed for the memory functions */

static void increment(Count *this)
{
    this->count++;
}

static WORD query(Count *this)
{
    return this->count;
}

Count *count_(void)
{
    Count *this;

    if((this=(Count *)malloc(sizeof(Count)))==NULL)
        error_handler();
    this->count=0;
    this->increment=increment;
    this->query=query;
    return this;
}

void count__(Count *this)
{
    free(this);
}
```

The constructor count_() is significantly modified from the earlier version. Here the memory space for the object is allocated, and the attribute count is initialized to zero. In this case the two method members of the structure are initialized with pointers to the functions increment() and query() defined earlier in the implementation file. Therefore, any access to these functions must take the form

```
Count *a=count_();
.
.
.
(*a->increment)(a);
.
.
```

It may seem like double jeopardy that the pointer to an instance of the object must be used twice in each method call. The first is to get to the individual function, and the second is to identify the specific object being worked upon. If several objects are defined, the pointer to the object in the function name can be a pointer to any of the several objects instantiated. Each object will have a pointer to all object methods within the object definition. Every like object will contain these pointers, and their values will all be the same. That is one of the inefficiencies of this approach. There is the extra baggage of pointers to each object method contained in each instance of the object. Each object will therefore be somewhat longer than one would think necessary. We will see in the next example, however, that there are benefits to be obtained from this seeming waste of memory space.

A test program is shown below. In this case, two instances of the object are created. Both of these instances are incremented 12 times, and then the a instance is incremented an additional six times.

```
#include "counter2.h"
#include <stdio.h>


main()
{
    Count *a=count_();
    Count *b=count_();
    int i;


    for(i=0;i<12;i++)
    {
        (*a->increment)(a);
        (*b->increment)(b);
    }
    for(i=0;i<6;i++)
    {
        (*a->increment)(a);
    }
    printf("a=%d and b=%d\n",(*a->query)(a),(*b->query)(b));
    count__(a);
    count__(b);
}
```

The output from this program is

```
a=18 and b=12
```

as it should be.

The class above will be counter2. counter2 satisfies the requirements established earlier. It has the ability to be incremented at arbitrary times, and the number of times that it was incremented can be determined at any time. The program can create an arbitrary number of counters, and the interface between the counter and the program is uniform. Admittedly, the interface is somewhat different, depending on the type of class that has been used, but once this choice has been made, access to each of the methods associated with the class is uniform. In the final version, the method names are hidden within the scope of the file in which they are created. Therefore, there can be several objects that have the same method names, and there will be no name conflicts in the program. The version called counter1 will not afford this benefit. In that case the method names are global and it is easily possible to have name conflicts with different classes in the program. As mentioned above, the price associated with this method name hiding is that each object must contain pointers to each of the class methods, making the size of the object larger than with the approach used in counter1. There is, however, an additional benefit beyond name hiding. That benefit is that with the method used in counter2, it is possible to implement inheritance.

The class Counter is a simple recording counter that can be incremented and queried to determine the number of increments. Suppose that we need to expand the capabilities of our counter to allow not only increment and query, but also decrement. There is a very important distinction at this point. This class and the objects instantiated are counters. The basic nature of the operation of the class is unchanged. If we call this system an **up/down counter,** we can say without fear of contradiction that the up/down counter is a counter. If a program is to use inheritance, the programmer must be able to say that the class inherited from the super class is of the same basic nature as the super class. Otherwise, a different programming approach probably should be used. Since an up/down counter is a counter, we may safely conclude that the up/down counter can inherit the characteristics of counter and we will see a classic case of class inheritance.

The header file for the up/down counter is shown below. The up/down counter is to be inherited from counter2, so counter2.h must be included in the header file. Recall that in counter2.h, a define statement defined COUNT, which contained all the attributes and methods needed to implement that version of the counter. In this header, new structure members are defined for the up/down counter. First, the members of COUNT are included in the definition of UDCOUNT. Additionally, the function prototype for the decrement function is included in the definition. UDCOUNT defines all the attributes and methods of COUNT along with the new decrement function. This define statement is then used as the argument of the struct udcount, which is typedefed as the new type Udcount. This is our new class and the header file is saved in counter3.h.

```
#ifndef UDCOUNT_H
#define UDCOUNT_H

#include "defines.h"
#include "counter2.h"

#define UDCOUNT \
    COUNT \
    void (*decrement)(struct udcount *);

typedef struct udcount
{
    UDCOUNT
}Udcount;

Udcount *udcount_(void);
void udcount__(Udcount *);

#endif
```

The functions increment() and query() used in the definition of counter2 are still valid functions for this class. Therefore, the new class must define only the function decrement(). decrement() is the first function defined in the implementation file.

The constructor is somewhat different from that in counter2. The attributes and methods of an instance of Count as defined by counter2 are use as a base class to udcount. A temporary instance of an object Count will be created by execution of the count_() constructor. Dynamic allocation is used via malloc() to create a memory space large enough to hold the new Udcount object. The contents of the temporary Count object are then moved to the newly created Udcount object, and the temporary Count is deleted by execution of its destructor. Finally, a pointer to the function decrement is placed in the proper location in the object, and a pointer to the new object is returned to the calling program. Pointers to increment() and query() are contained in the object created by the constructor count_(). Therefore, these methods from the base class will be used as methods for Udcount. Also, count_() initializes the count to zero, so when an object of the type Udcount is instantiated, it will have its own version of decrement() and will share the code from Count for increment() and query(). This new object will also have its own location count, in which the number of increments less the decrements is stored.

```
#include "counter3.h"
#include <stdlib.h> /* for memory function access */

static void decrement(Udcount *this)
{
    this->count--;
}
```

```
Udcount *udcount_(void)
{
    Udcount *this;
    Count *temp=count_();

    if((this=(Udcount *)malloc(sizeof(Udcount)))==NULL)
        error_handler();
    memmove(this,temp,sizeof(Count));
    count__(temp);
    this->decrement=decrement;
    return this;
}

void udcount__(Udcount *this)
{
    free(this);
}
```

The test function shown below demonstrates all operations of Udcount. Two instances of Udcount are instantiated. These instances are a and b. Both instances are incremented 12 times, and the values of the results are printed out. Then a is incremented an additional six times while b is decremented six times.

```
#include "counter3.h"
#include <stdio.h>

main()
{
    Udcount *a=udcount_();
    Udcount *b=udcount_();
    int i;

    for(i=0;i<12;i++)
    {
            (*a->increment)(a);
            (*b->increment)(b);
    }
    printf("a=%d and b=%d\n",(*a->query)(a),(*b->query)(b));
    for(i=0;i<6;i++)
    {
        (*a->increment)(a);
        (*b->decrement)(b);
    }
    printf("a=%d and b=%d\n",(*a->query)(a),(*b->query)(b));
    udcount__(a);
    udcount__(b);
    return 0;
}
```

The output from this program is as follows:

```
a=12 and b=12
a=18 and b=6
```

which is the expected result. Here Udcount has inherited all the methods and attributes of Count and extends the operation of the object to include a decrement as well as the increment and query associated with Count. Actually, one could have created an Udcount with all the necessary methods. However, this approach could require more code than is needed above because, in a program where both Count and Udcount are needed, the code for the methods in Count would not need to be repeated for Udcount. This ability to share code is one of the important benefits found with inheritance. Additionally, Udcount is another instance of a counter, and it is used in much the same way as Count. We have been able to build onto a base class another class that has all the base class characteristics, with some new characteristics of its own.

POLYMORPHISM AND VIRTUAL FUNCTIONS

With the background as described above, both polymorphism and virtual functions written in C can be examined. The basic idea of polymorphism is to allow several functions that execute similar but different functions for different inherited classes to have the same name. The choice as to which function will be used by the different classes cannot be made at the time of linking. This choice must be made when the program is run. Thus the name **late binding** or **run-time linking** is also assigned to polymorphism. It should be noted that a virtual function is not really bound at run time. In reality, the means by which a virtual function is created is to use a level of indirection in the choice of a function to be executed. Therefore, all the functions referred to as virtual are really accessed by pointers to the specific function to be executed rather than by the function name. Let us examine this concept further in the following discussion.

We begin by defining a class Graph that in essence defines a point. However, this class is really a dummy class that will never be instantiated with a regular program. Such a class is called an abstract class; the purpose of this type of class is to be a parent or a super class that will be used to inherit other useful classes. Consider the class shown below.

```
#ifndef GRAPH_H
#define GRAPH_H
#include "defines.h"

/* elements and methods of the class graph */
#define GRAPH_CLASS\
```

```
          int     x,\
                  y,\
                  background, \
                  foreground; \
          Boolean visible,\
                  (* is_visible)(struct graph*);\
          void    (* show)(struct graph*),\
                  (* hide)(struct graph*),\
                  (* move)(struct graph*, int, int);


    typedef struct graph
    {
         GRAPH_CLASS
    } Graph;


    Graph* graph_(int x,int y,int background,int foreground);


    void graph__(Graph*);


    #endif
```

GRAPH_CLASS is defined and contains all the members of the class Graph. The struct graph members then constitute the single statement GRAPH_CLASS. The class definition above will be saved in a file graph.h.

It is not necessary to include parameter names in a function prototype as was done above. In the prototypes for the constructors there are frequently several parameters, and it is a good idea to include some type of descriptive name for each parameter. For example, in the case above, x and y are the coordinates of the graphics point. The parameter background is the background color and the foreground is the foreground color. With these parameters named in the constructor prototype, it is not necessary to examine the implementation file to determine the meanings of these several parameters.

The implementation file for this class is shown below. We include the file graph.h to make available to the program all the information shown above. The constructor and destructor programs shown later are a part of this file. The code has been moved here to keep the descriptive text near the code. With this version of object management, it is necessary to pass a pointer to the specific instantiation of an object to each method whenever a method is called. Therefore, you will note below that the first argument of each method is a pointer to a type Graph. This pointer selects the specific object that the method will operate upon. (This approach may seem strange for object-oriented programming. If you examine the C code generated by a cfront, you will find that this is exactly the way that the different instantiations of the same object are kept separated.)

```
#include "graph.h"

static Boolean is_visible(Graph* this) /* is visible */
{
      return this->visible;
}

static void hide(Graph* this)      /* hide */
{
}

static void show(Graph* this)      /* show */
{
}

/* move to a new location */

static void move( Graph* this, int new_x, int new_y)
{
      (*this->hide)(this);
      this->x=new_x;
      this->y=new_y;
      move_to(new_x,new_y);
      (*this->show)(this);
}
```

The foregoing methods are straightforward and simple, as you would expect with object-oriented programming. All the methods are static, limiting visibility to the file in which they are defined. Therefore, if another class would use methods with the same name, there would be no name resolution problems. The first method, is_visible(), returns the state visible for the object specified. hide() and show() are stub functions that have no code for the abstract function. These functions are the virtual functions of the abstract class and they will be completed in any class that uses Graph as a super class. The method move() first hides the pixel, establishes a new position, and then shows the new point.

The code for the constructor of Graph is shown below. This constructor will return a pointer to the type Graph that will be associated with the particular instantiation of the object through the entire program. In the constructor, the variable *this* is a pointer to a type Graph. There is no memory allocated where the object can be stored. Since we cannot know how many objects of different types will be created, dynamic allocation is used to create memory for these variables. The malloc() function call will provide a pointer of the type void to a memory space the size of Graph. The pointer is cast onto a pointer to a type Graph and then assigned to *this*.

```
/* graph constructor */

Graph* graph_(int x, int y, int background,
                    int foreground)
{
       Graph* this;

       if((this=(Graph *)malloc(sizeof(Graph)))==NULL)
           error_handler();
       this->is_visible=is_visible;
       this->show=show;
       this->hide=hide;
       this->move=move;
       this->x=x;
       this->y=y;
       this->background=background;
       this->foreground=foreground;
       this->visible=FALSE;
       return this;
}
```

The next four statements in the code above place the addresses of the class methods into the proper locations in the newly defined object. The following four statements place the argument values into the proper location in the object, and finally, the new object is marked as invisible. The pointer to this specific object is then returned to the calling program.

The object destructor is shown below. This function has as a parameter a pointer to the type Graph. The memory space for this particular object is freed by the destructor after its image is removed from the screen.

```
/* graphics point destructor */

void graph__(Graph* this)
{
       hide(this); /* hide before destroying */
       free(this);
}
```

The class definition above cannot be used for a demonstration. The essential functions hide() and show() are merely stubs. These functions are essential to the operation of the class. Let us examine inheritance first and then demonstrate the use of a Graph as well as that of its child.

Many graphics objects can be inherited from Graph. Potential graphics objects include a circle, a point, and a rectangle. The common link that connects the items is that they are all Graph items. It is entirely possible that we could have an object that has many of the attributes of Graph but is still not a Graph item. For example, consider a golf ball. A golf ball could have a location, an x and a y; it could have a foreground color against a background color, and the methods hide, show, and move are excellent choices of functions to operate on a golf ball. Also, is_visible() is a perfect method for the operation of a golf ball that might be hiding in the rough. So a golf ball would have attributes and classes exactly the same as a Graph item. However, a golf ball is not a Graph item, so a golf ball should not be created as a descendent of a Graph.

If we should look at the definition files for some practical descendent classes—Point, Circle, and Rectangle—we would see that they share common methods and attributes as well as being Graph objects. Some of the characteristics of these classes are best shown as depicted in Figure 2.1. Observe in this figure that the first nine members of each class are the same, and in fact these nine members are identical to the corresponding members of the class Graph. These classes are extensions of the class Graph, and the three classes Point, Circle, and Rectangle are each merely slight variations of the base class Graph. They each meet the "is a" requirement that allows them to inherit the characteristics of Graph. As such, the nine common members, including the nonvirtual methods is_visible() and move() from the base class, can be used by the derived classes. The virtual classes are each unique to the derived classes and must be written specifically for each derived class.

The rewritten classes to include the inheritance are shown in Figure 2.2. The base class Graph is shown above the three derived classes, and the derived classes are shown in boxes below. Each of these classes has the needed parts of any class. Note that the point class has no unique members that differ from those of the base class. The circle class has some unique members because it needs both a radius and the grow() functions that are not a part of the base class. Here a new method, *grow,* and a new attribute, *radius,* complete a circle. The rectangle class needs a new method called *resize* and two new attributes needed to define uniquely the location of a rectangle on the screen.

The members of GRAPH_CLASS are used as the basis for creation of each new class. GRAPH_CLASS is extended in each case to include new members essential to the new class. Also, each constructor prototype is altered to have an appropriate number of arguments. Let us look at the implementation files for these classes.

Observe that the elements of Point are already found in Graph. Therefore, the implementation must supply only the functions that are the virtual functions not provided in the implementation of Graph. Of course, each implementation file must contain both a constructor and a destructor. The code for the Point implementation file is as follows:

```
#include "point.h"
static void hide(Point* this)           /* hide */
{
        this->visible=FALSE;
        pen_color(this->background);
        setpixel(this->x,this->y);
}
```

```
static void show(Point* this)          /* show */
{
       this->visible=TRUE;
       pen_color(this->foreground);
       setpixel(this->x,this->y);
}


/* point constructor */

Point* point_(int x, int y, int background,
int foreground)
{
       Graph* temp=graph_(x,y,background,foreground);
       Point* this;

       if((this=(Point *)malloc(sizeof(Point)))==NULL)
              error_handler();

       memmove(this,temp,sizeof(Graph));
       graph__(temp);
       this->show=show;
       this->hide=hide;
       return this;
}

       /* graphics point destructor */

       void point__(Point* this)
       {
              hide(this); /* remove from screen before
              destroying */
              free(this);
       }
```

The implementation of circle is typical for an inherited class. If a method is unique to the inherited class, it must be redone in the implementation. If it is not different from the code in the base class, the code in the base class can be used without change in the descendent class. For example, the only methods that need to be changed in Circle are the methods hide() and show(). These methods must draw circles on the screen while the same methods in Graph merely drew a pixel on the screen. Therefore, these two methods must be rewritten for Circle. The method move() is unchanged when linked into either Graph or Circle. Therefore, it need not be repeated in Circle. The new method grow() is also included.

```
#include "circle.h"

static void hide(Circle* this)
{
      this->visible=FALSE;
      move_to(this->x,this->y);
      circle(this->radius,this->background);
}

static void show(Circle* this)
{
      this->visible=TRUE;
      move_to(this->x,this->y);
      circle(this->radius,this->foreground);
}

static void grow(Circle* this, int del_radius)
{
      (*this->hide)(this);
      this->radius+=del_radius;
      (*this->show)(this);
}
```

The constructor circle_() shows the typical approach to use of inheritance. Here, two objects are needed, one of the type Graph* and the other of the type Circle*. An instance of the type Graph is created using the constructor graph_(). This instance will have the x and y locations of the center of the circle, and on a screen with a background and foreground specified for the circle. Then the memory for the type Circle is allocated, and the data contained in the instantiation of Graph are copied onto this memory location. At that point there is no longer a need for temp, so it is destroyed by a graph__(temp) call.

```
Circle* circle_(int x, int y, int radius,
                  int background, int foreground)
{
      Graph* temp;
      Circle* this;

      temp=graph_(x,y,background,foreground);
      if((this=(Circle*) malloc(sizeof(Circle)))==NULL)
            error_handler();

      memmove(this,temp,sizeof(Graph));
      graph__(temp);

      this->hide=hide;
      this->show=show;
```

```
        this->grow=grow;
        this->radius=radius;
        return this;
}
void circle__(Circle* this)
{
        hide(this); /* hide before destroying */
        free(this);
}
```

The new methods are now placed into the new instance of the object. A pointer to this new object is returned to the calling program. The class Circle here has inherited all of the members of the class Graph. In those instances where the methods of Graph are not usable in Circle, new methods are inserted. Methods and attributes unique to Circle have been added so that Circle is a complete class by itself. It is interesting that one of the main benefits from inheritance and polymorphism in C++ will be found here. Careful use of inheritance will reduce the code size. The code in a base class that is not changed by inheritance will be used by all classes inherited from the base. Therefore, the code in move() will not be repeated in the classes inherited from Graph unless there is something unique to the class that will not allow use of the base class methods.

```
#ifndef RECTANGLE_H
#define RECTANGLE_H
#include "defines.h"
#include "graph.h"


/* elements and methods of the class graph */
#define RECTANGLE_CLASS\
            GRAPH_CLASS\
    void    (* resize)(struct rectangle*,int,int);\
    int     x1;\
            y1;

typedef struct rectangle
{
    RECTANGLE_CLASS
} Rectangle;

Rectangle* rectangle_(int,int,int,int,int,int);
void rectangle__(Rectangle*);

#endif
```

The class Rectangle remains to be implemented. The basic approach to the creation of this class is quite similar to that used above with Point and Circle. The header file is written above, and the implementation file is shown below. Note here that we have created a special function that is equivalent to a private method in C++. This function, draw_rectangle(), is used by both hide() and show(). There is no reason that this function should be called by any part of the program other than by these two methods. Therefore, this static function can be seen in the implementation file only and is hidden from the rest of the program. Of course, the only way that hide() and show() can be accessed is through the method function pointers contained within the instantiations of Rectangle objects.

```
#include "rectangl.h"
static draw_rectangle(int,int,int,int);

static void hide(Rectangle *this)
{
        this->visible=FALSE;
        pen_color(this->background);
        draw_rectangle(this->x,this->y,this->x1,this->y1);
}

static void show(Rectangle *this)
{
        this->visible=TRUE;
        pen_color(this->foreground);
        draw_rectangle(this->x,this->y,this->x1,this->y1);
}

/* x_new and y_new are the new rectangle sides */
static void resize(Rectangle *this,int x_new,int y_new)
{
        Boolean see=this->visible;

        hide(this);
        this->x1=this->x+x_new;
        this->y1=this->y+y_new;
        if(see)
                show(this);
}

static move(Rectangle *this,int x_new,y_new)
{
        int delx,dely;

        delx=x_new-this->x;
        dely=y_new-this->y;
        hide(this);
```

```
        this->x=x_new;
        this->y=y_new;
        this->x1+=delx;
        this->y1+=dely;
        show(this);
}

static draw_rectangle(int x1, int y1,int x2, int y2)
{
        move_to(x1,y1);  /* start at one corner */
        line_to(x2,y1);  /* and draw a line around */
        line_to(x2,y2);  /* the rectangle */
        line_to(x1,y2);
        line_to(x1,y1);
}
```

The constructor and destructor are shown below.

```
Rectangle* rectangle_(int x, int y, int x1, int y1,
                  int background, int foreground)
{
        Graph* temp;
        Rectangle* this;

        temp=graph_(x,y,background,foreground);
        if((this=(Rectangle*) malloc(sizeof(Rectangle)))==NULL)
              error_handler();

        memmove(this,temp,sizeof(Graph));
        graph__(temp);

        this->hide=hide;
        this->show=show;
        this->move=move;
        this->resize=resize;
        this->x1=x1;
        this->y1=y1;
        return this;
}

void rectangle__(Rectangle* this)
{
        hide(this); /* hide before destroying */
        free(this);
}
```

The following test program uses each of the objects above. Note that each of the various header files is included in this program. Within main() the variables foreground and background are given values corresponding to white and black, respectively. An instance of each of Point, Circle, and Rectangle is created. The point is at the center of the screen, which is also the center of the circle. The circle has a radius of 80° and the rectangle is placed around the circle. The rectangle, a square in this case, is made one pixel larger than the circle in each dimension. The computer is put into a graphics display mode, and these objects are then shown followed by a getch(), which will freeze the image on the screen. After a key is hit, the rectangle is moved to the right and the circle with its center point is moved to the left. Then the image is again frozen until a key is hit. After a key is hit the second time, the rectangle is resized.

```
#include <graphics.h>
#include "point.h"
#include "circle.h"
#include "rectangl.h"


main()
{
      int foreground=15,background=0;
      Point *pt=point_(320,240,background,foreground);
      Circle *cir=circle_(320,240,80,background,foreground);
      Rectangle *rect rectangle_(241,321,401,161,background,
      foreground);

      setvmode(VGA_16);
      (*pt->show)(pt);
      (*cir->show)(cir);
      (*rect->show)(rect);
      getch();
      (*rect->move)(rect,401,321);
      (*cir->move)(cir,240,240);
      (*pt->move)(pt,240,240);
      getch();
      (*rect->resize)(rect,100,-100);
      getch();
      setvmode(DEFAULTMODE);
}
```

All of the numbers in the example above seem fine, with the exception of the y value in the rectangle resize call. In that case, the new y value is –100 rather than what intuition would say should be 100. The problem here is that the location of the origin of the screen is in the upper left-hand corner rather than the lower left-hand corner as one would have with a graph. Therefore, all of the increasing y values will move toward the bottom of the screen rather than toward the top. If you want the new rectangle to have its locked corner at its lower left-hand corner as these objects assume, you must use negative numbers to move toward the top of the screen.

TOWARD BETTER OBJECT INTERFACE

There are two additional considerations that should be examined now. First, we have made no provisions for the inclusion of an in-line function, and second, there is another way for the virtual and inherited functions to be written that will allow a more uniform interface with the object methods. Both of these considerations involve the use of C macros, which is anathema to most C++ programmers. One of the most sacred considerations that will be found with C++ is the strict type checking that is always in force. On the other hand, C might seem to have relatively strict type checking, but in reality, there are areas in which the type checking is completely lax. The most prominent place where type checking falls down in C is through the macro. A **macro** is a character substitution scheme. With macros, constants can be defined, but these constants are nothing more than character strings that are substituted at the time of compilation. The type of the constant is then taken in terms of the context of its use in the program. There is no rigidly defined type for any defined constant.

Similarly, functions defined by macros are also completely untyped, so the programmer can get into trouble very easily when using macro-defined functions. As an example, consider the following macro definition for a simple function:

```
#define max(a,b) ((a)>(b)) ? (a) : (b)
```

The clear intent of this function is to determine the parameter with the largest value and to return this value to the calling program. As long as both a and b are of the same type, the function works well. The return will be of the same type as both a and b. Suppose, however, that the program sent a type int for a and a float for b. In this case, when a is larger than b, an int will be returned to the calling function. When b is greater than a, max will return a float! We cannot tell for certain the type of the return from a macro, even though the calculations that take place will be correct. The macro is rarely used in C++, but it is still a convenient device for C programming. Just be careful when using macros and remember that they can be the source of some difficult problems when you are not careful with the types that are being used for parameters to the macro functions.

Let us go back and revisit the program saved in counter2.h and counter2.c These files are listed below for convenience.

```
#ifndef COUNT_H
#define COUNT_H
```

```
#include "defines.h"

#define COUNT \
WORD count; \
void (*increment)(struct cnt *);\
WORD (*query)(struct cnt *);


typedef struct cnt
{
COUNT
}Count;

Count *count_(void);
void count__(Count *);

#endif
```

The implementation file for this class is shown below.

```
#include "counter2.h"
#include <stdlib.h>     /* needed for the memory functions */

static void increment(Count *this)
{
    this->count++;
}

static WORD query(Count *this)
{
    return this->count;
}

Count *count_(void)
{
    Count *this;

    this=(Count *)malloc(sizeof(Count));
    this->count=0;
    this->increment=increment;
    this->query=query;
    return this;
}

void count__(Count *this)
{
    free(this);
}
```

We will make a few simple changes in these files that simplify the use of the methods of the object. First, the names of the methods will be changed. Then new functions will be defined as macros that have the names of the original functions. These macros will make a function call, with the appropriate indirection included, to the proper functions. We will have the two additional macros in the header file, and the implementation file will have functions with slightly different names.

```
#ifndef COUNT_H
#define COUNT_H

#include "defines.h"

#define COUNT \
    WORD count; \
    void (*inc)(struct cnt *);\
    WORD (*que)(struct cnt *);


typedef struct cnt
{
    COUNT
}Count;

#define increment(a)   (*(a)->inc)((a))
#define query(a)       (*(a)->que)((a))

Count *count_(void);
void count__(Count *);

#endif
```

The code above is saved in counter5.h. The modified implementation file is shown below. The function names have been changed in this file, but there is no other change from the original.

```
#include "counter5.c"
#include <stdlib.h>    /* needed for the memory functions */

static void inc(Count *this)
{
    this->count++;
}

static WORD que(Count *this)
{
    return this->count;
}
```

```
Count *count_(void)
{
    Count *this;

    if((this=(Count *)malloc(sizeof(Count)))==NULL)
    error_handler();
    this->count=0;
    this->inc=inc;
    this->que=que;
    return this;
}

void count__(Count *this)
{
    free(this);
}
```

There is not much change in the routines above. However, if you will examine the following test program, you will find that all of the method calls are now simplified and are identical to those calls found in earlier routines where no indirection was needed with the method calls.

```
#include "counter5.c"
#include <stdio.h>

main()
{
    Count *a=count_();
    Count *b=count_();
    int i;

    for(i=0;i<12;i++)
    {
        increment(a);
        increment(b);
    }
    for(i=0;i<6;i++)
    {
    increment(a);
    }
    printf("a=%d and b=%d\n",query(a),query(b));
    count__(a);
    count__(b);
}
```

The significant advantage of this approach is that you can accomplish the major goal of having a completely uniform interface between the calling programs and the class, or object, methods. The funny function calls via a pointer to the function are hidden from the programmer even though they are retained through the use of a macro. The function call can have as many parameters as needed. In the example above, the parameter passed is a pointer to a specific object. If other parameters are needed, they should be included in the definition of the function found in the header file.

A word of caution. Because the functions *increment* and *query* in the class above are now macro functions, they cannot be name protected by the static qualifier. Therefore, the names of functions defined like those above must be chosen carefully to prevent multiple defined symbols in the program. An in-line function is created by the use of a macro. Whenever, you wish an in-line function, you should create a macro definition of the function. The function will be created in-line with no function call and return overhead each time that it is accessed in the program. If a function is small and is called only a few times in the program, it is probably best to make it an in-line function.

There remains one major problem with the objects created using the foregoing techniques. Each object is contained in memory. The memory needed for an object is sufficient to hold all the object attributes along with space for pointers to each of the object methods. When we move to more complicated objects, the size of the objects can grow beyond sensible bounds because of the inclusion of the method pointers in each object. An approach, shown below, can be used to reduce the size of each object. This approach uses a table that contains all the pointers to the object methods. Each instance of the object contains only a pointer to the table rather than pointers to each of the several object methods.

The method pointer table could be in the form of an array or structure. The problem with an array table is that the types of the members of an array must all be the same. In the case of a structure, the members can be of different types. Thus it is possible to have members with different types, as is really needed.

One of the disadvantages that attends the use of a method table is the increased complication of method calls. The table approach requires two levels of indirection to find a method associated with an object. Thus we have introduced a third mechanism for access to methods. Fortunately, this added complexity is all within the class code and hidden completely from the application or maintenance programmer. Another major advantage that you will find with object-oriented programming is that the code for the objects themselves can be changed without affecting the code of the program using the objects. If you begin coding with instantiable objects and the macro call to access the object methods, later you can, for example, add a method table (as shown below) to your classes without change to the remainder of the program code. Of course, the program must be recompiled to be able to use any modification. At this level of complexity, it is highly recommended that you use a macro approach to access the methods along with a method table if there is any concern about object size. Such an approach is shown in the following header file. Notice that a define statement is used to identify the contents of a structure that contains all the methods. This approach allows the extension of the method structure needed to implement inheritance similar to that found with the object attributes.

```
#ifndef COUNT_H
#define COUNT_H

#include "defines.h"

#define METHODS    \
      void (*incr)(); \
      WORD (*quer)();

typedef struct
{
      METHODS
} Methods;

#define COUNT \
    WORD count; \
    Methods *methods;

typedef struct cnt
{
    COUNT
}Count;

#define increment(a)   (*((a)->methods->incr))((a))
#define query(a)       (*((a)->methods->quer))((a))

Count *count_(void);
void count__(Count *);

#endif
```

The type of methods structures is defined as Methods, and the member name of the methods table pointer in the structure type Count is methods. If there is a specific instance of an object named obj, access to one of the methods must be by a function call such as

```
(*(obj->methods->incr))(obj);
```

Such function calls throughout a program would create great confusion among the maintenance programmers. The macro definition of a function call such as

```
#define increment(a) (*((a)->methods->incr))((a))
```

will reduce the function call above to

```
increment(obj);
```

which is easily understood by a maintenance programmer.

The implementation file is shown below. Two static items are added to the file: an instance of the structure Methods named *meth* and a single flag. In the constructor program, memory is allocated to hold the object. In this case it must be enough memory to hold an unsigned int and a pointer to the methods table. The contents of the methods table must be initialized the first time that an object is created. The flag is used to assure that the table is filled the first time only. One word of warning: Make certain that you fill the object members in proper order. For example, if you should attempt to initialize the method pointer table as is done below prior to putting the address of meth into this->methods, you will have incorrect performance when the first object is initialized.

```
#include "counter6.h"
#include <stdlib.h>    /* needed for the memory functions */

static void inc(Count *this)
{
    this->count++;
}

static WORD que(Count *this)
{
    return this->count;
}

static Methods meth;
static Boolean count_flag=FALSE;

Count *count_(void)
{
    Count *this;

    if((this=(Count *)malloc(sizeof(Count)))==NULL)
    error_handler();
    this->count=0;
    this->methods=&meth;
    if(!count_flag)
    {
          count_flag=TRUE;
          this->methods->incr=inc;
          this->methods->quer=que;
    }
    return this;
}

void count__(Count *this)
{
    free(this);
}
```

The test program in this case is identical to the one for counter5, as shown below. The result of the program is also identical.

```
#include "counter6.c"
#include <stdio.h>

main()
{
    Count *a=count_();
    Count *b=count_();
    int i;
    for(i=0;i<12;i++)
    {
        increment(a);
        increment(b);
    }
    for(i=0;i<6;i++)
    {
        increment(a);
    }
    printf("a=%d and b=%d\n",query(a),query(b));
    count__(a);
    count__(b);
}
```

We have now seen that it is possible to include pointers to all the class methods in a single table, and a pointer to this table is the only access needed to be included in each instance of objects of this class. Judicious use of macro functions will simplify the interface to the class methods so that the maintenance programmer will not be confused by overly complicated double-indirection-type operations to find the method addresses. Throughout, the maintenance programmer is assumed to be a person who will deal with the final program but will probably not have need to get into the code associated with the objects. We are creating two classes of programmers: those capable of creating classes and those capable of writing code that makes use of the objects instantiated from the classes. It is assumed that senior programmers will create classes and junior programmers will be charged with maintenance.

Note in the simple test program above that the internal workings of the class are completely hidden from the programmer. There is no need to know how increment() or count__() does its job. It is sufficient for the programmer to know that they work without bad side effects. There is also no reason to expect that over the life of the program the class methods will remain unchanged. The class programmer should be free to upgrade and improve any class method when it is needed. The only limitation placed on the class programmer is that the performance of the method, regardless of the implementation, will remain unchanged to the outside world.

IMPROVED INTERFACE WITH INHERITANCE AND VIRTUAL FUNCTIONS

Let us now apply these same ideas to inheritance. Remember that with inheritance the base class could contain some of the methods, while the derived classes would contain their own unique methods along with the virtual functions needed. A single method table cannot suffice in such a case. Probably the easiest approach here is to use a method table for each derived class. The method table in the derived classes will be filled the first time a derived class is instantiated, just as with the base class above. We will see below examples where the derived classes each have a method table identical to the method table for the base class. In instances where the derived classes need additional methods of their own, these methods will be handled by placing a pointer to the methods in the object rather than adding additional pointers to the derived class method pointer table. It is an easy matter to add additional pointers to the method table if needed, so the memory cost of the extra method pointers associated with each object can be eliminated if necessary.

Let us return to our graphics program above to be used as an example. If you examine the header file for the abstract class graph1 shown below, you will see that the only substantial change is addition of the macro method functions. These functions each employ a double indirect access to the specific function. The first pointer is to the object itself, the second is to the methods table, and the final pointer is to the individual function pointer in the table. It is this messy code that we are trying to hide through the use of macro methods. The remainder of the header file is unchanged.

```
#ifndef GRAPH_H
#define GRAPH_H
#include "defines.h"

/* elements and methods of the class graph */
#define GRAPH_METHODS \
    Boolean (* is_vis)(struct graph*);\
    void    (* sho)(struct graph*),\
            (* hid)(struct graph*),\
            (* mov)(struct graph*, int, int);

typedef struct
{
       GRAPH_METHODS
} Graph_Methods;

#define GRAPH_CLASS \
    int     x,\
            y,\
            background, \
```

```
            foreground; \
    Boolean visible; \
    Graph_Methods *methods;


typedef struct
{
    GRAPH_CLASS
} Graph;

#define show(a) (*((a)->methods->sho))((a))
#define hide(a) (*((a)->methods->hid))((a))
#define is_visible(a) (*((a)->methods->is_vis))((a))
#define move(a,b,c) (*((a)->methods->mov))((a),(b),(c))


Graph* graph_(int x0,int y0,int background,int foreground);

void graph__(Graph*);

#endif
```

We see below the implementation file for the class graph1. The methods hid() and sho() are merely stubs that will be given useful functions in the derived classes. The methods is_vis() and mov() are identical to the similar functions seen earlier. There is significant modification to the constructor. This modification is quite similar to that seen above when we developed the method tables. You should have little trouble following these changes.

```
#include "graph1.h";

static void hid(Graph* this)        /* hide */
{
}

static void sho(Graph* this)        /* show */
{
}

static Boolean is_vis(Graph* this)
{
return this->visible;
}


    /* move to a new location */
static void mov( Graph* this, int new_x, int new_y)
{
```

```
        (*this->methods->hid)(this);
        this->x=new_x;
        this->y=new_y;
        move_to(new_x,new_y);
        (*this->methods->sho)(this);
}

Graph_Methods graph_methods;
static Boolean graph_flag=FALSE;

/* graph constructor */

Graph* graph_(int x, int y, int background,
              int foreground)
{
        Graph* this;

        if((this=(Graph *)malloc(sizeof(Graph)))==NULL)
                error_handler();
        this->x=x;
        this->y=y;
        this->background=background;
        this->foreground=foreground;
        this->visible=FALSE;
        if(!graph_flag)
        {
                graph_flag=TRUE;
                this->methods=&graph_methods;
                this->methods->sho=sho;
                this->methods->hid=hid;
                this->methods->mov=mov;
                this->methods->is_vis=is_vis;
        }
        return this;
}
/* graphics point destructor */

void graph__(Graph* this)
{
        hid(this); /* hide before destroying */
        free(this);
}
```

You will find that there is no change in the point header file used in the following example from that one used to discuss inheritance. There is no needed change because the derived class has no methods of its own beyond the methods identified in the base class. In later derived classes such as circle and rectangle, the derived class has some unique methods that will require the identification of macro methods in the header file.

```
#ifndef POINT_H
#define POINT_H
#include "defines.h"
#include "graph1.h"

/* elements and methods of the class point */
#define POINT_CLASS \
            GRAPH_CLASS

typedef struct
{
    POINT_CLASS
} Point;

Point* point_(int x,int y,int background,int foreground);
void point__(Point*);

#endif
```

There are substantial changes in the implementation file for Point. The reasons that these changes are necessary are to incorporate the method table for Point. In the base class graph, note that the definition of the method table was not labeled static. It is not static because this table must be visible to each of the derived classes. Note, for example, that the methods hid() and sho() below, along with the external instance of the methods table and the flag, are all static. These names have file scope and thus cannot be seen outside the implementation file. Because the method table for Point is the same as the method table for Graph, we can use the type Graph_Methods to create a new method table to be used for Point. Inside the constructor function point_(), an instance of graph is created and this class is moved into the newly created memory space that will be the instance of Point. Also, the contents of the graph methods table are moved into the point methods table. When the first instance of Point is created, a pointer to the point methods table is moved into the location methods in the object at the same time that the virtual functions are placed in the point methods table.

```
#include "point1.h"

static void hid(Point* this)        /* hide */
{
      this->visible=FALSE;
      pen_color(this->background);
      setpixel(this->x,this->y);
}
```

```
static void sho(Graph* this)        /* show */
{
      this->visible=TRUE;
      pen_color(this->foreground);
      setpixel(this->x,this->y);
}

/* point constructor */

static Graph_Methods point_methods;
static Boolean point_flag=FALSE;
extern Graph_Methods graph_methods;

Point* point_(int x, int y, int background,
                  int foreground)
{
      Graph* temp=graph_(x,y,background,foreground);
      Point* this;

      if()this=(Point *)malloc(sizeof(Point)))==NULL)
            error_handler();

      memmove(this,temp,sizeof(Graph));
      memmove(&point_methods,&graph_methods,
                  sizeof(graph_methods));
      graph__(temp);
      if(!point_flag)
      {
            point_flag=TRUE;
            this->methods=&point_methods;
            this->methods->sho=sho;
            this->methods->hid=hid;
      }
      return this;
}

/* graphics point destructor */

void point__(Point* this)
{
      hid(this); /* remove from screen before destroying */
      free(this);
}
```

There is little difference to note about the class Circle. This header file does contain the macro method grow(a,b).

```
#ifndef CIRCLE_H
#define CIRCLE_H
#include "defines.h"
#include "graph1.h"

/* elements and methods of the class circle */
#define CIRCLE_CLASS\
              GRAPH_CLASS \
    void      (* gro)(struct circle*,int);\
    int       radius;

typedef struct circle
{
    CIRCLE_CLASS
} Circle;

#define grow(a,b) (*((a)->gro))((a),(b))

Circle *circle_(int x0,int y0,int radius,int background,
                    int foreground);

void circle__(Circle*);

#endif
```

The implementation file for Circle is shown below. The changes in this routine are all around the creation and filling of the circle methods table. You will note here that the extra function pointer to the method *gro* is included in the class instance. This method could, of course, be appended to the method table.

```
#include "circle1.h"

static void hid(Circle* this)
{
      this->visible=FALSE;
      move_to(this->x,this->y);
      circle(this->radius,this->background);
}

static void sho(Circle* this)
{
      this->visible=TRUE;
      move_to(this->x,this->y);
      circle(this->radius,this->foreground);
}

static void gro(Circle* this, int del_radius)
{
      hid(this);
```

```
        this->radius+=del_radius;
        sho(this);
}

/* Circle constructor */

static Graph_Methods circle_methods;
static Boolean circle_flag=FALSE;
extern Graph_Methods graph_methods;

Circle* circle_(int x, int y, int radius,
                int background, int foreground)
{
        Graph* temp;
        Circle* this;

        temp=graph_(x,y,background,foreground);
        if((this=(Circle*) malloc(sizeof(Circle)))==NULL)
                error_handler();

        memmove(this,temp,sizeof(Graph));
        memmove(&circle_methods,&graph_methods,sizeof(graph_meth
                ods));
        graph__(temp);
        if(!circle_flag)
        {
                circle_flag=TRUE;
                this->methods=&circle_methods;
                this->methods->hid=hid;
                this->methods->sho=sho;
        }
        this->gro=gro;
        this->radius=radius;
        return this;
}

void circle__(Circle* this)
{
        hid(this); /* hide before destroying */
        free(this);
}
```

Finally, we come to the class Rectangle. This header file contains the macro method resize(). There is no other change from the earlier version of this header.

```
#ifndef RECTANGLE_H
#define RECTANGLE_H
```

```
#include "defines.h"
#include "graph1.h"

/* elements and methods of the class graph */
#define RECTANGLE_CLASS\
             GRAPH_CLASS\
    void     (* resiz)(struct rectangle*,int,int);\
    int      x1;\
             y1;

typedef struct rectangle
{
    RECTANGLE_CLASS
} Rectangle;

#define resize(a,b,c) (*((a)->resiz))((a),(b),(c))

Rectangle* rectangle_(int x0,int y0,int x1,int y1,
                      int background,int foreground);

void rectangle__(Rectangle*);

#endif
```

The rectangle implementation file shown below has the additional code needed to create and fill the methods table.

```
#include "rectang1.h"

static draw_rectangle(int x0,int y0,int x1,int y1);

static void hid(Rectangle *this)
{
      this->visible=FALSE;
      pen_color(this->background);
      draw_rectangle(this->x,this->y,this->x1,this->y1);
}

static void sho(Rectangle *this)
{
      this->visible=TRUE;
      pen_color(this->foreground);
      draw_rectangle(this->x,this->y,this->x1,this->y1);
}

/* x_new and y_new are the new rectangle sides */
static void resiz(Rectangle *this,int x_new,int y_new)
{
      Boolean see=this->visible;
```

```
        hid(this);
        this->x1=this->x+x_new;
        this->y1=this->y+y_new;
        if(see)
              sho(this);
}

static mov(Rectangle *this,int x_new,y_new)
{
        int delx,dely;

        delx=x_new-this->x;
        dely=y_new-this->y;
        hid(this);
        this->x=x_new;
        this->y=y_new;
        this->x1+=delx;
        this->y1+=dely;
        sho(this);
}

static draw_rectangle(int x1, int y1,int x2, int y2)
{
        move_to(x1,y1);  /* start at one corner */
        line_to(x2,y1);  /* and draw a line around */
        line_to(x2,y2);  /* the rectangle */
        line_to(x1,y2);
        line_to(x1,y1);
}

/* the Rectangle class constructor */

static Graph_Methods rectangle_methods;
static Boolean rectangle_flag=FALSE;
extern Graph_Methods graph_methods;

Rectangle* rectangle_(int x, int y, int x1, int y1,
                  int background, int foreground)
{
        Graph* temp;
        Rectangle* this;

        temp=graph_(x,y,background,foreground);
        if((this=(Rectangle*) malloc(sizeof(Rectangle)))==NULL)
              error_handler();

        memmove(this,temp,sizeof(Graph));
        memmove(&rectangle_methods,&graph_methods,
```

```
                                    sizeof(graph_methods));
        graph__(temp);

        if(!rectangle_flag)
        {
                rectangle_flag=TRUE;
                this->methods=&rectangle_methods;
                this->methods->hid=hid;
                this->methods->sho=sho;
                this->methods->mov=mov;
        }
        this->resiz=resiz;
        this->x1=x1;
        this->y1=y1;
        return this;
}

void rectangle__(Rectangle* this)
{
        hid(this); /* hide before destroying */
        free(this);
}
```

The test program shown below exercises each of the several methods derived in a single program. The important items to note here is that there is no interaction between the several objects even though they are all derived from a common base class.

```
#include <graphics.h>
#include "point1.h"
#include "circle1.h"
#include "rectang1.h"


main()
{
       int foreground=15,background=0;
       Point *pt=point_(320,240,background,foreground);
       Circle *cir=circle_(320,240,80,background,foreground);
       Rectangle *rect=rectangle_(241,321,401,161,
                                  background,foreground);

       setvmode(VGA_16); /* turn on the graphics mode */
       show(pt);           /* show the graphics items */
       show(cir);
       show(rect);
       getch();            /* wait for a keystroke */
```

```
        move(rect,401,321); /* move rectangle to new location */
        getch();
        move(cir,238,240); /* now the circle */
        getch();
        move(pt,238,240);   /* and finally the point */
        getch();
        resize(rect,100,-100);/* resize the rectangle and circle */
        grow(cir,100);
        getch();            /* wait for keystroke and */
        setvmode(DEFAULTMODE);/* shut down */
}
```

SUMMARY

In this chapter we have seen that the C language supports many of the basic concepts of object-oriented programming. The important concepts of inheritance and polymorphism can be implemented exactly. It is not possible to hide attributes of a class from the remainder of a C program. It is possible to hide the method names by means of the static modifier for the various methods. Therefore, when the program needs inheritance and polymorphism, all the methods can be attached to the class and they cannot be used with any other portion of the program.

Several classes were developed to show how they are implemented in C. These classes were all based on a counter each of which contained a new concept of OOP in C. To show the potential of both code reduction and reuse of base classes, a series of graphic classes were defined. These simple classes provide the ability to draw a point, a circle, or a rectangle on the screen. These several different graphic classes were all derived from a basic class that had all the characteristics of an abstract class. The base class was never intended to be instantiated: It is used as a class from which other useful classes will be inherited. It was shown that some methods of the base class could be used in descendant classes with no modification. Other methods needed to be class specific. Polymorphism, virtual functions, and inheritance were all demonstrated with this set of classes.

Two sections of this chapter were devoted to techniques that can be employed to simplify program interface with objects that have been written in C. Most of these ideas employ C macros. The person doing function or method naming must use care to avoid multiple definitions of functions. Also, there is no type checking on a macro function call. Therefore, the programmer must be cautious when using these functions. An attempt to create smaller objects necessitated multiple indirection to access object methods. This level of indirection would put a serious burden on any programmer not experienced with this type of programming. Again, the use of C macros afforded an approach that helped simplify the use of these objects.

In the next chapter we look at the development of several classes in C. These classes have specific applications in writing code for microcontrollers.

3

SOME USEFUL CLASSES

One fact discourages many experienced programmers of microcontrollers when they examine object-oriented programming. Most texts and articles on OOP are directed toward data structures that are converted to objects. Linked lists, tree structures, containers, even complex arithmetic are data structure items that have little use in the world of the microcontroller. Unfortunately, OOP can have a great impact on the design and programming of these embedded controllers, and most programmers never allow these advantages to be employed in their programs. In these cases, the class probably best represents a peripheral or perhaps a control function. It should be the goal of the programmer to provide a program that is clean, reusable, easy to understand and maintain and meets the need of the program specification. We must consider the good and bad of OOP and other techniques when writing our code and then decide the programming approach that best suits each application. In this chapter we look at several potential classes that can be used with microcontrollers. Most of these items will be used either to interface with on-board peripherals or to provide exclusive access to a peripheral from each of several tasks running in the machine.

Several tasks? As we work through the remainder of this book, the concept of multiple tasks will be explored and developed. To begin, let us simply admit that a single controller can process several independent programs simultaneously or at least appear to execute various programs at the same time. There will be no attempt here to develop a complete multitasking operating system. However, we shall use multiple tasks that must work cooperatively to accomplish the goal of the program. Therefore, some concepts that belong to multitasking operating systems will show up in our programs. As an aside, if the program being developed requires many of the features found in a standard multitasking operating system, it is probably the best choice to purchase one of the several available operating systems to use on the machine. These programs are complicated, large, and very specialized and have been developed by specialists with vast experience in the field. It makes little sense to redevelop all of this code when it has been done for you. To begin with, though, let us look at some features that will be needed by the basic system and see how these features can be used as classes from which we can create useful objects.

In Chapter 2 we saw how a class can be derived that will support inheritance and virtual functions. There is a cost to our making these features available to the class. The earilier version, which allowed several instantiations of each object, had only the attributes contained within the class structure. The more general class had to contain not only all the class attributes, but each object contained pointers to the methods pertaining to the class. When instances of objects are created, memory space for the object location is taken from the program heap. The heap is an undedicated block of RAM accessible by the program. Where there is an operating system, the allocation of heap space is made by the operating system, not the program. Every instantiation of an object requires RAM, and RAM is usually a limited resource on any microcontroller. Therefore, when using objects, the programmer will usually attempt to minimize the RAM use.

On the other hand, the objects that use the least RAM can provide neither inheritance nor virtual functions. Another important feature is lost. Recall that in the later implementations of our class methods it was possible to make the methods static, thus limiting them to file scope. The method names could be used elsewhere in the programs with no danger of multiple defined function names at link time. The latter problem can be overcome easily by using method names that are unlikely to be found elsewhere in any program. The class name should be a part of the name of any method attached to the class.

SEMAPHORE

A class that is very useful is the **semaphore,** a flag or token that can be made a part of any resource. When a process or task needs exclusive access to a resource, it must attach the resource semaphore before access to the resource is permitted. The semaphore is then assigned to the resource. As long as the resource is attached to the initial process, no other process can access the resource. When finished with the resource, the semaphore is released and another process can use the resource.

Listed below is a header file for a semaphore. The class structure contains only one member, sem. There are four methods. Each method has the word *semaphore* in its name. There should be little danger of multiple definitions with these names. At this time there is no intent to use semaphore as a base class. Therefore, the use of global functions for the semaphore methods is indicated. This approach will use the least memory space for each instance of a semaphore. The function calls will all be direct to the functions rather than through pointers contained in the object. Therefore, the actual code will be simpler and smaller than would be obtained if we had used the more complicated form of the class.

```
#ifndef SEMAPHORE_H
#define SEMAPHORE_H

#include "defines.h"

typedef struct semaphor
{
    Boolean sem;
}Semaphore;

Boolean attach_semaphore(Semaphore *);
void release_semaphore(struct semaphor *);
Boolean semaphore_status(struct semaphor*);
void wait_for_semaphore(struct semaphor*);

Semaphore* semaphore_(void);
void semaphore__(Semaphore *);
#endif
```

The implementation file is shown below. The first method listed is attach_semaphore( ). There are a couple of pieces of business that must be taken care of in this method, which has no counterpart in the language C or C++. Therefore, we will use assembly language inserts in the C program. The first line of code is actually two assembly instructions. The first pushes the content of the condition code register on the stack for later access. It then performs the logical OR of the condition code register contents with a value 0x00e0. Those familiar with the M68HC16 will recognize that this operation has disabled the interrupts of the microcontroller. This approach avoids a potential problem that could allow two processes attached to the same semaphore in error.

```
#include "semaphor.h"

Boolean attach_semaphore(Semaphore *s)
{
    _asm("pshm ccr\norp #00e0H\n"); /*disable the interrupts */
    if(s->sem==FALSE)
    {
        s->sem=TRUE;
        _asm("pulm ccr\n"); /* enanble interrupts */
        return TRUE;
    }
    else
    {
```

```
            _asm("pulm ccr\n"); /* enanble interrupts */
            return FALSE;
        }
}

void release_semaphore(Semaphore *s)
{
    s->sem=FALSE;
}

Boolean semaphore_status(Semaphore *s)
{
    return s->sem;
}

void wait_for_semaphore(Semaphore *s)
{
    while(semaphore_status(s));
    attach_semaphore(s);
}

Semaphore *semaphore_(void)
{
    Semaphore *this

    if(!(this=(Semaphore*)malloc(sizeof(Semaphore))))
            error_handler();
    this->sem=FALSE; /* default is unattached */
    return this;
}

void semaphore__(Semaphore *this)
{
    free( this);
}
```

After the interrupts are disabled, the content of s->sem is examined, and if it is FALSE it is set to TRUE. It is at this point in the code that a problem could have occurred. Suppose that the program is executing the line of code

```
if(s->sem==FALSE)
```

The compiled version of this code is shown below. The two instructions on lines 18 and 19 load the contents of s->sem into the d register and the conditional branch is then taken, depending on the value of s->sem. Assume that it is FALSE. Suppose that during the execution of the code in line 19, an interrupt would occur. Further suppose that as a result of that interrupt, another process is launched and it needs the use of the resource protected by the semaphore being attached in the code being examined. The second process would access s->sem and find it to be FALSE because the first process had not yet marked the semaphore as TRUE. The second process would then claim the semaphore and the resource as its own and proceed. As time passes and program executes, the first process would eventually regain control of the program and would start execution where it left off. At that point, process 1 would discover that s->sem is FALSE, the value saved just prior to the interrupt, and would claim the semaphore as its own and proceed forward to disaster because two processes would each have exclusive access to the same resource.

```
17                   ;    6        if(s->sem==FALSE)
18    000A  CD02           ldy     OFST+2,x
19    000C  9500           ldd     0,y
20    000E  B606           bne     L1
```

The line of code that disables all the system interrupts will prevent the simultaneous access of more than one process to an exclusive resource. The interrupts are disabled while lines 18 and 19 above are executed, so the problem described above cannot happen. Immediately following the test and set of the semaphore, the interrupts are enabled so that normal processing can continue.

The remainder of the semaphore methods are straightforward. The semaphore is available whenever s->sem is FALSE. release_semaphore( ) simply sets s->sem to FALSE so that the semaphore can be made available to another process. The method semaphore_status( ) returns the Boolean value of s->sem. Finally, wait_for_semaphore( ) holds the calling process in the wait_for_semaphore( ) method until the semaphore becomes available. When the semaphore becomes available, it is given to the waiting process immediately and control is returned to that process. The constructor allocates memory space for the semaphore and sets its value to FALSE. The destructor destroys the semaphore.

There are other types of semaphores called counting sempahores, which can be implemented readily by the means described above. We will use the simple semaphore described above in several instances later in the book. The semaphore will be used whenever it is necessary to grant exclusive access of a resource to one of several competing processes, each of which requires the resource.

LINKED LIST

Many object-oriented-programming texts stress creation of objects that are in reality data structures. One seen often is the code associated with a list of some sort. Lists, queues, stacks, singly linked list, doubly linked list, circular lists, and so on, are all derivatives of common list operations. These lists are easily implemented as classes and lend themselves to object-oriented programming.

We start with a very practical list operation. This class will be a doubly linked list and will make use of some advanced programming techniques to simplify the code being generated. Such a list will contain three separate classes. The first is a class that when instantiated will be an object to be stored in the list. The first class is called an object. The second class implements a simple node that contains a pointer to the object being stored and two pointers needed to implement the links. This class is named link. Finally, the linklist class contains the collections of links and the code necessary to add, delete, and exercise the objects linked together in the linked list.

Object Class

It is important that flexibility be maintained when creating different types of classes. It is possible, for example, that one could specify in some detail the type of object that is to be stored in our linked list. Such an approach would lock the linked list into the use of the specified object only, and modifications of the content of the list would force serious reprogramming. Such an approach is quite inflexible and should be avoided whenever possible.

The single most effective mechanism for maintaining flexibility in the program is to use pointers to objects that are being used in all outside objects rather than the objects themselves. A pointer is simply a single entry in an object, while an object could be many bytes of code. Therefore, additional instantiations of the object will be smaller because the object need not contain a reproduction of the object, but rather, a pointer to it is sufficient. You will find pointers used extensively in the following sections.

The base object is a thing to be put into the list. That object can be anything, and we will see instances later where the base object can be a delay in time or perhaps a representation of a task that must execute sometime. It is not necessary that the objects stored on the list be of the same type. When all the objects are of the same type, there will probably be a common operation that each object will require. These common operations should be methods for the base object. Any attempt to associate the common operations with the link or the linklist objects complicates the code and makes it extremely difficult to sort out errors.

For this example we are going to create a link list of objects that merely create a delay. At the end of the specified delay, the computer bell operation will be executed. Therefore, you can hear how the program is progressing. Such an object needs one attribute, the amount of time for the delay, and one method that will cause the delay to be executed. The following header file defines such an object. The attribute is named *count*, and the method is named *exercise*. Note that the method is defined in the structure content definition statement as a pointer to a function.

```
#ifndef OBJECT_H
#define OBJECT_H
```

```
#include "defines.h"

#define OBJECT \
      void (*exercise)(struct object*);\
      long count;

typedef struct object
{
      OBJECT
} Object;

Object *object_(long count);
void object__(Object *);

#endif
```

The new type Object is defined as a struct object. Function prototypes of both the object constructor and destructor are also included in the header file. The implementation file follows. Note that the method exercise() is defined as a static function so that visibility to the function and the name exercise is limited to the implementation file. The operation contained in the exercise function is merely to execute the while loop count times to cause a delay in the program. Then a bell signal is sent out from the computer.

```
#include "object.h"

static void exercise(Object *this)
{
    long i=this->count;
    while(i–) /* kill some time */
        ;
    putch(0x07); /* send out a signal */
}

Object *object_(long count)
{
    Object *this=(Object *)malloc(sizeof(Object));

    this->count=count;
    this->exercise=exercise;
    return this;
}

void object__(Object *this)
{
    free(this);
}
```

The constructor first allocates a memory space to hold the object and then the parameter count is placed in the object followed by the placement of a pointer to the static function exercise in the proper location in the object. Finally, the destructor merely deallocates the memory that was allocated for the object.

Link Class

The link header file link.h is shown below. This file includes a reference to the object header file along with the defines header file shown in Chapter 2. The structure body definition statement contains three attributes that are each pointers to other objects. The first is a pointer to the object class associated with this particular link. The remainder of the pointers are to the previous and next links in the list. There is no use for these link pointers in this class. Use for these pointers is reserved for the linklist class that follows. The remainder of this header file is standard and follows the approach always used to include prototypes for the constructor and destructor methods.

```
#ifndef LINK_H
#define LINK_H

#include "defines.h"
#include "object.h"

#define LINK_CLASS \
          struct object *current_object; \
          struct link *previous_link; \
          struct link *next_link;

typedef struct link
{
      LINK_CLASS
} Link;

Link * link_(void *object);
void link__(struct link *);

#endif
```

The link implementation file contains the code for the link constructor and destructor. The constructor allocates memory for the link object and places the object pointer that is passed in as a parameter into the location current_object. Both previous_link and next_link are assigned a value NULL. The pointer to the object, *this*, is returned to the calling program. Finally, the destructor merely frees the memory allocated for a specific object.

```
#include "link.h"

Link* link_(Object *obj)
{
    Link *this;

    this=(Link *)malloc(sizeof(Link));
    this->current_object=obj;
    this->previous_link=NULL;
    this->next_link=NULL;
    return this;
}

void link__(Link *this)
{
    free(this);
}
```

Linklist Class

Linklist is an interesting class. It works by manipulating the values contained in previous_link and next_link in the several link objects stored in the list. The link list must be started by entering a NULL object into the list. A NULL object is what you will get if you exercise object_(NULL), which is the object constructor with a NULL parameter. This object will have a NULL pointer to each of its three attributes. When a link is added, in this case, it will be placed at the head or beginning of the list. The NULL object will always be found at the end or tail of the list, and the list exists as long as this NULL object exists. The way that the list is destroyed is to delete all the list objects along with the NULL object that deliniates the end of the list. Then the linked list can be deleted. Conversely, the linked list object is created by creating a linked list, a NULL object, a NULL link, adding the NULL link to the linked list, and then adding objects needed to the list.

The class definition contains only one entry, the attribute that is a pointer to the void type head. This parameter points to the beginning of the linked list. It is possible to complete a linked list without this attribute, but then it is a requirement that the program using the linked list keep track of the beginning of the list, which will change as links or nodes are added to or removed from the list.

Three class methods are needed for the linklist class. The first method is called walk_list. This method is given a parameter that is a pointer to the linked list. It will execute the method exercise() for every object stored in the list. The method add_link() places the new method at the beginning of the list, and delete_link will search the list for the specified old_link and remove this link from the list.

```
#ifndef LINKLIST_H
#define LINKLIST_H
```

```
#include "defines.h"
#include "object.h"
#include "link.h"

#define LINK_LIST void *head;

typedef struct
{
      LINK_LIST
}     Link_list;

Link_list *link_list_(void);
void link_list__(Link_list *);
void walk_list(Link_list *list);
int add_link(Link_list *list,Link *new_link);
int delete_link(Link_list *list, Link *old_link);

#endif
```

When the program enters the method add_link(), the value list is a pointer to the link list. The new link will be placed at the head of the list. Figure 3.1 shows a layout of a link list that contains two objects with a proper terminating null link at its end. Each link object contains three pointers: object, next_link, and previous_link. When the list is created, a NULL link with all three attributes equal to a NULL is added to the list. As additional links are added, the previous_link pointer NULL link is pointed to the newly added link. The next_link pointer in the new object is pointed to the NULL link. The previous_link pointer in the new link will be unaltered from the NULL value assigned to it when it was created. Siimilarly, the next_link pointer of the NULL link will point to a NULL, as it always will. Additional links can be added merely by changing the contents of the next_link and previous_link pointers.

A new link is added to a linked list easily. The contents of the previous_link of the head of the list is set to the address of the new link. The attribute next_link of

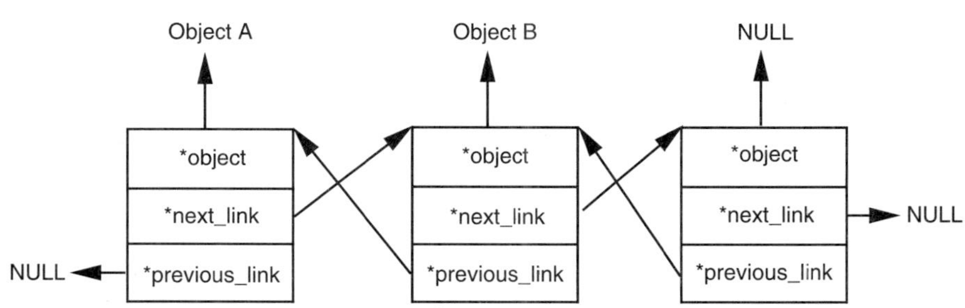

Figure 3.1 Complete Link List

the new link is set the address of the old list head. These operations are shown in Figure 3.2.

The code required to add a new link to the head of the list is shown below. This code merely executes the ideas listed above. There must be a special treatment to handle the addition of a link when the list is newly created. The first entry must be a NULL link. A test is completed when there are no entries in the list, to assure that the first entry is a NULL link. Then a functioning link can be added at the head of the list. The parameter head found in the object list is a pointer to the first link in the list. This method will return a TRUE if it executes with no error and a FALSE otherwise.

```
int add_link(Link_list *list,Link *new_link)
{
        Link *start;

        start=list->head;
        if(start==NULL) /* got an empty list */
        {
                if(new_link->next_link !=NULL)
                        return FALSE;/* got an error—no NULL link for
the end */
                else
                {
                        list->head =new_link;
                        return TRUE;
                }
        }
        else
        {
                new_link->next_link=start;
                start->previous_link=new_link;
                list->head=new_link;
                return TRUE;
        }
}
```

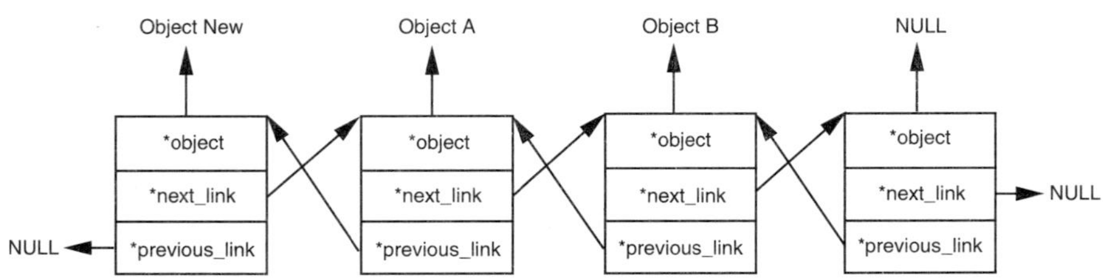

Figure 3.2 Result of Adding a New Link to the List

Removal of a link from a list involves adjustment of pointers in the two links adjacent to the link being deleted. The value in the next_link of the link being removed is moved into the next_link pointer of the preceding link. Also, the value of the previous_link in the removed link is placed in the previous_link of the link following the one being removed. At that time, the destructor for the link should be executed to free the allocated memory for later use. Note that the object pointed to by the link is not deleted by this operation. It is necessary to remove the object with code in the program that created the object in the first place (see Figure 3.3).

The code that implements removal of an arbitrary link from the list is shown below. If the first link is being removed, it is merely necessary to make the previous_link of the second link equal to a NULL. This operation does not work out so nicely when working with other links, so removal of the first link is handled specially. The first link is to be removed whenever the old_link, the link to be removed, equals the list->head, which is the address of the first link. Upon completion of this business, the first link is destroyed by a call to link__(old_link).

```
int delete_link(Link_list *list, Link *old_link)
{
       Link *start;

       start=list->head;
       if(start==old_link) /* first list entry */
       {
         start->next_link->previous_link=NULL;
              list->head=start->next_link;
       }
     else
     {
         while(start != old_link && start->next_link!=NULL)
         {
                    if(start->next_link==NULL) /* link not in list
                    */
                           return FALSE;
                    else
                    start=start->next_link;
```

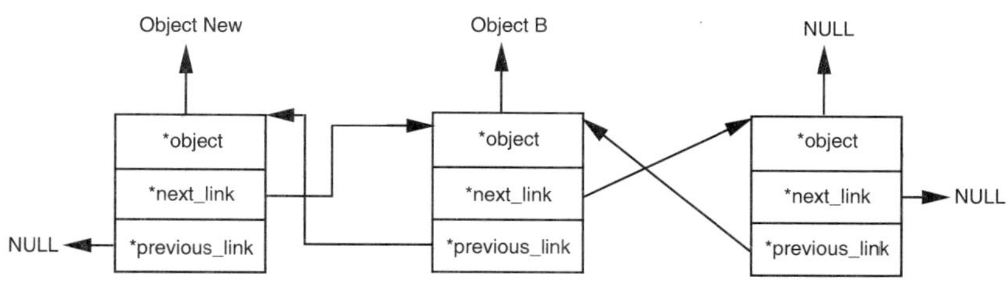

Figure 3.3 Removing a Link from a List

```
        }
        start->previous_link->next_link=start->next_link;
        start->next_link->previous_link=start->previous_link;
    }
    link__(old_link);                    /* destroy the old link */
    return TRUE;
}
```

Otherwise, the value of old_link is compared with the pointers to the list objects in the link list until a match is found. When the match is attained, pointers in next_link and previous_link of the adjacent links are altered to bypass the link to be removed. Then old_link is destroyed by the destructor function link__(old_link). An error condition occurs when there is no matching link to be found in the list. In such a case, a FALSE is returned from this method. When there is no error, TRUE is returned.

The final concern with the linked list at this time is the routine walk_list(). In some applications to which a linked list might be applied, it is desirable to execute some function for each entry in the list. The method walk_list() does exactly this operation. When walk_list() is executed, the function exercise() found with object will be executed for each object contained in the list. We will see applications of this type of operation later in the text. Some care should be exercised when attempting to design an operation like a walk_list(). One of the most common errors that will occur when designing this type of class is to place an operation that belongs in the class object here in the linklist class. For example, the code shown below contains the necessary operations to select the proper object link from the link list and then execute the specific method associated with the object. Since the program has a pointer to the current object, one might be tempted to place the code executed in the method exercise() right here in the linklist object. With the pointer to the current object, all methods and attributes of the current object are available to the linklist program.

Such an approach would be a mistake. The way that the classes are laid out here with exercise a method of the class object provides generality that would be lost with the approach above. The thought here is that exercise is a part of the class object, it works on object attributes, it is unique to the class object, and it will probably change with different classes whose objects might be stored in the linked list. Therefore, to place any object specific code within the boundaries of the linked list program would limit use of the linked list object to the specific object type that it was written for, and it would be completely nongeneral.

In the code shown below, it is assumed that a linklist exists. The program is cycled through each link and the specific method exercise() is executed for each object on the list. The method parameter is the value stored in the current object. It is assumed here that the required method parameter is a pointer to the current parameter. The execution of the walk is terminated when the next_link pointer contains a NULL.

```
void walk_list(Link_list *list)
{
```

```
    Link *start;

    start=list->head;
    while(start->next_link != NULL)
    {
        (*start->current_object->exercise)(start->current_ob-
        ject);
        start=start->next_link;
    }
}
```

With the exception of the constructor and the destructor, we have completed the discussion of the code for the linklist implementation file. The code for the parts of this file have been presented piecemeal above. The entire program, including the constructor and destructor, is presented below.

```
#include "linklist.h"

/*  This routine receives a list pointer and a pointer to a new
    link that is to be added to the list.  The new link will be
    placed at the head of the linked list.  If the list is empty
    and there is no NULL link to start the list, there is an
    error and the function returns FALSE.  */

int add_link(Link_list *list,Link *new_link)
{
      Link *start;

      start=list->head;
      if(start==NULL) /* got an empty list */
      {
            if(new_link->next_link !=NULL)
                  return FALSE; /* got an error—no NULL link for
                  the end */
            else
            {
                  list->head =new_link;
                  return TRUE;
            }
      }
      else
      {
      new_link->next_link=start;
      start->previous_link=new_link;
            list->head=new_link;
            return TRUE;
      }
```

```
}
/*  This routine removes a link.  The linked list is searched
    from start to the end.  When the link old_link is found, it
    is removed from the list and then the link destructor is exe-
    cuted.  If the link is not found on the list, a FALSE is re-
    turned to the calling function. Otherwise, the function re-
    turns a TRUE.  */

int delete_link(Link_list *list, Link *old_link)
{
      Link *start;

      start=list->head;
      if(start==old_link) /* first list entry */
      {
       start->next_link->previous_link=NULL;
           list->head=start->next_link;
      }
      else
      {
         while(start != old_link && start->next_link!=NULL)
         {
                 if(start->next_link==NULL) /* link not in list
                 */
                        return FALSE;
                 else
                 start=start->next_link;
            }
         start->previous_link->next_link=start->next_link;
         start->next_link->previous_link=start->previous_link;
      }
      link__(old_link); /* destroy the old link */
      return TRUE;
}

void walk_list(Link_list *list)
{
      Link *start;

      start=list->head;
    while(start->next_link != NULL)
    {
        (*start->current_object->exercise)(start->current_ob-
        ject);
        start=start->next_link;
    }
}
```

```
/* The constructor */

Link_list *link_list_(void)
{

        Link_list *this;

        this=(Link_list *)malloc(sizeof(Link_list));
        this->head=NULL; /* start with empty list */
        return this;
}

void link_list__(Link_list *this)
{
        free(this);
}
```

The constructor and destructor for the linked list are simple. link_list_() shown above merely allocates space to hold the member of a linked list and places a NULL pointer in the head attribute. There are no other attributes or internal member functions for this method. The destructor frees the memory allocated for this list.

This linked list program is a primitive list that will probably need change. Among the changes that might be desirable is that of adding some attributes to the class. What changes would we need? The list as it is constructed here can be a stack or a last-in first-out operation. Here, new links are added to the head of the list, and links are removed from the head of the list. There are other operations that might be desirable. A queue, or a first-in first-out operation, would require that new links be added to the head of the list and links removed from the list would come from the end or the tail of the list. Our linked list can be either a stack or a queue, but there is no really good code to find the tail of the list. A potential attribute of a linked list might contain a pointer to the end of the list. Yet another attribute might be the length, the number of links, of the list. These additional attributes would make finding the tail easy, so that a queue would be more easily implemented. More of these ideas will be explored as they are needed.

A simple example will test the performance of the linked list. The code shown below creates a linked list with five entries. Each link entry contains an object with a different value for count. The link is walked. As the routine exercise() is executed for each value of count and the computer signal is actuated, you can measure the time required to execute the count in each instance.

Five objects are created: no1, no2, ..., no5. Also, six links are created. They are bel1, bel2, ..., bel5, and nil. The first five links will receive the corresponding objects, and the final link, nil, will be the NULL link that terminates the list. The objects are instantiated with different values of count. The links are created. The NULL link nil is constructed with a NULL parameter. The remainder of the links are created with objects as parameters. The linked list is then created by adding the links to the list with add_link() commands. After this business is completed, each value of count, extracted from the link list, is printed on the screen. The list is then walked with walk_link(). With the parameters used and the computer on which this program was tested, a count of 5,000,000 will yield about a 7-second delay. Therefore, the difference in delays is easily sensed. After completion of the walk_list() operation, the links bel5 and bel3 are removed from the list. After their corresponding objects are destroyed, the values of count are again printed out. walk_list() is again executed for the list, and you, the operator, can accuractly sense that the links and their corresponding objects have been removed from the list.

```
#include <stdio.h>
#include "object.h"
#include "link.h"
#include "linklist.h"


main()
{
    Link *bel1,*bel2,*bel3,*bel4,*bel5,*nil;
    Object *no1,*no2,*no3,*no4,*no5;
    Link_list *list=link_list_();
    Link *start;
    int i;


    no1=object_(1000000);     /* create the objects */
    no2=object_(2000000);
    no3=object_(3000000);
    no4=object_(4000000);
    no5=object_(5000000);


    nil=link_(NULL);          /* create the links */
    bel1=link_(no1);
    bel2=link_(no2);
    bel3=link_(no3);
    bel4=link_(no4);
    bel5=link_(no5);


    add_link(list,nil);     /* link the links into a linked list */
    add_link(list,bel1);
    add_link(list,bel2);
    add_link(list,bel3);
    add_link(list,bel4);
    add_link(list,bel5);
```

```
    printf("got here 1\n"); /* do some tests */
    start=list->head;
    for(i=0;i<5;i++)
    {
        printf("%ld\n",start->current_object->count);
        start=start->next_link;
    }
    walk_list(list);


    delete_link(list,bel5); /* delete a couple of links */
    delete_link(list,bel3); /* and repeat the tests */
    object__(no3);
    object__(no5);
    printf("got here 2\n");
    start=list->head;
    for(i=0;i<3;i++)
    {
        printf("%ld\n",start->current_object->count);
        start=start->next_link;
    }
    walk_list(list);
}
```

A note of caution. It may seem silly to delete the object in the code above. When the program is completed, all of the objects created by the program are destroyed anyway. Therefore, there is really never a need to execute a destructor in a program like the one above. True! However, as your programs become more complicated, and when you are working within the limited RAM constraints of a microcontroller, the occasional neglect of execution of the destructor can eventually lead to RAM filled completely with unneeded objects. When this happens, the program will crash on any attempt to create a new object. In Chapter 2 we began to test for the successful allocation of memory each time a new object was instantiated. That practice is absolutely required for all microcontroller code: perhaps not so important on a desktop machine that has essentially infinite memory for the programs that we are executing. If your code will ever be used on a microcontroller, make certain that each malloc() is tested to determine if a proper allocation was completed. Otherwise, the program must enter some type of error recovery routine. Also, make certain that you destroy any object when it goes out of scope. Such a habit will keep the maximum amount of RAM available to the program at all times.

You might note that the test program above was written to run on a desktop computer. All of the code, with the exception of the test program, has also been compiled to run on an M68HC16, and this code executes properly. You might note that there is no change needed when moving the linklist program from your PC to a microcontroller.

LOOK-UP TABLE

In many instances, some sort of a nonlinear transfer function is used to operate on input data to generate a desirable transformation of the data. This transform can be in the form of an equation, a limiting operation, a rounding operation, or even an empirical transform that depends on measured data. Sometimes the work required to execute this transform is minimal, but if a transform consists of a high-order equation, it might require significant computer time to calculate the output value. One approach that will allow the approximation of an equation or empirical data is the look-up table. With a look-up table, a series of samples over the range of the input and their corresponding outputs are either calculated or measured. These inputs and outputs are placed in a table, and the transformation is calculated by finding the nearest point to the input data and then interpolating between the adjacent points in the table to provide better resolution than the basic table represents. The interpolation is usually a linear interpolation, so the calculation is simple. Usually, four additions or subtractions, one multiplication, and one division are needed to execute the interpolation. We shall also see a different way to generate the look-up table that will simplify the interpolation calculation to two additions and one multiplication for each interpolation. Such a look-up table is a good example of an object application that can have significant use in embedded systems.

When dealing with control systems or other embedded applications, most data inputs are communicated to the computer through either serial inputs or other approaches, such as analog-to-digital converters. Most of the time the data format found for these inputs is eight-bit unsigned data. In other words, the range of the input data is from 0 to 255 in steps of 1. In such cases, it is probably wise simply to use an unsigned char to contain the data values. It is not expected that the required resolution of the interpolated data should be finer than 1, and the output data range should not seriously exceed the input range.

A header file for a look-up table object is shown below. The look-up table itself must be defined in some manner in this header. The approach chosen here is to build the table of a series on *n* two-BYTE entries. With this approach, the table can be created in either RAM or ROM, and a pointer to the beginning of the table will be passed to the object when it is created. Also, the length of the table will be passed. This approach allows complete flexibility because the size of the table is in no way limited by the class construction. It is also important because the table can be placed in ROM or some type of programmable ROM, where it will usually be found in an embedded application. To simplify the association of the two-BYTE entry idea, a new type named Entry is created. This type contains two BYTEs, an x and a y value. (Recall that the name BYTE is defined in the header file as a type unsigned char.) The look-up class definition statement needs only two entries, the number of entries in the table and a pointer to the first two-BYTE pair in the table. The new type Look_up is defined by the next struct statement.

```
#ifndef LUTOBJ_H
#define LUTOBJ_H
```

```
#include "defines.h"

/* table used below is a pointer to an array of the type Entry.
   The number of entries in the array must be equal to x_length.
   Each entry contains two values which are of the type BYTE */

typedef struct
{
   BYTE x,y;
}Entry;

#define LOOK_UP_CLASS \
            int x_length; \
            Entry *table; \

typedef struct LUT
{
            LOOK_UP_CLASS
} Look_up;

Look_up *look_up_(int x_length, Entry *table);
void look_up__(Look_up * this);
BYTE get_value(struct LUT *this, BYTE value);
BYTE interpolate(BYTE value,BYTE x0,BYTE y0,BYTE x1,BYTE y1);

#endif
```

There are three method prototypes associated with this class. The constructor and destructor are the usual form. The method get_value() is the only method that will be needed for the class. Interpolate is an internal function that does not necessarily need to be defined to the outside world. If, however, there are more than one type of look-up table to be employed, for example, a three-dimensional rather than a two-dimensional table such as we are developing here, the interpolation routine could be used elsewhere. Therefore, the interpolate() routine is not hidden from the remainder of the program. The routine interpolate has five parameters. The parameter value above is the input value for which the output is to be calculated. The remainder of the parameters are two adjacent points in the look-up table. The parameter value must lie between x0 and x1. The interpolation routine does not test for this input range. The interpolation routine returns a type BYTE to the calling program.

The method get_value() receives a pointer to the look-up table object along with the input value to be transformed. It returns the interpolated value from the table.

```
#include "lutobj.h"
#include <stdlib.h>

BYTE get_value(Look_up *this, BYTE value)
{
```

```
    int i=0;
    while(this->table[i].x<=value)
        i++;
    --i;                    /* the search has gone too far */
    if(this->table[i].x==value)
        return this->table[i].y;
    else
        return interpolate(value,
                           this->table[i].x,
                           this->table[i].y,
                           this->table[i+1].x,
                           this->table[i+1].y);
}

/* the constructor's name ends with a single underscore _ */

Look_up *look_up_(int x_length, Entry *table)
{
    Look_up *this;
    if(!(this=(Look_up*)malloc(sizeof(Look_up))))
        error_handler();
    this->x_length=x_length;
    this->table=table;
    return this;
}

/* the destructor's name ends with a double underscore __ */

void look_up__(Look_up *this)
{
    free(this);
}

/* interpolate() function can be used by other look-up tables,
   such as a three-dimensional look-up.  This function works only
   for unsigned numbers, both inputs and outputs.  It is assumed
   that x progresses monotonically, but y need not. */

BYTE interpolate(BYTE value,BYTE x0,BYTE y0,BYTE x1,BYTE y1)
{
    WORD v=(WORD)value,xx0=(WORD)x0,yy0=(WORD)y0,
             xx1=(WORD)x1,yy1=(WORD)y1;

    if(yy1 > yy0)
        return yy0+(v-xx0)*(yy1-yy0)/(xx1-xx0);
    else
        return yy0-(v-xx0)*(yy0-yy1)/(xx1-xx0);

}
```

The code for interpolate() bears some discussion. All the data passed into the the routine are of the type BYTE. For this discussion we will assume that characters are eight bits and words are 16-bits. The product of two chars, two eight-bit objects, either unsigned or signed is a 16-bit result. C specifies that the product of two chars is also a char, and the result is the least significant eight bits of the result. To produce a 16-bit result, we must first cast each BYTE factor onto a WORD type prior to the multiplication. The product will be a 16-bit unsigned int type or a WORD. Since the factors have only eight significant bits each the resulting product can have no more than 16 significant bits. Such a 16-bit result can be divided by an eight-bit quantity, that has been cast onto a type WORD, and the result will be a number that is unsigned and has no more than eight significant bits. This number can be added to v which is derived from value and when cast onto a type BYTE it can be returned to the calling program.

The test program that follows sets up three look-up tables and exercises the object methods in two manners. The first is to calculate the table look-up value for a range of inputs that covers the complete dynamic range of inputs in steps of ten. The second covers the range of inputs that surround a break point in the data to show how the interpolation function handles the data near the breaks. The tables themselves are quite arbitrary. In the first table y is monotonically increasing in x, and it saturates at a fixed value before the end of the table is reached. In the second table, y is quite flat in x, but still monotonic. The third table contains a y range that increases and then decreases as x values increase.

```
#include "lutobj2d.h"
#include <stdio.h>

const Entry taba[]={
        0,0,
        96,40,
        144,68,
        166,128,
        221,160,
        255,160 };

const Entry tabb[]={
        0,0,
        96,128,
        144,139,
        166,158,
        221,178,
        238,184,
        255,255 };

const Entry tabc[]={
        0,0,
        96,162,
```

```
          144,117,
          166,196,
          221,255,
          238,184,
          255,178 };

void main(void)
{
     int i;
     Look_up *a=look_up_(6,taba), /* create three look-up tables */
             *b=look_up_(7,tabb), /* named a, b, and c */
             *c=look_up_(7,tabc);


     for(i=0;i<255;i+=10)
          printf(" %d\t%d\t%d\t%d\n", i,get_value(a,i),
                    get_value(b,i),get_value(c,i));
     getch();
     printf("\n");
     for(i=210;i<230;i++)
          printf(" %d\t%d\t%d\t%d\n", i,get_value(a,i),
                    get_value(b,i),get_value(c,i));
     look_up__(a); /* destroy all objects when no longer needed*/
     look_up__(b);
     look_up__(c);
}
```

The tables are constructed as simple linear arrays of the type Entry. In the main program, a variable i is created. Three look-up tables are created by execution of the look_up_() constructor function, and pointers to these tables are assigned to the variables a, b, and c. There are two simple printout loops. The first gives i a value range of zero to 250 and prints the values of i and get_value(table, i) for each table. When this routine is completed, it prints out the same values for a range of i between 210 and 230 in steps of 1 to show the operation as the input passes through a break point in the table. The result of this calculation is listed below. The first value shown is i, the second is table a, and so on. The blank line is inserted between the two different calculations.

```
  0      0      0      0
 10      4     13     16
 20      8     26     33
 30     12     40     50
 40     16     53     67
 50     20     66     84
 60     25     80    101
 70     29     93    118
 80     33    106    135
```

```
 90      37     120     151
100      42     128     159
110      48     131     149
120      54     133     140
130      59     135     131
140      65     138     121
150      84     144     138
160     111     152     174
170     130     159     200
180     136     163     211
190     141     166     221
200     147     170     232
210     153     174     243
220     159     177     253
230     160     181     218
240     160     192     184
250     160     234     180

210     153     174     243
211     154     174     244
212     154     174     245
213     155     175     246
214     155     175     247
215     156     175     248
216     157     176     249
217     157     176     250
218     158     176     251
219     158     177     252
220     159     177     253
221     160     178     255
222     160     178     251
223     160     178     247
224     160     179     243
225     160     179     239
226     160     179     235
227     160     180     230
228     160     180     226
```

You must compare the table values with the outputs in each case above. You will note that the output ranges are smooth and appear to be nearly correct in the first table. There is no good way of knowing without calculating the correct values by hand. If you should do these calculations, you will find that the computed values are accurate when you recognize that integer arithmetic rounds all fractional results down, toward zero. Calculation of the data through a break point is shown in the second output. Note that there is a break at 221 in the input data. In each case the calculated value gives the specified table value at the break point, and the data to the left and right of the break point change correctly. Table a saturates at an input of

221, which is demonstrated in the output data. The data in table b are quite flat above the break point and less flat below the break point. This performance is seen in the tabular data. Finally, the output from table c peaks at the input value of 221 and falls on either side of the break, as shown in the data above.

A faster table search. In the code above, a simple linear table search to find the index into the table from which to start the interpolation was used. For short tables, this approach is probably the best choice. But what if there are a large number of entries into the table? In such a case, it is probably best if an alternative search method be used to find the table index rather than the straight linear search seen above. What are our choices? One choice stands out as good. This choice is the binary search.

All searches require compares. The important question that should be addressed is the average number of compares needed to determine the needed index into the table. The linear search will require, on average, a number of compares that is equal to one-half the length of the table if the input data are distributed uniformly over the input range. A binary search is a search that determines the location of the index by successively reducing the search space in half after each comparison. This approach leads to a number of searches that is proportional to the logarithm, base 2, of the length of the table. If the table has only four entries, the linear search will require an average of two comparisons and the binary search will also require a maximum of two comparisons. On the other hand, at eight entries, the linear search requires an average of four comparisons, and the binary search needs a maximum of only three comparisons. Above eight, the advantage of the binary search becomes much greater.

A binary seach is implemented as follows: The input data are assumed to be an array with its contents in order. The array is divided in half, and the data value is compared with the contents of the center of the array. If the data value is greater than the value found in the center, the lower half of the array is discarded and the search is restarted with the newly shortened array. Similarly, the larger half of the array is discarded if the data value happens to be less than the value of the center entry in the array. This routine is repeated until one of two things happen. First, the comparison test is to determine if the value is either greater or less than the center entry in the array. If it is neither, the value must equal the center value, and the search is completed with this value being returned to the calling program. Second, the search will continue until the value lies between two entries in the array. In this case, the lower index value is returned to the calling program. The implementation of this algorithm is shown below.

```
int table_search(Look_up *this,BYTE value)
{
    int top, bottom, middle;

    top=this->length - 1;
    bottom=0;
```

```
        while((top-bottom)>1)
        {
            middle=(top+bottom)/2;
            if(value>this->table[middle].x)
                bottom=middle;
            else if(value<this->table[middle].x)
                top=middle;
            else
                return middle;
        }
        return bottom;
    }
```

The three variables used in this function are *top, bottom,* and *middle*. The top of the array being tested is at *top*, the bottom is at *bottom*, and *middle* is the center between top and bottom. The value of *top* is started at one less than the length of the array, and *bottom* is at zero. The while loop in which all of the calculation is completed is exercised as long as *top* and *bottom* are separated by more than one. When *top* is one greater than *bottom*, value has been bracketed by the adjacent table entries corresponding to *top* and *bottom*. At this time, *bottom* is returned to the calling program. Otherwise, the value is compared with the central entry in the array. If it is larger than the center value, *bottom* is changed to the value of *middle* and the procedure is continued. Whenever the value is less than the central array entry, *top* is given the *value* of *middle*. In the event that the value is neither larger nor smaller than the value found at *middle*, it must equal the value at *middle*, and this index value is returned.

There is a subtle difference between this binary search and the one you usually see in textbooks. In those cases, the midpoint is excluded when the new values of *top* or *bottom* are calculated. The following lines of code show this difference.

```
if(value>this->table[middle].x)
    bottom=middle+1;
else if(value<this->table[middle].x)
    top=middle-1;
```

Here, *bottom* is given a value *middle* + 1 and *top* is given a value *middle* – 1; then the appropriate conditions are met. This approach assumes that the array data themselves are the desired result, not an interpolated value between two points in the array. When the code above is used with the table look-up, the range nearest the center point, *middle*, is excluded from the next test, and the program misses the correct result most of the time.

We can now see one of the big advantages of object-oriented programming. The modifications to the program above will be included in the header file and the implementation file for the look-up table objects. The header file needs to have a function prototype for the routine table_search(). The new header file follows.

```
#ifndef LUTOBJ_H
#define LUTOBJ_H

#include "defines.h"

/* table used below is a pointer to an array of the type Entry.
   The number of entries in the array must be equal to x_length.
   Of course, each entry contains two values which are of the
   type BYTE  */

#ifndef ENTRYF
#define ENTRYF
    typedef struct
    {
        BYTE x,y;
    }Entry;
#endif

#define LOOK_UP_CLASS \
            int length; \
            Entry *table; \

typedef struct LU
{
      LOOK_UP_CLASS
} Look_up;

Look_up *look_up_(int x_length, Entry *table);
void look_up__(Look_up * this);
BYTE get_value(struct LU *this, BYTE value);
BYTE interpolate(BYTE value,BYTE x0,BYTE y0,BYTE x1,BYTE y1);
int table_search(Look_up *,BYTE);
#endif
```

The next-to-last line in the code above is added for this part of the program. In the implementation file, the routine get_value() is modified so that the table_search() function is called rather than to execute the linear search above. Also, the code for the table_search() function is added to the implementation file. This function is made static so that there is no visibility to the routine outside the implementation file.

```
#include "lutobjnu.h"
#include <stdlib.h>

BYTE get_value(Look_up *this, BYTE value)
{
    int i;
```

```
    i=table_search( this,value);
    if(value==this->table[i].x)
        return this->table[i].y;
    else
        return interpolate(value,
                            this->table[i].x,
                            this->table[i].y,
                            this->table[i+1].x,
                            this->table[i+1].y);
}

/* the constructor's name ends with a single underscore _ */

Look_up *look_up_(int length, Entry *table)
{
    Look_up *this;

    if(!(this=(Look_up*)malloc(sizeof(Look_up))))
        error_handler();
    this->length=length;
    this->table=table;
    return this;
}

/* the destructor's name ends with a double underscore __ */

void look_up__(Look_up *this)
{
    free(this);
}

/* interpolate() function can be used by other look-up tables,
   such as the three-dimensional look-up. This function works
   only for unsigned numbers, both inputs and outputs. It is as-
   sumed that x progresses monotonically, but y need not. */

BYTE interpolate(BYTE value,BYTE x0,BYTE y0,BYTE x1,BYTE y1)
{
    WORD v=(WORD)value,xx0=(WORD)x0,yy0=(WORD)y0,xx1=(WORD)x1,
           yy1=(WORD)y1;

    if(yy1 > yy0)
        return yy0+(v-xx0)*(yy1-yy0)/(xx1-xx0);
    else
        return yy0-(v-xx0)*(yy0-yy1)/(xx1-xx0);
}
```

```
static int table_search(Look_up *this,BYTE value)
{
    int top, bottom, middle;

    top=this->length - 1;
    bottom=0;
    while((top-bottom)>1)
    {
        middle=(top+bottom)/2;
        if(value>this->table[middle].x)
            bottom=middle;
        else if(value<this->table[middle].x)
            top=middle;
        else
            return middle;
    }
    return bottom;
}
```

The names of these files were changed from lutobj2d.x to lutobjnu.x to keep them separate from earlier files. The test program used above can be used to test this version of the table look-up object. The only change in the test program is to change the lutobj2d.h to lutobjnu.h. Otherwise, the program is identical. We have made significant changes in the class code, but it is unnecessary to alter the program code at all to be able to realize these changes.

A different interpolate(). Every time that interpolate() is called, the code must execute a multiply, a divide, and four adds. It is possible to eliminate the divide operation and several of the adds in the interpolation. This form of interpolate() will be somewhat faster than the earlier version. Its use will, however, force a reevaluation of the entire approach to the look-up table. We examine this approach next.

The function interpolate() from the class definition above is shown here.

```
BYTE interpolate(BYTE value,BYTE x0,BYTE y0,BYTE x1,BYTE y1)
{
    WORD v=(WORD)value,xx0=(WORD)x0,yy0=(WORD)y0,
              xx1=(WORD)x1,yy1=(WORD)y1;
    if(yy1 > yy0)
        return yy0+(v-xx0)*(yy1-yy0)/(xx1-xx0);
    else
        return yy0-(v-xx0)*(yy0-yy1)/(xx1-xx0);
}
```

In both calculations, you will notice that the portion of the expression

```
(yy1-yy0)/(xx1-xx0)
```

or

```
(yy0-yy1)/(xx1-xx0)
```

are values that depend on the table values at the break points only and remain unchanged between the break points. Therefore, this calculation could be completed and included in the table data. These values are the slope of the line that join two adjacent points in the table. Another advantage of the use of the slopes is that we can use negative values for slopes and avoid the dual calculation above to account for either a positive or a negative slope with unsigned values. It is proposed that the value of slope be calculated and included in the look-up table. Then the interpolation will require multiplication of the partial distance between the points by the slope and then add the result to the y value at the point in the table.

We now have a problem. It is necessary to have some kind of fractional representation for slopes. It is impossible to consider rounding all slopes less than unity to zero because this range of slopes is too significant to discard. A means must be found to include fractional data in our table. We will create for this particular program a fixed-point fractional arithmetic system that will resolve all of our problems here. A new class of data along with all the methods needed to execute complete arithmetic on these data types could be created. In this case, though, we need only create some slopes and then multiply these values by an unsigned char value. This set of operations can be executed easily without resorting to the implementation of a full class and the appropriate objects. A fixed-point arithmetic scheme will be used. The basic numeric system in this case is a 16-bit number that from a programming standpoint is merely an int—if an int is a 16-bit number on your machine. A binary point will be placed between the two eight-bit portions of this number. The most significant byte of the number will be a standard integer number that has a range of −128 to +127. The least significant byte will be the fractional part of the number. If we start at the left, the first bit is the number of halfs in the fraction, the second bit is the number of quarters in the fraction, and so on, until we reach the eighth bit, which is the number of 256ths in the fractional portion of the number. This fractional portion of the number can represent any fractional value from zero to 0.99609375 in steps of 0.00390625. This range of fractional values will be satisfactory for calculation of the slopes between points in the table. These numbers are generated merely by multiplying the numerator by 256—0x100—prior to execution of a divide and then dividing the result of a product by the same value.

The look-up table will now require three entries per point rather than two as was used earlier. Each table entry will need an x value, a y value, and a slope value. This change in the program is significant enough that the test program must be altered to provide the new look-up tables. Also, the interpolation routine will require different arguments and a new routine in the class files, forcing modification of both the class header file and the class implementation file.

Prior to looking at these modifications, we should look at a little program that will receive the point values in the look-up table and calculate the slopes for each point. This seemingly simple program has a couple of pitfalls that will fool the best programmer and can cause errors to creep into the results. These errors might go undetected if you as a programmer do not stop to check the accuracy of the calculations from the program. In the following program, the type Entry is changed to include both the point location and the slope. The slope in this case is the slope from the current point to the next point in the table. Therefore, the last slope value will be meaningless. There will be an array of points to be entered into the program. The value defined for ENTRY is the maximum number of point entries that the program can handle. To enter the data, a simple routine that first requests the values for a point followed by an "x="prompt is sent to the screen. After the x value is entered, it is converted from an ASCII string to an integer value that is assigned to the current x Entry value in the array of Entry values named inputs. Then a "y=" prompt is sent to the screen. This value entered is converted to an integer and saved in the current inputs.y location. The value of the index value i is then incremented. This routine is repeated until i becomes equal to ENTRIES or a nondigit value is entered for y.

```
#include <stdio.h>
#include "defines.h"
#define ENTRIES 100

typedef struct
{
      BYTE x,y;
      int slope;
} Entry;

main()
{
      Entry inputs[ENTRIES];
      int i=0,j;
      char data[10];

      while(i<ENTRIES )
      {
            printf("Enter a point value x,y\n");
            printf("x=");
            gets(data);
            inputs[i].x=atoi(data);
            printf("y=");
            gets(data);
            if(isdigit(data[0]))
```

```
                    inputs[i++].y=atoi(data);
                else
                    break;
            }
            for(j=0;j<=i-1;j++)
            {
                inputs[j].slope=0x100*((signed long)((WORD)inputs
                                        [j+1].y)-
                                        (signed long)((WORD)inputs
                                        [j].y))/
                                          ((signed long)((WORD)inputs
                                          [j+1].x)-
                                           (signed long)((WORD)inputs
                                           [j].x));
                printf("\t%d\t%d\t0x%x\n", inputs[j].x, inputs[j].y,
                                                inputs[j].slope);
            }
    }
```

Upon successful completion of the data entry, the slope for each point is calculated and printed on the screen for the several points along with the point values. You might note that the input values are printed out as decimal values and the slope value is printed as a hexidecimal value. This choice is made so that the programmer will recognize that the numbers are in reality fixed-point fractions and the fractional point is between the two bytes of the number.

A few words about the calculation of the slope in the program above. The types of inputs.x and inputs.y are both unsigned char. If these numbers are cast onto the type unsigned int—WORD—the arithmetic involved with subtraction will give a correct value unless the number being subtracted is greater than 127. In that range, the compiler used extends the sign bit of the subtrahend, making the subtrahend negative, which causes an incorrect result. To avoid this problem, we cast these values onto the type signed long. This cast corrects the sign extension in the program above, which was executed for each of the look-up tables used in the earlier example. The results of these calculations are shown below. These values have been entered into the test program. You might note that the slope values are all positive in the first two tables, as you would expect with monotonic increasing curves. In the third table, the slope jumps from positive to negative to positive to negative again as the slopes in the curve jump around.

```
   0      0    0x6a
  96     40    0x95
 144    680    x2ba
 166    128    0x94
 221    160    0x0
 255    160
```

```
  0      0    0x155
 96    128    0x3a
144    139    0xdd
166    158    0x5d
221    178    0x5a
238    184    0x42d
255    255

  0      0    0x1b0
 96    162    0xff10
144    117    0x397
166    196    0x112
221    255    0xfbd3
238    184    0xffa6
255    178
```

The class definition files are seen below. In the header file, the type Entry has been changed to include the slope as was done above. Also, the function prototype for interpolate() has been changed to reflect the new approach.

```
#ifndef LUTOBJ_H
#define LUTOBJ_H

#include "defines.h"

/* table used below is a pointer to an array of the type Entry.
   The number of entries in the array must be equal to x_length.
   Of course, each entry contains two values which are of the
   type BYTE */

#ifndef ENTRYF
#define ENTRYF
    typedef struct
    {
        BYTE x,y;
        int slope;
    }Entry;
#endif

#define LOOK_UP_CLASS \
            int length; \
            Entry *table;

typedef struct LU
{
      LOOK_UP_CLASS
} Look_up;
```

```
Look_up *look_up_(int x_length, Entry *table);
void look_up__(Look_up * this);
BYTE get_value(struct LU *this, BYTE value);
BYTE interpolate(BYTE value,BYTE x0,BYTE y0,int slope);
int table_search(Look_up *,BYTE);
#endif
```

The routine interpolate() is changed in the implementation file shown below. Here *interpolate* receives the offset value, the point location of the point with an x value just less than the value and the slope between the point and the next point from the table. The interpolation is much simpler here than before. It is only necessary to multiple the offset distance between the two points that is passed in as value by the slope and add this product to the y value of the point. Note that the product involves a division by 256 to account for the fixed-point fractional number conversion to a char value.

```
#include "lutslope.h"
#include <stdlib.h>

BYTE get_value(Look_up *this, BYTE value)
{
    int i;

    i=table_search( this,value);
    if(value==this->table[i].x)
        return this->table[i].y;
    else
        return interpolate(value,
                           this->table[i].x,
                           this->table[i].y,
                           this->table[i].slope);
}

/* the constructor's name ends with a single underscore _ */

Look_up *look_up_(int length, Entry *table)
{
    Look_up *this;

    if(!(this=(Look_up*)malloc(sizeof(Look_up))))
        error_handler();
    this->length=length;
    this->table=table;
    return this;
}
```

```
/* the destructor's name ends with a double underscore __ */

void look_up__(Look_up *this)
{
    free(this);
}

/* interpolate() function can be used by other look-up tables,
   such as the three-dimensional look-up. This function works
   only for unsigned numbers, both inputs and outputs. It is as-
   sumed that x progresses monotonically, but y need not. */

BYTE interpolate(BYTE value,BYTE x0,BYTE y0,int slope)
{
    WORD v=(WORD)value,xx0=(WORD)x0,yy0=(WORD)y0;
    return yy0+(long)(value-xx0)*(long)slope/256;

}

static int table_search(Look_up *this,BYTE value)
{
    int top, bottom, middle;

    top=this->length - 1;
    bottom=0;
    while((top-bottom)>1)
    {
        middle=(top+bottom)/2;
        if(value>this->table[middle].x)
            bottom=middle;
        else if(value<this->table[middle].x)
            top=middle;
        else
            return middle;
    }
    return bottom;
}
```

The test program shown below contains the same executing code as the earlier test program. In this case the tables are changed to contain the slopes discussed above.

```
#include "lutslope.h"   /* saves link in the lutobj later. */
#include <stdio.h>

const Entry taba[]={
        0,0,0x6a,
        96,40,0x95,
```

```
        144,68,0x2ba,
        166,128,0x94,
        221,160,0x0,
        255,160 };

const Entry tabb[]={
        0,0,0x155,
        96,128,0x3a,
        144,139,0xdd,
        166,158,0x5d,
        221,178,0x5a,
        238,184,0x42d,
        255,255 };

const Entry tabc[]={
        0,0,0x1b0,
        96,162,0xff10,
        144,117,0x397,
        166,196,0x112,
        221,255,0xfbd3,
        238,184,0xffa6,
        255,178 };

void main(void)
{
    int i;
    Look_up *a=look_up_(6,taba), /* create three look-up tables
            */
            *b=look_up_(7,tabb), /* named a, b, and c */
            *c=look_up_(7,tabc);

    for(i=0;i<255;i+=10)
        printf(" %3d\t\t%3d\t\t%3d\t\t%3d\n", i,get_value(a,i),
                get_value(b,i),get_value(c,i));
    getch();
    printf("\n");
    for(i=210;i<230;i++)
        printf(" %3d\t\t%3d\t\t%3d\t\t%3d\n", i,get_value(a,i),
                get_value(b,i),get_value(c,i));
    look_up__(a);       /* destroy all objects when no longer
                                needed*/
    look_up__(b);
    look_up__(c);
}
```

It is suggested that you compile all the programs along with the class files shown in this section and see how they work. The results of each program should be identical. In the test programs, there have been minimal changes. Note between the first and second test programs that there is no substantial change—the only change here is the header file and hence the class implementation file linked to the program that is renamed. In the final test program, the new class files are used, and the tables are altered to contain the needed slopes. These minimal changes in the test program show one of the important benefits of object-oriented programming. The objects are divorced from the applications programs so that changes in the object or class implementation often require no modification of the applications programs.

SUMMARY

In this chapter three general types of objects are discussed. The main purpose of the chapter is to show the construction of some practical objects that can be used with microcontrollers or embedded systems. The first, the semaphore, is a device that allows assignment of a resource to a task, or process, until the task has completed its need for the resource. Such semaphores should be used whenever more than one process will need a given resource. We will see such applications several times in subsequent chapters.

A linked list is the basis for many popular objects. A derivative of the linked list might be a stack, a queue, a circular list, a string, a tree— the potential seems endless. The list code shown in this chapter is for a minimal linked list, and it will probably need expansion to meet the need of any application. We will see the linked list in Chapter 5, where it is used to hold several delays that are each associated with a given timer. Another application for the linked list would be to hold the tasks or processes in a multiple tasking system. Here a task would probably consist of a task control block and the list would have to be searched to determine the next task to execute, which task to delete, and so on.

Finally, we discussed a table look-up scheme. Look-up table classes were created, and several important modifications of the operation of the objects were implemented. It was seen that each of these modifications had minimal impact on the test program while implementing significant changes in the object performance. This separation of the implementation of objects and applications where they are used is one of the important benefits of object-oriented programming. We will see other applications where this dichotomy is very useful and important.

4

ASYNCHRONOUS SERIAL PORT

The main focus of this chapter is the asynchronous serial communications system in the MC68HC16Y1. There is one point that should be considered outside the serial services that can be placed here. Access to and creation of all peripheral devices can cause errors. We will need a clean error handling system to help recover from these errors.

ERROR HANDLER

In the earlier chapters, occasions involving access to an error handler were pointed out, but the error handling routines were stubbed out when it came to functioning programs. Here we are beginning to write code for real microcontrollers, and it is now time to consider the ramifications of a real error handler. This handler will be used with the asynchronous serial communications systems here, and in fact, it is general enough that it can be used in support of any peripheral object devices developed in this book.

There are two types of errors that we consider. The first type comes about when the system itself is in trouble, and the second type occurs when there is some type of peripheral failure. For example, a NULL return from a malloc() transaction indicates that there is no memory left on the system heap when more memory is needed. This type of error is quite serious in that the program cannot continue operating in its current state. Such an error is of the first type. On any serial communications system, it is possible that the computer system will not get around to servicing some data until those data are no longer valid. Serial input data can reside in a buffer only until the next character has arrived in the input shift register. At that time, either the old data must be overwritten by the new character, or the next character arriving will destroy the contents of the shift register before it is transferred into the input buffer. Either event causes the input data stream to have an overrun error, but neither event is catastrophic in regard to the ability of the system to continue its designated operation. We shall call errors of the first type TYPE_1 errors, and noncatastrophic errors will be called TYPE_2 errors.

An error handler will have to do different things for these types of errors. In the first case, something must be done that attempts to restore the integrity of the system. In the second case, it is probably satisfactory to log the fact that an error occurred and proceed with the program. Of course, in the event that there is a plan to correct for this type of error, the plan will be put into effect. For example, a TYPE_2 error in a serial communications driver can be corrected. A message could be sent which requests that the last block of data be resent in an attempt to correct the error. In the absence of a specific plan, we will assume that the program merely logs the error and returns to its normal business.

TYPE_1 errors, on the other hand, require some additional consideration. Any TYPE_1 error indicates that there is a system failure and normal processing cannot proceed. In such an event, the response should probably be similar to that one would choose with a watchdog or computer operating properly (COP) time-out. Most computer systems cannot distinguish between a power-on reset and a COP reset. We have an advantage here in that we can direct the code to wherever we please when the TYPE_1 error occurs and are not limited to the code contained in the reset initialization portion of the program.

What should be done when a TYPE_1 error occurs? One thing is clear, most memory operations should be initialized and the stack pointer reset to its initial value. Unfortunately, the error handler itself requires some global memory, and it would be counterproductive to initialize this memory in the event of a TYPE_1 error. Part of this memory is an error log that should be available for later diagnosis of the system performance, so this memory cannot be initialized by an error-based restart. Actually, we will see that this problem is simplified somewhat by putting the initialization of the error log into the constructor for the error handler and controlling the initialization by a flag that is reset during the power-on reset. This flag cannot be reset during an error-based reset, but it must be reset during a power-on reset.

How the error handler should be incorporated into the program is a serious question. One of the popular approaches is to use a setjmp() and longjmp() function that is a part of the language. This approach permits a transfer of control from anywhere in the program to a specified location. Of course, the specified location in this case would be the error handler. This approach is fine for TYPE_1 errors, but there is no convenient mechanism for returning to the program that generated the error as is needed for a TYPE_2 error. An alternative approach that is certainly in line with object-oriented programming is to place the error handler into a base class like the class object in Chapter 3. Then new classes created for the program are each inherited from the base abstract class. With this approach, each object will have its own access to the error handler and there will be no problems with longjmp() or other calls to global functions. With a TYPE_1 error, the error handler will transfer control of the program to a point in the initialization program that follows global memory initialization for the program but precedes the initialization of the stack pointer. Important external memory contents needed for the error logging will thus be saved, but the program will be restarted otherwise. The TYPE_2 error will merely increment the appropriate entry in the error log and return to the program where the error occurred.

A header file for error is shown in Listing 4.1. The error handler will be a descendent of the class Object. We will see interesting uses for this approach in later chapters. The ERROR_HANDLER define statement contains no attributes, a reference to the #defined macro OBJECT found in the object.h header, and a single pointer to the error_hand() function. A macro defines the function error_handler(a,b,c) which will be used to access this object from any program. The first parameter, a, is a pointer to the object in which the error has occurred. The param-

```
#ifndef ERROR_H
#define ERROR_H

#include "defines.h"
#include "object.h"

enum {TYPE_1,TYPE_2};

#define ERROR_HANDLER \
      OBJECT            \
      void (*error_hand)(void*,int,Error_source);
typedef struct err
{
      ERROR_HANDLER
} Error_handler;

#define error_handler(a,b,c) (*a->error_hand)(a,b,c)

Error_handler *error_(void);
void error__(Error_handler *);

#endif
```

Listing 4.1 Error Handler Class Definition File

eter b is the error type, and the parameter c is a numeric identifier of the class that generated the error.

The error manager implementation file is shown in Listing 4.2. For the moment it is assumed that the maximum number of different error sources is 10. There is a small function named restart() contained within this class, and it is to be private to the error manager, so it is declared to be static. This little function is a jump to the location error1 declared as an external destination. Such a program must be written in assembly language, and it requires but a single instruction and the external reference to the address as seen in the function.

The error handler function examines type. If the error is TYPE_1, the appropriate error log array entry is incremented and the program is restarted. If it is TYPE_2, the error log entry is incremented, and the program control is returned to the program that called the error handler. Otherwise, if type is neither TYPE_1 nor TYPE_2, the error handler was called by error and the program is restarted. The error handler class is made a descendent of the class Object by inclusion of a copy of an Object in the class Error.

In the files above, there is frequent use of the void type where one might expect the Error_handler type. The void type in these cases defines a generic pointer. The parameter in each case must be a pointer, but we will later use the type of inherited objects to access the error manager. In these cases a specific type of pointer in the basic error manager code would cause the compiler to report an error whenever the inherited object type would attempt to access functions in the base type object. This little subterfuge avoids problems where types are frequently miscast with the coding approach we are using here.

As many error handlers as are needed can be instantiated in a program. Regardless of the number of error handlers, there can be only one error log. The error handler is created with a malloc() call to allocate space for the object. When the program is started, the variable error_log will be contained in a memory area that is initialized to zero. Therefore, whenever the error_() routine is executed the first time after program initialization, error_log will be zero and the calloc() routine will be called. This function allocates a memory space large enough to hold an array of ERROR_SOURCES unsigned integer variables. Because the variable error_log is declared to be static, it will work exactly the same as does a static variable found in C++. Only one copy of this variable is created, regardless of the number of error handlers instantiated. This copy of the variable will be visible to all the error handlers. Therefore, there will be one copy of the array error_log, and regardless of the number of error handlers created, error_log is the record of transactions for all the error handlers.

The remainder of the constructor and the destructor function are straightforward. The function restart() contains three assembly lines. The first is a jump instruction to the 20-bit location named _error1 and the next two are external declarations of the 20-bit field _error1. These values are filled in by the linker at link time for the program.

```
#include "error.h"

#define ERROR_SOURCES 10 /* max number of error sources */

static void restart(void);
static int *error_log;

static void error_hand(Error_handler *error,
                       int type,
                       Error_source error_source)
{
      if(type==TYPE_1)
    {
          ++error_log[error_source];
          restart();
    }
    else if(type==TYPE_2)
          ++error_log[error_source];
    else
          restart();

}
Error_handler *error_(void)
{
      Error_handler *this;
      Object *temp=object_();

      this=(Error_handler *)malloc(sizeof(Error_handler));
      if(!error_log)
            error_log=(int*)calloc(ERROR_SOURCES,sizeof(int));
      memmove(this, temp, sizeof(Object));
      this->error_hand=error_hand;
      object__(temp);
      return this;
}

void error__(Error_handler *this)
{
      free(this);
}

static void restart(void)
{
      _asm("jmp _error1\n");
      _asm(".external _error1\n");
      _asm(".external ._error1\n");
}
```

Listing 4.2 Error Handler Class Implementation File

DEVELOPMENT ENVIRONMENT

The programs developed in the remainder of this book will all be compiled, debugged, and tested. All of the code will be compiled primarily for the MC68HC16Y1 microcontroller. The user's manual for this part can be obtained from Motorola.* This chip is based on the CPU16 core, which is an expanded version of the MC68HC11. The CPU16 is truly a 16-bit processor with 20-bit data and program address spaces. The CPU16 works with the intermodual bus structure, which is also used with the M68300 family of components. The peripheral devices placed on these two families of parts are identical. Therefore, the interface approach to these peripherals is identical on these two families.

The MC68HC16Y1 has several built-in peripheral components. These peripherals include:

- Analog-to-digital converter
- Multichannel communications interface
- General purpose timer
- Timer processor unit
- Standby RAM

We will be building software components that access these peripherals as components. All of the code developed here has been compiled using the Cosmic HC16 compiler. Access to this compiler is described in Appendix A. There you will find some command files that aid in compilation of your programs with this compiler.

The code has been debugged using the M68HC16Y1EVS evaluation system. The debug code that was used is supplied by P&E . This program is available from the Motorola Freeware Bulletin Board 512 891 3733. Also, the program ICD16 will work. All of the debugging was done in the background debug mode (BDM), which allows noninvasive debugging of a program. The debugger does not reside in the microcontroller memory, so the only time that the debugger is active is when the computer enters the BDM. Otherwise, the microcontroller runs at full speed without any notice of the presence of a debugging environment.

A photograph of the M68HC16Y1EVS is shown in Figure 4.1.

SERIAL DRIVER

A serial communications driver requires that the calling program send quite a bit of data to the driver when setting up the communications system and doing the serial transfer. There are different ways that these parameters can be delivered to the

*Motorola M68HC16 Family MC68HC16Y1 User's Manual MC68HC16Y1UM/AD can be obtained from Motorola Literature Distribution Center, P.O. Box 20912, Phoenix, AZ 85036.

Fig. 4.1 A photograph of the M68HC16Y1EVS.

driver. The first is to have several argument values for the functions that will be needed. A second is to build a table and communicate a pointer to the table as the function parameter. The table contains all the important parameters needed to establish the communications or complete the communications, whichever is needed. We use both approachs here.

The serial communications device on the MC68HC16Y1 is called the multichannel communications interface (MCCI). The MCCI contains two asynchronous serial communications interfaces (SCIs), along with a synchronous serial peripheral communications interface (SPI). We work with the asynchronous system in this chapter. Our software must address both SCI ports, but the SPI is treated elsewhere. Since we are using a class/object approach to the interface design, is it desirable to design the class so that several different instances of the serial interface can be established at the same time? Of course, we can establish more serial communications driver objects than there are ports, but no more than two serial ports can be worked at the same time. We now look at building a serial communications driver for a single SCI port and plan to extend the code later to the second port.

The serial i/o header file shown in Listing 4.3 contains components similar to all the classes that we have developed so far. There is also some serial port control business that should be included in the header file to control any serial port. These additional peripherial specific entries in the header files will become more common now that the code being written is specifically addressing peripheral components. The first included file is the error header file, and the serial driver will be a descendent class of the error handler. Next you will observe a #define statements that defines an important value for the program. The EOM (end of message) value is zero.

The enum{} construct has not been used much until now. This useful scheme assigns numerical values to the various arguments, starting at zero and incrementing the value for each additional argument. They are very useful for assigning values to mnemonics where the value is not important—just having a unique value for each name is important. There are two enum{} statements in this header. Two commands are used by the serial i/o programs, INPUT and OUTPUT. The enum io_command defines these two values. Finally, several possible errors can occur in the serial i/o programs. These errors are given values in the enum io_errors.

Whenever a serial i/o takes place, the program must receive several parameters; also, the program can receive several parameters from the driver program. As mentioned above, these parameters are all collected into a single structure called an input/output control block. This structure is declared and type defined as a type io_command_block. The first three parameters, io_command, buffer, and buffer_length, are each parameters sent to the serial driver by the calling program. The last three parameters, characters_transferred, call_complete, and error, are parameters returned to the calling program by the serial driver. The meanings of these various parameters are straightforward.

In the implementation file for the serial i/o shown in Listing 4.3, a header file iodefs.h is included. A listing of this file is

```
#define MCCI_IARB 3
#define MCCI_LEVEL 3
#define MCCI_INTV 0x40 /* MCCI vector at 0x40 */
```

There are three constants that are values used in the setup of the MCCI on the microcontroller. It may seem excessive to have a series of definition statements for such parameters, but it is extremely important for good programming practice to avoid the use of “magic” values.

```
#ifndef SERIO_H
#define SERIO_H

#include "error.h"
#include "iodefs.h"
#include "defines.h"

#define EOM            0       /* End Of Message */

#define SERIO_METHODS \
            void (*do_rec)(void); \
            void (*do_trans)(void);

typedef struct
{
      SERIO_METHODS
} Serio_Methods;

enum io_commands{INPUT,OUTPUT };

enum io_errors{NO_ERROR,
               BUFFER_OVERFLOW,
               COMMAND_ERROR};

/* i/o command block */

typedef struct /* See enumerates above for commands and error
returns */
{
    int io_command;                  /* input parameters */
    BYTE *buffer;
    int buffer_length;
    int characters_transferred;      /* output parameters */
    Boolean call_complete;
    int error;
} io_command_block;
```

Listing 4.3 Serial Input/Output Class Definition File

```
#define SERIAL_IO\
    BYTE (*i_o)(struct serio *,io_command_block *);

typedef struct serio
{

      ERROR_HANDLER
      SERIAL_IO
} Serial_io;

#define serial_io(a,b) (*a->i_o)(a,b)

/* Function prototypes */
Serial_io *serial_io_(int baud_rate,int vector,int iarb,int
int_level);
void serial_io__(Serial_io *);
static BYTE getch(void);
static void putch(BYTE ) ;
static void do_receive(void);
static void do_transmit(void);

#endif
```

Listing 4.3 (continued)

Use will be made of virtual functions in this class. Therefore, the first entries in the serio header file are those items necessary to create a virtual function table. This table will have two entries.

The SERIAL_IO define statement contains a single pointer to a function that returns a type BYTE and takes two arguments. The first argument is a pointer to the serial i/o object being activated, and the second argument is a pointer to the io command block that contains the information needed to process the i/o. The type Serial_io is created as a combination of the SERIAL_IO statement and the ERROR_HANDLER statement found in the error.h header.

The constructor has four arguments. These are needed to set up the serial port on the microcontroller. Note that the program required to set up the serial port does not depend in any way on the parameters needed in the io control block. Therefore, the io control block is not a part of the constructor. The destructor function prototype is similar to all seen before. Several internal functions are included in this class. The functions getch() and putch() do exactly as you would expect. These functions either get a character from or put a character to the serial port. The functions do_receive() and do_transmit() are virtual functions that can be changed by inherited classes.

Until now, there has been little reference to the microcontroller being used for these programs. We must now consider the microcontroller in some detail. The header files included in the serio.c file shown below include the header for the MC68HC16Y1 along with the header for the multichannel communications interface module in the MC68HC16Y1. Listings of these two header files, provided in Appendix B, contain important definitions of values used for programming these parts.

Two internal functions are needed for the serial port driver. These functions are both declared as static and are the functions getch() and putch(). getch() reads a single character from the input of the serial port, and putch() sends a single character out of the serial port. Although there is no error checking within these two functions, it is here where overrun errors, parity errors, framing errors, and noise errors can be detected. These errors are all TYPE_2 errors, and the strategy for handling these errors should be included within these functions. In this case, these errors were ignored. Perhaps, in a real application, these error events should be considered as more important than they were here.

The next function, i_o(), is the object method call that establishes an input or output. This function receives an io_command_block and the identification of a specific serial input output object that has already been created. Within this function, commands are evaluated and the port is established as either an input or an output. By the way, there is no reason that the program could not process an input and an output at the same time. Separate calls to i_o() with different io_commands will be needed to set up simultaneous input and output transactions. The main work that takes place inside this function is controlled by a case statement that selects the proper code based on the io_command found in the block parameter.

There are two static pointers to the type io_command_block. These pointers are used to save the pointers to the two possible command blocks that are being used currently. It is assumed that all i/o transactions are block oriented. In other words, a block of data is transferred with a single transaction. This block is passed to i_o() as a buffer along with the length of the message contained in the buffer.

In both cases, input or output, the output parameters that are contained in the io_command_block are given proper values. The characters transferred are set to zero, the call complete flag is set FALSE, and the error value contained within the command block is set to NO_ERROR. These are each values that will be changed as the input or output proceeds. These parameters in the command block are the three output parameters. The remaining three parameters are input parameters that pass data into this function.

The receiver and the transmitter are usually kept in the OFF condition and are turned ON only when they are needed. Similarly, the receiver and transmitter interrupts are kept OFF until needed. These flags are set in the microcontroller by the code in either the INPUT or OUTPUT setup areas. After these appropriate bits are set, the function returns NO_ERROR to the calling program.

All the setup code for either the INPUT or OUTPUT command is directed by a case statement. There are only two choices, INPUT or OUTPUT. If another command is sent to the i_o() program, a COMMAND_ERROR is returned to the calling program.

```
#include "serio.h"
#include "hc16y1.h"
#include "mcci.h"

/* ISR prototypes */
@port void SCR_Isr(void) ;

/* This function reads in a single character from the SCI */
static BYTE getch(void)
{
    while(SCSRA.RDRF==OFF)    /* wait until data are available */
        ;
    return SCDRA.DATA;        /* and reset RDRF bit */
}

/* This function sends a single character to SCI */
static void putch(BYTE x)
{
    while(SCSRA.TDRE==OFF)    /* wait until register is empty */
        ;
    SCDRA.DATA=x;             /* and send out the data */
}                             /* which resets TDRE bit */
io_command_block *giob, *goob;  /* used in ISR */
static BYTE i_o(Serial_io * this, io_command_block *block)
{
    switch(block->io_command)
    {
        case INPUT : giob=block;
                     giob->characters_transferred=0; /* none sent
                     yet */
                     giob->call_complete=FALSE; /* reset when
                     done */
                     giob->error=NO_ERROR;
                     SCCR1A.RE=ON; /* enable receiver*/
                     SCCR1A.RIE=ON; /* enable receiver interrupt
                     */
                     return NO_ERROR;

       case OUTPUT : goob=block;
                     goob->characters_transferred=0; /* none sent
                     now */
                     goob->call_complete=FALSE; /* reset when
                     done */
                     goob->error=NO_ERROR;
                     SCCR1A.TE=ON; /* enable transmitter */
                     SCCR1A.TIE=ON; /* enable transmit interrupt
                     */
                     return NO_ERROR;
```

```
            default : return COMMAND_ERROR;
        }
    }
```

The next code that we observe is the serial_io_() constructor. This constructor must do several things that we have not seen before. It is necessary to set up many of the internal components within the controller when we need to use these modules. There are four special considerations that must be set up in this serial system. If you examine the code that follows, you will find that there are four parameters, int_level, iarb, vector, and baud rate, that are put into specific registers in the part. The interrupt level is a number between one and seven. The higher-level interrupt will be processed before a lower-level interrupt, and level-seven interrupts are non-maskable. The iarb is a number between 1 and 15. This number is used to resolve simultaneous interrupts that occur at the same level. In the event that more than one interrupt occurs at the same time and on the same interrupt level, these interrupts must have come from separate modules. In that event the module with the largest iarb will be processed first. If a module has an iarb of zero, there will be no response to an interrupt from that module.

The interrupt vector must be placed in two different locations. First, the vector is placed in the interrupt vector field in an interrupt-level serial communications interface register field named INTV. In the M68HC16 family of parts, the interrupt vector and the address of the interrupt vector are related by a factor of 2. The location in the vector table of a specific interrupt service routine address, is at twice the vector number. The macro vector() places the interrupt service routine address at the specified address, which in this case is twice the value of vector.

The next business is to select the proper baud rate for the serial communications. The three baud rates chosen here are 4800, 9600, and 19,200. Of course, the SCI can be used at faster baud rates, but for our purposes here it is neither necessary nor desirable. One problem with the use of faster baud rates: This particular driver will use interrupts to notify the processor of the need for service. Faster baud rates will increase the number of interrupts per unit time. With a system that must be doing more than just servicing a serial port, the increase in interrupts can overload the computer and leave no time for other services. If the processor must handle very fast baud rates, it is recommended that the communications services take over the computer completely during communications. Interrupts have an interrupt latency which is time lost from processing. This lost time is avoided by the use of polling. Use a polling technique to determine the need for data transactions rather than interrupting the processor will allow faster communications.

The remainder of the constructor follows our usual approach. The i/o class is inherited from the error class, so an instance of an error object is created. A memory block large enough to contain a complete copy of a Serial_io is allocated, and the copy of the error object is copied into this memory location. The error object is no longer needed, so it is destroyed. The address of the function i_o() is copied into the object location i_o and the pointer to the new i/o object is returned to the calling program.

It will be advantageous to be able to change the interrupt service routine code at times when using the serial i/o system. To provide this advantage, we will make the interrupt service routine code for both the input and the output routines virtual. Recall from Chapter 2 that when creating a virtual function, the base class must build a globally available virtual function table. The contents of this table can be changed by any class constructor that inherits from the base class. The serial methods table is filled during the course of creating an object of this class. The serio_flag is used to prevent refilling this table each time a new object is instantiated from this class.

```
/* the serial io port constructor */

Serio_Methods serio_methods;
static Boolean serio_flag=FALSE;

Serial_io *serial_io_(int baud_rate, int vector, int iarb, int
int_level)
{
    Error_handler *temp; /* the object from which inheritance
    takes place */
    Serial_io *this; /* this object */
    /* The following instructions set values in the micro-
    controller needed to establish the proper communications */

    MCCI_MCR.IARB=iarb;      /* unique iarb for each module */
    ILSCI.ILSCIA=int_level;/* interrupt level in place */
    ILSCI.INTV=vector;     /* interrupt address is twice the
    vector*/
    vector(SCR_Isr,VAL*vector); /* set the vector */
    switch(baud_rate)/* set the component baud rate—assume 16.77
    mHz */
    {
        case 4800 : SCCR0A.BR=BAUD_4800;
                    break;
        case 9600 : SCCR0A.BR=BAUD_9600;
                    break;
        case 19200: SCCR0A.BR=BAUD_19K;
    }

    temp=error_(); /* create error object */
    this=(Serial_io*)malloc(sizeof(Serial_io)); /* make new
    object */
    if(this==NULL) /* a malloc() error */
        error_handler(this,TYPE_1,SERIAL);
    memmove(this,temp,sizeof(Error_handler));/* move in inher-
    ited object */
    error__(temp); /* get rid of the error object */
```

```
        this->i_o=i_o;
        if(!serio_flag)
        {
            serio_flag=TRUE;
            serio_methods.do_rec=do_receive;
            serio_methods.do_trans=do_transmit;
        }
        return this;
    }
```

One might expect that the destructor for a serial_io object would be more complicated than shown below. However, more complication is not really needed here. The main idea is that even though interrupt vectors and iarbs and interrupt levels have been established, it is not necessary to alter these parameters inside the microcontroller when they are no longer needed. The most important single consideration is the interrupt enable for the transmitter and the receiver. If every i/o transaction is allowed to proceed to its completion, these interrupts are disabled. It is not really necessary to undo the setup for the interrupts when destroying the object. The destructor is an orderly operation that will occur within the program. There should never be an occasion when the destructor is executed during an i/o transaction.

```
void serial_io__(Serial_io *this)
{
      free(this);
}
```

The final portion of the serial i/o object is its interrupt service routine. The time required to send a single character to the output or to read a single character is almost insignificant, perhaps less than 1 microsecond. On the other hand, at 9600 baud, the transaction time for a single character is about 1 millisecond. There is no reason for the processor to be unable to do other business while waiting for another character to be either sent out or received. The approach that allows full use of the computer is to use interrupts to process the data as they need to be handled. There are two interrupts that are used to process the serial i/o module of the MC68HC16Y1. These two interrupts are actually processed through a single interrupt vector and hence have a single interrupt service routine. When properly enabled, the interrupts occur when either the receiver data register is full of new data or when the transmit data register is empty. These two conditions are the only ones that will cause a serial port interrupt. Inside the interrupt service routine, the program must determine the type of interrupt and process the data appropriately.

Note in the routine shown below that the first executable statement determines if SCSRA.RDRF==ON. This flag bit in the serial communications status register is called the receive data register full flag. If this bit is on, data have been received and need processing. Otherwise, since the only other possible source for the interrupt is the transmitter, it is unnecessary to examine the SCSRA.TDRE bit. If the RDRF bit is not set, the TDRE (transmit data register empty) bit must be set.

```
@port void SCR_Isr(void) /* The serial port interrupt handlers
                            */
{

   if(SCSRA.RDRF==ON) /* got an input interrupt */
       (*serio_methods.do_rec)();
   else  /* ready to send another character out */
       (*serio_methods.do_trans)();
}
```

Assume that the RDRF bit is ON so that we have an input interrupt. In that case the do_receive() method will be executed to read in the new data as soon as possible. When these data are read in, the RDRF bit is reset automatically, and the Receive Data Register, SCDRA.DATA, is emptied. Once the data are read in and saved, two tests are performed: first, if the data character received is not an EOM (end of message) and second, if the number of characters read in and saved is less than the size of the available buffer into which it will be stored. If these two conditions are satisfied, the valid character is saved in the buffer. At this time control is returned to the interrupted program. Otherwise, the end of the message as indicated by either receiving an EOM or a possible data buffer overflow has been reached. In either case, another character cannot be received. If an EOM has been received, the EOM which is a zero will be inserted into the buffer. Then the call_complete flag is set to TRUE and the receiver is disabled by resetting both the receiver interrupt enable bit and the receiver enable bit. Then a test is performed to make certain that the buffer length has not in some manner grown to greater that the available buffer. If it has, a buffer overflow error is set in the io_command_block by making error equal to BUFFER_OVERFLOW. Otherwise, the error message in the io_command_block is set to NO_ERROR.

```
static void do_receive(void)
{
    BYTE cr;
    if((cr=getch())!= EOM && giob->characters_transferred++ <
                        giob->buffer_length)
        *giob->buffer++=cr;
    else
    {
        if(cr==EOM)
        {
            giob->characters_transferred++;
            *giob->buffer=cr;
        }
        giob->call_complete=TRUE;
        SCCR1A.RIE=OFF;      /* turn the receiver interrupt off */
```

```
        SCCR1A.RE=OFF;          /* and disable the receiver */
        if(giob->characters_transferred >=giob->buffer_length)
            giob->error=BUFFER_OVERFLOW;
        else
            giob->error=NO_ERROR;
        giob=NULL;              /* get rid or iocb */
    }
}
```

In the event that the RDRF flag is not found to be set in the interrupt service routine, the TDRE (transmitt data register empty) flag must be set. In that event the following method is executed. The transmit interrupt service routine is very similar to the receive routine. Here the next character in the buffer is obtained and immediately sent out the serial port. The characters_transferred is incremented and two checks are completed. First, the characters transferred must be less than the buffer length, and second, the character sent should not be an EOM. In either of these cases, there are more data to be transmitted, so control is returned to the interrupted program until the next time that the transmit data register is empty. Otherwise, we have reached the end of the message being transmitted, and the transmitter must be turned off. The code needed to turn the transmitter off are the instructions SCCR1A.TIE=OFF and SCCR1A.TE=OFF. The first instruction disables the transmitter interrupt, and the second turns the transmitter off. The code that follows these instructions sets the call_complete flag in the io_command_block equal to TRUE and puts the correct value in the error flag. In both this case and above in the receiver service routine, the last piece of business is to put a NULL into the io_command_block pointer.

```
static void do_transmit(void)
{
    BYTE ct;
    putch(ct=*goob->buffer++); /* send out the character */
    goob->characters_transferred++;
    if(goob->characters_transferred<goob->buffer_length &&
    ct!=EOM)
        ; /* go back if more data to be sent */
    else
    {
        SCCR1A.TIE=OFF;  /* disable the transmitter interrupt */
        SCCR1A.TE=OFF;   /* and also disable the transmitter */
        goob->call_complete=TRUE;
        if(goob->characters_transferred>goob->buffer_length)
            goob->error=BUFFER_OVERFLOW;
        else
            goob->error=NO_ERROR;
        goob=NULL;       /* delete iocb */
    }
}
```

The implementation file for the serial i/o class has been broken into several parts above. To help avoid confusion, this file is shown in its entirety in Listing 4.4.

```
#include "hc16y1.h"
#include "mcci.h"
#include "serio.h"

/* ISR prototypes */
@port void SCR_Isr(void) ;

/* This function reads in a single character from the SCI */

static BYTE getch(void)
{
    while(SCSRA.RDRF==OFF) /* wait until data are available */
         ;
    return SCDRA.DATA;     /* and reset RDRF bit */
}

/* This function sends a single character to SCI */

static void putch(BYTE x)
{
    while(SCSRA.TDRE==OFF) /* wait until register is empty */
         ;
    SCDRA.DATA=x;          /* and send out the data */
}

io_command_block *giob, *goob; /* used in ISR */

static BYTE i_o(Serial_io * this, io_command_block *block)
{
    switch(block->io_command)
    {
        case INPUT : giob=block;
                     giob->characters_transferred=0; /* none sent
                     yet */
                     giob->call_complete=FALSE; /* reset when
                     done */
                     giob->error=NO_ERROR;
                     SCCR1A.RE=ON; /* enable receiver*/
                     SCCR1A.RIE=ON; /* enable receiver interrupt
                     */
                     return NO_ERROR;
```

Listing 4.4 Serial Input/Output Class Implementation File

```
        case OUTPUT : goob=block;
                      goob->characters_transferred=0; /* none
                      sent now */
                      goob->call_complete=FALSE; /* reset when
                      done */
                      goob->error=NO_ERROR;
                      SCCR1A.TE=ON; /* enable transmitter */
                      SCCR1A.TIE=ON; /* enable transmit interrupt
                      */
                      return NO_ERROR;


        default : return COMMAND_ERROR;
    }
}

/* the serial io port constructor */

Serio_Methods serio_methods;
static Boolean seric_flag=FALSE;

Serial_io *serial_io_(int baud_rate, int vector, int iarb, int
int_level)
{
    Error_handler *temp; /* the object from which inheritance
    takes place */
    Serial_io *this; /* this object */

    /* The following instructions set values in the microcon-
    troller needed to establish the proper communications */

    MCCI_MCR.IARB=iarb;      /* unique iarb for each module */
    ILSCI.ILSCIA=int_level;/* interrupt level in place */
    ILSCI.INTV=vector;     /* interrupt address is twice the vec-
    tor*/
    vector(SCR_Isr,VAL*vector); /* set the vector */
    switch(baud_rate)/* set the component baud rate--assume 16.77
    mHz */
    {
        case 4800 : SCCR0A.BR=BAUD_4800;
                    break;
        case 9600 : SCCR0A.BR=BAUD_9600;
                    break;
        case 19200: SCCR0A.BR=BAUD_19K;
}
```

Listing 4.4 (continued)

```
temp=error_(); /* create error object */
this=(Serial_io*)malloc(sizeof(Serial_io)); /* make new object */
if(this==NULL) /* a malloc() error */
    error_handler(this,TYPE_1,SERIAL);
memmove(this,temp,sizeof(Error_handler));/* move in inherited ob-
ject */
    error__(temp); /* get rid of the error object */
    this->i_o=i_o;
    if(!serio_flag)
    {
        serio_flag=TRUE;
        serio_methods.do_rec=do_receive;
        serio_methods.do_trans=do_transmit;
    }
    return this;
}

@port void SCR_Isr(void) /* The serial port interrupt handlers */
{

    if(SCSRA.RDRF==ON) /* got an input interrupt */
        (*serio_methods.do_rec)();
    else /* ready to send another character out */
        (*serio_methods.do_trans)();
}

static void do_receive(void)
{
    BYTE cr;
    if((cr=getch())!= EOM && giob->characters_transferred++ <
                    giob->buffer_length)
        *giob->buffer++=cr;
    else
    {
        if(cr==EOM)
        {
            giob->characters_transferred++;
            *giob->buffer=cr;
        }
        giob->call_complete=TRUE;
        SCCR1A.RIE=OFF; /* turn the receiver interrupt off */
        SCCR1A.RE=OFF; /* and disable the receiver */
        if(giob->characters_transferred >=giob->buffer_length)
            giob->error=BUFFER_OVERFLOW;
        else
```

Listing 4.4 (continued)

```
            giob->error=NO_ERROR;
        giob=NULL;      /* get rid of iocb */
    }
}

static void do_transmit(void)
{
    BYTE ct;
    putch(ct=*goob->buffer++); /* send out the character */
    goob->characters_transferred++;
    if(goob->characters_transferred<goob->buffer_length &&
    ct!=EOM)
        ; /* go back if more data to be sent */
    else
    {
        SCCR1A.TIE=OFF;  /* disable the transmitter interrupt */
        SCCR1A.TE=OFF;   /* and also disable the transmitter */
        goob->call_complete=TRUE;
        if(goob->characters_transferred>goob->buffer_length)
            goob->error=BUFFER_OVERFLOW;
        else
            goob->error=NO_ERROR;
        goob=NULL; /* delete iocb */
    }
}
```

Listing 4.4 (continued)

What has been accomplished so far with this exercise? We have created a class that is a complete input/output system that communicates with the computer through port A of the multichannel communications interface module on the MC68HC16Y1 microcontroller. With this piece of code behind us, we can use this channel very easily from any program. The important items that must be included in any program that makes use of this class are as follows:

1. The serio.h header file must be included.
2. An io_command_block must be created and appropriately initialized. This block is used to pass control information to and from the i/o object .
3. An instance of a Serial_io object must be created and its pointer is used in the remainder of the program.
4. The serial_io_() constructor must be executed to set up the communications channel.
5. The i/o is accomplished by execution of the method serial_io() for the object and with the proper io_control_block pointer as an arugment.

A test program is shown in Listing 4.5. This program is quite simple. It repeatedly sends a message to the screen of a terminal attached to the MC68HC16Y1 evaluation module. The message is defined as a constant BYTE and is given the name pszMessage[]. An instance of an io_command_block and a pointer to an io_command_block are created. Inside the main() program, a pointer to a type Serial_io is defined. This machine is a microcontroller, so some additional business must be taken care of whenever the component is brought into use. The next three lines of executable code set up the part to run at 16.78 megahertz (MHz), disable the system watchdog, and establish that the memory needs no wait states. Next the serial_io_() constructor is executed. The parameters here are a baud rate of 9600, an interrupt vector of 0x40, an iarb of 10, and an interrupt level of 3. The pointer oob1 is given the value of the address of ob1. This block pointer will be used to send a message to the serial_io() method of *sio. A loop is then set up. Inside this loop the input parameters of the io_command_block are given proper values. The command is OUTPUT, the buffer is pszMessage, and the buffer size is sizeof pszMessage. The serial_io(sio,oob1) is executed, and when the function returns, it enters a while loop that will hold off any additional processing until the call complete flag in oob1 is set to TRUE. This flag is set in the interrupt service routine.

```
#include "hc16y1.h"
#include "scim.h"
#include "defines.h"
#include "serio.h"

#define SERIO_BAUD_9600 9600
#define SERIO_INT_VECTOR 0x40
#define SERIO_IARB 10
#define SERIO_INT_LEVEL 3

const BYTE pszMessage[]="Here is a pretty long message, in fact
                        \n"
                        "it is about one hundred milliseconds long
                        \n"
                        "at 9600 baud. Of course, the processor \n"
                        "is working only a small fraction of its \n"
                        "time sending out this message.\n\n";

io_command_block *oob1,ob1;

void main(void)
{
    Serial_io *sio;

    /* initialize the SIM registers */
    SYNCR.X=ON;      /* set the system freq to 16.78 mHz */
```

Listing 4.5 Serial Input/Output Test Program

```
    SYPCR.SWE=OFF;  /* disable the watchdog */
    CSORBT.DSACK=0; /* zero wait-state */

    /* set up the serial communications */
    sio=serial_io_(          /* open serial i/o object */
                    SERIO_BAUD_9600,     /* the baud rate */
                     SERIO_INT_VECTOR,   /* interrupt vector */
                     SERIO_IARB, /* iarb */
                    SERIO_INT_LEVEL);   /* and interrupt level */
cli();                 /* enable the system interrupts */

/* set up and fill the io block */
oob1=&ob1;
/* do the outputs--loop forever here and do the output */
FOREVER
{
        oob1->io_command=OUTPUT; /* prepare the io command block
                                 */
        oob1->buffer=pszMessage;
        oob1->buffer_length= sizeof pszMessage;
                serial_io(sio,oob1); /* message to the i/o object
                */
                while(!oob1->call_complete)
                    ;           /* wait until transmission is
                                done */
    }                           /* the processor spends essen-
                                tially */
}                               /* all of its time in this
                                while() */
```

Listing 4.5 (continued)

It was mentioned earlier that the MCCI on the MC68HC16Y1 contains two serial communications interfaces. A single object could be created that would serve as a driver for both these devices. However, it would probably be counter-productive to attempt to build both into a single class. First, the constructor would have to have an additional parameter to specify the particular serial port. The constructor code would be more complicated because different paths through the constructor would be needed to set up the serial port properly. Also, the getch() and putch() would have to be duplicated to accommodate the additional serial port. Finally, the second interrupt service routine needed for the second serial port would have to execute exactly the same operations as seen above. In fact, it appears as if the best approach to integrating the two objects in a case like this one is to create a PORTA object and a PORTB object. The code above is the PORTA object code, and the proper modifications to this code could create the PORTB object code. We will see in Chapter 5 an example where the object is expanded beyond its most basic capability to encompass as many as four timers within a single class.

Another approach that we might consider is the inclusion of a semaphore as part of the i/o sequence. Here the first time that the Serial_io object is created, a semaphore is also created by the calling program and sent to the constructor. From that point on, the state of the semaphore would indicate whether the serial port is being used.

5

TIMERS

The timer subsystem on the MC68HC16Y1 consists of two parts. The first is the general purpose timer (GPT), and the second is the timer processor unit (TPU). This chapter is devoted to use of the GPT.* The GPT has four output compare units, three input capture units, and one timer that can be programmed as either. We shall write a code module that provides program access to all four input captures, and code will be written that permits input capture system measurement of relative event times. Input capture control code will be written to cover the three independent input capture timer subsystems. The single timer that can be programmed as either an input capture or an output compare will not be programmed. It is an easy matter to add this channel to either input or output classes, depending on the system need. This addition can be done by inheritance.

OUTPUT COMPARE SUBSYSTEM

Operation of an output compare timer is simple. The basic timer has a free-running counter that is being clocked at some fraction of the system clock frequency. This register is called the timer counter register (TCNT) and is used as a time base for the entire timer subsystem. A value is placed in one of several output compare registers. These registers are given the names OC1..., OC4. With only minor exceptions, these registers are the same in both function and operation. When the content

*This unit is described in detail in the Motorola Document GPTRM/AD, *Motorola Microcontroller Family General Purpose Timer.*

of the TCNT matches the value in the output compare register, several things can happen depending on the setup of the system. An internal flag is set to indicate that the output compare has occurred. This flag can be polled by the program to determine whether the output compare event has occurred, the corresponding output pin can change to a programmed state, and if properly enabled, an interrupt can be requested. All of these events happen synchronous with match of the TCNT contents with that of the appropriate OCx register.

Both the TCNT and the OCx registers are 16-bit registers. The timer subsystem prescaler can cause the TCNT to be incremented at any binary division of the system clock frequency between 4 and 256. The default prescaler value is 4. There is only one TCNT, so all clocking functions for the general purpose timer subsystem must work from the same time base.

OC1 has some unique properties. This subsystem can be coupled to any other output compare. When OC1 occurs in these cases, the coupled OCx pin will go to a programmed state. This type of operation is very convenient for operations such as a pulse-width modulator. In this case OC1 will be used to establish the base time period of the PWM system, and the coupled output compare will be used to determine the duty factor. With this arrangement, output pulses as small as one timer clock cycle can be created.

Here is a case where several on-board devices operate similarly, and a class can be created that will allow the programmer to make use of any output compare subsystem selected. This choice is made by making an appropriate constructor call. Remember that in Chapter 4, we saw a case of several similar peripheral components on the microcontroller. We decided there that a special class should be written for each of the two SCI interfaces rather than attempt to create a single class that could create instances of either of the two hardware serial ports. Here all the components are set up by a single class. The timer class will embody the complete output compare system and demonstrate that a class can provide complete coverage and control of a peripheral.

TIMER CLASS

What are we going to do with these timers? I do not know now, and in fact, there is no way to know, so an approach must be used that will allow for very flexible extension of the basic timer classes. This flexibility will permit the connection of objects instantiated from other classes, or perhaps standard applications code created by the programmer. This flexibility is implemented by the inclusion of two attributes in the timer object. One is a call to an external function and the other is a parameter to be passed to this function. With these external accesses, the actions that can be performed by the timer during an interrupt service routine are essentially unlimited.

The header file for the class timer is shown in Listing 5.1. Six parameters must be passed to the timer constructor. These parameters are pulled together into a single structure type and a pointer to this structure is passed to the constructor. The five parameters found in the Timer_parameter structure are all that are needed to set up completely any of the four output compare subsystems. The first value, number, is simply the number of the timer and can have a value between 1 and 4. The second parameter, tick, is the value added to the specific output compare register whenever there is an interrupt caused by an output compare. The next parameter determines the output that will occur whenever there is an output compare on OC2 through OC4. Table 5.1 summarizes the possible actions that can occur. The contents of action will be given a value of 0 through 3 and the proper bits in the timer registers will be set to cause the action shown in the table to occur.

The contents of Table 5.1 are collected into an enumeration in the header file so that the programmer can use mnemonic descriptions of the output rather than trying to remember the meanings of the several numbers above.

Output compare 1 works somewhat differently from the remainder of the output compares. OC1 can be connected to any other output compare, and when OC1 occurs, the connected output compare will go to a designated state. The parameter OC1_connect is given a value of 0 to 4. If the value is 0, the OC1 is connected to neither an output nor another output compare. If it is 1, OC1 is connected to its own output pin. Otherwise, the number is the output compare to which OC1 is connected. The connect_data input will be given a value of ON or OFF, which is the state that the connected output compare will go to when OC1 occurs.

The last entry in the type Timer_parameters is a Boolean value named interrupt. This parameter can have a value of TRUE or FALSE, or YES or NO as defined in the defines.h file. If the value is YES, an interrupt will be set up to occur when the proper output compare occurs. Otherwise, there will be no interrupt, and either the program or perhaps the external hardware must respond to the occurrence of the output compare.

The timer class is derived from the error handler, and it has three attributes: who_am_I, ms_tick, and a pointer to a type void called a hook_object. There are two class methods. The first is identified as a pointer to hook_method and the second is a pointer to an internal function called reset. The timer class is defined as Timer, and it has both a constructor and a destructor. The constructor requires a parameter that is a pointer to a type Timer_parameters.

There are two methods needed to assign values to hook_object and hook_method. These functions are created as macros which are included in the header file. As such, the two assign functions will always be used as inline code rather than function calls. In addition to the usual two functions, the constructor and the destructor, an additional class method is needed. This method, reset(), will be used to reset a particular timer so that the output compare will occur a specified time

Table 5.1 OMx,OLx Bits

OMx-OLx	Action Taken on Compare
00	Timer disconnected from output (default)
01	Toggle OCx line
10	Clear OCx line to zero
11	Set OCx line to 1

Source: Motorola Microcontroller Family General Purpose Timer, Motorola Document GPTRM/AD.

```
#ifndef TIMER_H
#define TIMER_H

#include "defines.h"
#include "error.h"

#ifndef GPT_IARB
      #define GPT_IARB 12   /* iarb value of 12 for the GPT */
      #define GPT_VBA 5    /* GPT vectors start at 0x50 */
      #define GPT_LEVEL 6  /* use interrupt level 6 */
#endif

typedef enum BYTE
{
      DISCONNECT,
      TOGGLE,
      CLEAR,
      SET
}Output;
enum output_compares(OC1=1,OC2,OC3,OC4);
typedef struct
{
      WORD   number,
             tick;
      Output action;
      BYTE   OC1_connect,
             connect_data;
      Boolean  interrupt;
} Timer_parameters;

#define TIMER_CLASS \
        ERROR_HANDLER \
        WORD who_am_I;\
        WORD ms_tick; \
        void (*reset)(struct time *); \
        void *hook_object;\
        void (*hook_method)(void*);

typedef struct time
{
TIMER_CLASS
}Timer;
#ifndef ATTACH
#define ATTACH
      #define attach_object(a,b) ((a)->hook_object=(b))
```

Listing 5.1 Timer Class Definition File

```
        #define attach_method(a,b) ((a)->hook_method=(b))
#endif

Timer* timer_(Timer_parameters *);
void timer__(Timer*);
#endif
```

Listing 5.1 (continued)

after the current time. The reset also forces an output event to the outside world (if it is set up to be delivered to the outside) when the reset method is executed. It does not cause the output compare flag to be set or an output compare interrupt to occur.

Several pieces of business must be completed whenever the timer subsystem is to be used. The interrupt arbitration level, the vector base address, and the interrupt level have all been seen before. It was decided in this case that these values would be assigned specific values. If this approach is not acceptable, it is an easy matter to expand the number of parameters passed to the constructor to include these values. It is important to note that these three values must remain the same for each of the different timers, so perhaps it is best to preassign these values and not worry about them any further. There are four interrupt service routines, each named OCxIsr(). There is also a static function named do_hook(). The prototypes for these several functions are listed next in the file below.

```
#include "hc16y1.h"
#include "gpt.h"
#include "timer.h"

#define GPT_IARB 12         /* iarb value of 12 for the GPT */
#define GPT_VBA 5       /* GPT vectors start at 0x50 */
#define GPT_LEVEL 6     /* use interrupt level 6 */
#define OC1_offset 4     /* output compare vector offsets */
#define OC2_offset 5
#define OC3_offset 6
#define OC4_offset 7
@port void OC1Isr(void);
@port void OC2Isr(void);
@port void OC3Isr(void);
@port void OC4Isr(void);
static void do_hook(Timer *);
```

The reset function is shown below. If instantiated as objects, each of the four timers can be reset. A reset will cause an output compare to occur if an external connection between the output compare and its output pin is set up or there is a connection between OC1 or any other output compare. Also, a reset will calculate a new value that is equal to the current content of the timer counter register plus the object specified tick value and place this value in the proper output compare register. The code to implement these operations is shown below.

```
static void reset(Timer *this)
{
        switch(this->who_am_I)
        {
              case 1 : TOC1=TCNT+this->ms_tick; /* restart output
                                                   comp count */
                       CFORC.FOC1=ON;    /* and force an output
                                                   compare */
                       break;
              case 2 : TOC2=TCNT+this->ms_tick;
                       CFORC.FOC2=ON;
                       break;
              case 3 : TOC3=TCNT+this->ms_tick;
                       CFORC.FOC3=ON;
                       break;
              case 4 : TOC4=TCNT+this->ms_tick;
                       CFORC.FOC4=ON;
                       break;
        }
}
```

The constructor for the output compare subsystem is shown below. There are four pointers to the type Timer defined as external variables. These variables will hold pointers to the four possible instances of timer objects. They are needed to implement the basic interrupt service routines that follow. The first executable code in the constructor is a series of tests that check for appropriate parameter values. If a parameter is found that is out of the acceptable range, a FALSE value is returned to the calling program, indicating that there has been a program error. Memory is allocated to hold the new object; an error object is instantiated, the error object is copied onto the new timer object, and the error object is destroyed. The preassigned values of IARB, LEVEL, and VBA are placed in the appropriate registers in the timer subsystem. Note in the preceding listing that copies of hc16y1.h and gpt.h were included. It is in these files that the parameters such as GPT_MCR and IARB are defined. The parameters passed as arguments to the constructor are next put into the attributes locations. Here *number* is the number of the output compare and can have a value of 1 through 4. The value ticks is the number that is added to the content of the output compare register with each interrupt. This number sets the basic timing of the timer being instantiated. If it is intended to connect the output of OC1 to another timer, this connection is made and the output action of the connection is put into place at this point in the code. The parameters hook_object, a pointer to a type void, and hook_method, a pointer to a void function, are each assigned the value of a NULL which is a pointer with a value zero. These parameters will be changed when it is necessary to connect an applications function to the timer.

```
Timer *OC1_T,*OC2_T,*OC3_T,*OC4_T;

Timer* timer_(Timer_parameters *tp)
{
    Timer* this;
    Error_handler *temp = error_();

    if(tp->number >4)  /* error must be between 1 and 4 */
            return FALSE;
    if(tp->OC1_connect>4)
            return FALSE;          /* got a bad OC1_connect */
    if(tp->connect_data >4)
            return FALSE;          /* got bad connect_data*/
    this=(Timer*) malloc(sizeof(Timer));
    if(this==NULL)
            error_handler(temp,TYPE_1,TIMER);
    memmove(this, temp, sizeof(Error_handler));
    error__(temp);
                              /* initialize the GPT  */
    GPT_MCR.IARB=GPT_IARB; /* pick an IARB for the timers */
    ICR.IRL=GPT_LEVEL;     /* interrupt level 6 */
    ICR.VBA=GPT_VBA;       /* vectors start at 0x50 */
    this->who_am_I=tp->number; /* save the number of the timer */
    this->ms_tick=tp->tick;
    this->reset=reset;     /* put reset function in place */
    if(tp->OC1_connect>=2 && tp->OC1_connect>=4) /* set up the */
                                           /* OC1 connections */
    {
            switch(tp->OC1_connect)
            {
               case 1 : OC1M.OC1M3=ON;
                        OC1D.OC1D3=tp->connect_data;
                              break;
               case 2 : OC1M.OC1M4=ON;
                        OC1D.OC1D4=tp->connect_data;
                              break;
               case 3 : OC1M.OC1M5=ON;
                        OC1D.OC1D5=tp->connect_data;
                              break;
               case 4 : OC1M.OC1M6=ON;
                        OC1D.OC1D6=tp->connect_data;
                              break;
            }
    }
```

```
    this->hook_object=NULL;
    this->hook_method=NULL;
    switch(tp->number)
    {
            case 1: TFLG1.OC1F=OFF;      /* reset event flag */
                   TOC1=TCNT+tp->tick;     /* set output compare
                                           register */
                    vector(OC1Isr,VAL*(GPT_VBA*0x10+OC1_offset));
                                         /* put vector in place */
                    if(tp->interrupt) /* do we need an interrupt?
                                        */
                        TMSK1.OC1I=ON; /* enable the interrupt*/
                    OC1_T=this; /* keep Timer pointer */
                    break;
            case 2: TFLG1.OC2F=OFF;
                    OMLREG.OML2=tp->action; /* put action in
                    place */
                    TOC2=TCNT+tp->tick;
                    vector(OC2Isr,VAL*(GPT_VBA*0x10+OC2_offset));
                    if(tp->interrupt)
                        TMSK2.OC2I=ON;
                    OC2_T=this;
                    break;
            case 3: TFLG1.OC3F=OFF;
                    OMLREG.OML3=tp->action;
                    TOC3=TCNT+tp->tick;
                    vector(OC3Isr,VAL*(GPT_VBA*0x10+OC3_offset));
                    if(tp->interrupt)
                        TMSK2.OC3I=ON;
                    OC3_T=this;
                    break;
            case 4: TFLG1.OC4F=OFF;
                    OMLREG.OML4=tp->action;
                    TOC4=TCNT+tp->tick;
                    vector(OC4Isr,VAL*(GPT_VBA*0x10+OC4_offset));
                    if(tp->interrupt)
                        TMSK2.OC4I=ON;
                    OC4_T=this;
                    break;
    }
    return this;
}
```

The switch statement shown above is used to set up the proper interrupt for the specific output compare being instantiated. The value of OCxF is turned off to avoid an immediate entry into an unwanted interrupt when the interrupt mask is enabled later in the code. For output compares 2 through 4, the action value passed in through the parameter block is placed in the proper OMx and OLx bits in the TCTL1 register. This register has been given the duplicate name of OMLREG to ease the proper setting of the control bits. The proper output compare is given a value equal to the contents of the TCNT register plus the tick value. The next interrupt for this timer will occur when TCNT equals this value. The statement

```
vector(OCxIsr,VAL*(GPT_VBA*0x10+y))
```

invokes the vector macro found in the header hc16y1.h. Table 5.2 shows the interrupt vector layout for the timer subsystem. Each vector address starts with a $X, indicating that this value is programmable. X is replaced by the value found in the ICR.VBA bit field. We earlier put the #defined value GPT_VBA into this bit field. The value y in the expression above will have a value 4 through 7. Therefore, the term

```
GPT_VBA*0x10+y
```

is the correct vector for the interrupt and the vector is converted into an address when it is multiplied by the value VAL. VAL is either 2 or 4, depending on the microcontroller being used, and is defined in the core microprocessor header file. The address of the OCxIsr interrupt service routine is placed at this location by the macro vector().

The remainder of the setup for the several interrupts is completed when the corresponding interrupt enable bit is set by an instruction

```
TMSK1.OCxI = ON;
```

Table 5.2 Timer Interrupt Priorities and Vectors

Name	Interrupt Source Function	Priority	Vector
	Adjusted channel	0 (highest)	$X0
IC1	Input capture 1	1	$X1
IC2	Input capture 2	2	$X2
IC3	Input capture 3	3	$X3
OC1	Output compare 1	4	$X4
OC2	Output compare 2	5	$X5
OC3	Output compare 3	6	$X6
OC4	Output compare 4	7	$X7
IC4/OC5	Input capture 4/output compare 5	8	$X8
TOF	Timer overflow flag	9	$X9
PAOVF	Pulse accumulator overflow flag	10	$XA
PAIF	Pulse accumulator input flag	11 (lowest)	$XB

Source: Motorola Microcontroller Family General Purpose Timer, Motorola Document GPTRM/AD, Table 7-1.

and the value of this is saved in the external variable OCx_T. This value is needed to execute the interrupt service routine properly.

Next to follow is the destructor. In this case the destructor must free the memory allocated to the object, and it must also disable the interrupt for the object being discarded. The switch statement selects the proper interrupt to disable, and the free(this) function call deletes the memory allocation.

```
void timer__(Timer* this)
{
    switch(this->who_am_I)
    {
       case 1 : TMSK1.OC1I=OFF; /* turn off the timer interrupt
                                 */
                break;
       case 2 : TMSK1.OC2I=OFF;
                break;
       case 3 : TMSK1.OC3I=OFF;
                break;
       case 4 : TMSK1.OC4I=OFF;
                break;
    }
    free(this);
}
```

The interrupt service routines are quite simple. In each case the corresponding interrupt flag bit is turned OFF. Then the contents of TOC1 is incremented by the corresponding tick value so that the next interrupt will occur when expected. Finally, the function do_hook(OCx_T) is executed. There are four interrupt service routines: one for each of the four output compare subsystems.

```
/* interrupt service routines */

@port void OC1Isr(void)
{
    TFLG1.OC1F=OFF;
    TOC1+=OC1_T->ms_tick;
    do_hook(OC1_T);
}

@port void OC2Isr(void)
{
    TFLG1.OC2F=OFF;
    TOC2+=OC2_T->ms_tick;
    do_hook(OC2_T);
}
```

```
@port void OC3Isr(void)
{
    TFLG1.OC3F=OFF;
    TOC3+=OC3_T->ms_tick;
    do_hook(OC3_T);
}

@port void OC4Isr(void)
{
    TFLG1.OC4F=OFF;
    TOC4+=OC4_T->ms_tick;
    do_hook(OC4_T);
}
```

Each instance of a timer contains two attributes that can be altered by the program that instantiates the timer. The functions attach_object() and attach_method() place a value and a pointer to a function into the locations hook_object and hook_method in the object attribute list. It is assumed that (*hook_method)() is a function that can use hook_object as a parameter. If these values have been provided by the calling program, it is possible for the interrupt service routine to execute any practical function associated with the calling program as a part of the interrupt service routine. When program control returns after execution of this function, the control of the computer is returned to the program interrupted.

The function do_hook() that is executed in each interrupt service routine is shown below. This simple program executes the corresponding (*hook_method)() function with hook_object as a parameter. This function is executed only if the value of hook_method is not a NULL. We will see a couple of examples in the programs that follow where functions or objects are attached to the timer interrupt service routines.

```
static void do_hook(Timer *time)
{
    if(time->hook_method !=NULL)
       (*time->hook_method)(time->hook_object);
}
```

The description of the timer implementation file above has been broken into several small pieces to help with description of the various parts. Listing 5.2 is a complete, contiguous listing of the program.

The basic timer class above will provide a starting point for several other classes developed in the following examples. Timer is a very good example of a software component. It will be used in conjunction with several other classes that are all based on working in time. Assuming that the class has been debugged completely, an object of the type Timer can be used without fear of either failure to perform its designated task or unexpected side effects caused by leakage between

```
#include "hc16y1.h"
#include "gpt.h"
#include "timer.h"

#define GPT_IARB 12          /* iarb value of 12 for the GPT */
#define GPT_VBA 5       /* GPT vectors start at 0x50 */
#define GPT_LEVEL 6     /* use interrupt level 6 */
#define OC1_offset 4     /* output compare vector offsets */
#define OC2_offset 5
#define OC3_offset 6
#define OC4_offset 7

@port void OC1Isr(void);
@port void OC2Isr(void);
@port void OC3Isr(void);
@port void OC4Isr(void);
static void reset(Timer *);
static void do_hook(Timer *);

Timer *OC1_T,*OC2_T,*OC3_T,*OC4_T;

static void reset(Timer *this)
{
      switch(this->who_am_I)
      {
            case 1 : TOC1=TCNT+this->ms_tick; /* restart
                                                   outputcomp count */
                     CFORC.FOC1=ON; /* and force an output
                                                           compare */
                     break;
            case 2 : TOC2=TCNT+this->ms_tick;
                     CFORC.FOC2=ON;
                     break;
            case 3 : TOC3=TCNT+this->ms_tick;
                     CFORC.FOC3=ON;
                     break;
            case 4 : TOC4=TCNT+this->ms_tick;
                     CFORC.FOC4=ON;
                     break;
      }
}

Timer* timer_(Timer_parameters *tp)
{
```

Listing 5.2 Timer Class Implementation File

```
Timer* this;
Error_handler *temp = error_();


if(tp->number >4) /* error must be between 1 and 4 */


        return FALSE;
if(tp->OC1_connect>4)
        return FALSE;  /* got a bad OC1_connect */
if(tp->connect_data >4)
        return FALSE;  /* got bad connect_data*/
this=(Timer*) malloc(sizeof(Timer));
if(this==NULL)
            error_handler(temp,TYPE_1,TIMER);
memmove(this, temp, sizeof(Error_handler));
error__(temp);
/* initialize the GPT  */
GPT_MCR.IARB=GPT_IARB; /* pick an IARB for the timers */
ICR.IRL=GPT_LEVEL;     /* interrupt level 6 */
ICR.VBA=GPT_VBA;       /* vectors start at 0x50 */
this->who_am_I=tp->number; /* save the number of the timer */
this->ms_tick=tp->tick;
this->reset=reset;     /* put reset function in place */
if(tp->OC1_connect>0 && tp->OC1_connect<5)  /* set up the
                                               OC1  connections */
{
        switch(tp->OC1_connect)
        {
           case 1 : OC1M.OC1M3=ON;
                    OC1D.OC1D3=tp->connect_data;
                    break;
           case 2 : OC1M.OC1M4=ON;
                    OC1D.OC1D4=tp->connect_data;
                    break;
           case 3 : OC1M.OC1M5=ON;
                    OC1D.OC1D5=tp->connect_data;
                    break;
           case 4 : OC1M.OC1M6=ON;
                    OC1D.OC1D6=tp->connect_data;
                    break;
      }
}
this->hook_object=NULL;
this->hook_method=NULL;
switch(tp->number)
{
```

Listing 5.2 (continued)

```
        case 1: TFLG1.OC1F=OFF;         /* reset event flag */
                TOC1=TCNT+tp->tick;     /* set output compare
                                           register */
                vector(OC1Isr,VAL*(GPT_VBA*0x10+OC1_offset));
                                      /* put vector in place */
                if(tp->interrupt)     /* do we need an interrupt? */
                    TMSK1.OC1I=ON;    /* enable the interrupt*/
                OC1_T=this;           /* keep Timer pointer */
                break;
        case 2: TFLG1.OC2F=OFF;
                OMLREG.OML2=tp->action;
                TOC2=TCNT+tp->tick;
                vector(OC2Isr,VAL*(GPT_VBA*0x10+OC2_offset));
                if(tp->interrupt)
                    TMSK2.OC2I=ON;
                OC2_T=this;
                break;
        case 3: TFLG1.OC3F=OFF;
                OMLREG.OML3=tp->action;
                TOC3=TCNT+tp->tick;
                vector(OC3Isr,VAL*(GPT_VBA*0x10+OC3_offset));
                if(tp->interrupt)
                    TMSK2.OC3I=ON;
                OC3_T=this;
                break;
        case 4: TFLG1.OC4F=OFF;
                OMLREG.OML4=tp->action;
                TOC4=TCNT+tp->tick;
                vector(OC4Isr,VAL*(GPT_VBA*0x10+OC4_offset));
                if(tp->interrupt)
                    TMSK2.OC4I=ON;
                OC4_T=this;
                break;
        }
    return this;
}


void timer__(Timer* this)
{
    switch(this->who_am_I)
    {
       case 1 : TMSK1.OC1I=OFF; /* turn off the timer interrupt
                                 */
                break;
       case 2 : TMSK1.OC2I=OFF;
                break;
```

Listing 5.2 (continued)

```
        case 3 : TMSK1.OC3I=OFF;
                 break;
        case 4 : TMSK1.OC4I=OFF;
                 break;
    }
    free(this);
}

/* interrupt service routines */

@port void OC1Isr(void)
{
    TFLG1.OC1F=OFF;
    TOC1+=OC1_T->ms_tick;
    do_hook(OC1_T);
}

@port void OC2Isr(void)
{
    TFLG1.OC2F=OFF;
    TOC2+=OC2_T->ms_tick;
    do_hook(OC2_T);
}

@port void OC3Isr(void)
{
    TFLG1.OC3F=OFF;
    TOC3+=OC3_T->ms_tick;
    do_hook(OC3_T);
}

@port void OC4Isr(void)
{
    TFLG1.OC4F=OFF;
    TOC4+=OC4_T->ms_tick;
    do_hook(OC4_T);
}

/* function that allows external access to isr */
static void do_hook(Timer *time)
{
    if(time->hook_method !=NULL)
       (*time->hook_method)(time->hook_object);
}
```

Listing 5.2 (continued)

memory areas. None of the attributes of Timer should be accessed except through the methods provided. If it becomes necessary to access an attribute, a separate method, perhaps created in an inherited class, should be created to handle this contingency. Usually, the code in a header file and its associated implementation file should never be changed. A case where we will allow such a change is for the addition of macro methods. These cases pose a dilemma. Such a change should be associated with the class code, and we do not want to alter the class code directly. Use inheritance in any but the most basic of changes, and then put any new macros into the header file of the affected class. Never change the implementation file. If it is necessary to change features in the implementation file, use inheritance to isolate the changed code from the known working and debugged code.

DELAY

The first example that will make use of Timer is to create a delay. Often, it is necessary to delay execution of a program by a specified amount of time. It is expected that in these cases, a Timer can be made available to effect the delay. Recall, Timer needs a tick value that is usually aimed to produce an event on a relatively short time basis. Certainly, the size of the number to be added to the output compare register should be represented in an unsigned integer that is the size of the timer counter register. With the microcontroller running at 16 MHz, the time required to overflow this register is 16 milliseconds. With proper setup of the timer prescaler, this time can be extended to approximately 4000 milliseconds. Therefore, most timers have periods that lie in this range of values. Also, you should have noted that if a Timer is instantiated properly, it will run periodically with an interrupt occurring each time the timer counter register matches the corresponding output compare register. This arrangement makes Timer a perfect base for a delay. A Timer will be created that has some convenient base frequency or time of interrupt. The delay is set up to count the number of interrupts, and when the specified number of interrupts occur, the delay is released. Here is a case where a semaphore (discussed in Chapter 3) can be used to an advantage. The calling program that initiates the delay will create a semaphore. This semaphore will be attached to the delay, and the calling program will be put into a wait_for_semaphore() call, which will stop execution of the calling program until the semaphore is released by the delay program. The delay program will wait until the proper number of ticks from the base Timer and then delete itself, which will release the semaphore automatically, allowing the calling program to proceed.

In the delay header file shown in Listing 5.3, you will note that these objects will access error.h, timer.h, semaphore.h, and defines.h. The class is set up to have delay inherit the error_handler. There are three attributes, the delay time, a pointer to the specified timer, and a pointer to the semaphore. These three parameters are passed to the delay constructor as arguments.

```
#ifndef DELAY_H
#define DELAY_H

#include "error.h"
#include "timer.h"
#include "semaphor.h"
#include "defines.h"

#define DELAY_CLASS \
                    ERROR_HANDLER \
                    unsigned int delay_time; \
                    struct time *Time;\
                    Semaphore *semaphore;

typedef struct delay
{
      DELAY_CLASS
}Delay;
struct delay *delay_(struct time*, Semaphore*,unsigned int);
void delay__(struct delay *);
#endif
```

Listing 5.3 Delay Class Definition File

The implementation of delay needs access to a function that we will call exercise(). The Timer interrupt occurs at a rate specified when the timer is instantiated. Normally, this rate is relatively fast, and when a program delay is needed, that time is usually longer than the timer interrupt rate. Therefore, we must pass a number to the delay that is the number of timer interrupts that need to be executed during the delay time. This number is the third argument of the delay constructor. This number, called delay_time, is stored in the object. The function exercise() decrements this number until it becomes zero. At that time, the delay object is deleted. The operations done during delete are discussed below.

The delay constructor, delay_(), follows the general plan used in most other constructors. Delay is inherited from the Error_handler, so a temporary Error_handler object is created. Space is allocated to hold the delay object, and the temporary Error_handler is moved into this space. The Error_handler is then deleted. The timer pointer and the semaphore pointer are moved into the newly created object and the semaphore is attached to the delay. The delay time passed into the constructor is stored in the delay_time location of the new object. A pointer to the delay is placed in the hook object location of the timer object, and a pointer to the function exercise is put into the hook method location in the timer object. Therefore, the function exercise for this delay will be executed during each timer interrupt service routine. Finally, a pointer to the newly created delay object is returned to the calling program.

```
#include "delay.h"

static void exercise(Delay *delay)
{
    if(--delay->delay_time==0)
    {
        delay__(delay); /* delete the delay */
    }
}

Delay* delay_(Timer *Time,Semaphore *sem, unsigned int
delay_time)
{
    Delay *this;
    Error_handler *temp=error_();

    this = (Delay* ) malloc(sizeof(Delay));
    if(this==NULL)
            error_handler(temp,TYPE_1,DELAY);
    memmove(this,temp,sizeof(Error_handler));
    error__(temp);
    this->Time=Time;
    this->semaphore=sem;
    attach_semaphore(this->semaphore); /* attach semaphore
                                          to process */
    this->delay_time=delay_time;
    attach_object(Time,(void*)this);  /* put hook object in
                                         place */
    attach_method(Time,exercise);  /* and the hook method */
    return this;
}
```

The delay destructor is a little different from most destructors discussed so far. Of course, the memory allocated to the delay must be released back to the system by execution of the free(this) function. Also, a semaphore attached to the delay object must be released so that the calling function will be able to proceed. Finally, since this delay will no longer exist after execution of the destructor, it is important to remove its presence from the timer object to which it was attached. The two calls attach_method(this->Time,NULL) and attach_object(this->Time,NULL) replace the data stored in hook_object and hook_method within the timer object with NULL, which is a pointer to a nonexistent memory location. When the timer interrupt service routine is executed, the value of hook_method is tested and there is no attempt to execute this function if it contains a NULL.

```
void delay__(Delay *this)
{
    release_semaphore(this->semaphore); /* Release the semaphore
                                         */
    attach_method(this->Time,NULL); /* release timer */
    attach_object(this->Time,NULL);
    free(this);
}
```

We next demonstrate the use of the delay class in a very simple program. This program will start execution, delay operation for 10 seconds, and quit. It will run on an MC68HC16Y1 chip. This chip has a general-purpose timer, so the timer class that we wrote earlier can be executed. We include the standard header files, which include the chip-related headers hc16y1.h and scim.h, along with the delay.h, semaphor.h, timer.h, and delay.h headers, which are class header files.

The next two lines of code define TIMECOUNT as 4000 and DELAY_TIME as 10,000. TIMECOUNT is the number of timer clock cycles that will be executed prior to each timer interrupt. DELAY_TIME is the number of interrupts that will occur during the total delay. One millisecond requires 4000 timer clock cycles. Therefore, there will be a timer interrupt each millisecond. The delay time of 10,000 interrupts will expire in 10 seconds.

```
#include "hc16y1.h"
#include "semaphor.h"
#include "timer.h"
#include "delay.h"
#include "scim.h"
#include "defines.h"

#define TIMECOUNT 4000
#define DELAY_TIME 10000
```

When running a timer, we must control the basic clock frequency of the system if the timing is to be accurate. This control is through the clock synchronization register, which is a part of the single chip integration module (SCIM). The SYNCR controls the operation of a frequency synthesizer. This synthesizer locks a high-frequency oscillator to the phase of a low-frequency crystal oscillator and allows the programmer or hardware engineer wide flexibility in choice of a system frequency. The SYNCR register is shown in Figure 5.1. The important bit fields in this register are the W, X, and Y fields. Depending on the crystal frequency, there are two equations that can be used to calculate the system frequency. When the crystal frequency, or reference frequency, is between 25 and 50 kilohertz, the following equation is used to determine the system frequency:

$$F_{\text{system}} = F_{\text{reference}}\ [4(\mathrm{Y} + 1)(2^{2\mathrm{W}+\mathrm{X}})]$$

SYNCR $####04

Bit 15	14	13	12	11	10	9	8	7	6	5	4	3	2	1	0
W	X	Y						EDIV	0	0	SLIMP	SLOCK	RSTEN	STSIM	STEXT
Reset															
0	0	1	1	1	1	1	1	0	0	0	U	U	0	0	0

Figure 5.1 Clock Synchronization Register

where W, X, and Y are the values contained in the corresponding bit fields. The most common crystal used in this frequency range is a watch crystal, which runs at 32,768 Hz. The default condition of these bit fields, after reset, are shown in the register description below. Note that both W and X contain a value 0 and Y contains a value 63. Therefore, if the crystal frequency is 32,768, the system frequency will be 32,768 × 256 or 8,388,608. If the operation requires a frequency near 16 MHz, this value must be doubled. It can be doubled easily by placing a value of 1 in the X-bit field of the SYNCR. This setup will cause the system frequency to be 16.777216 MHz.

Alternatively, it is possible to use a higher-frequency crystal. In this case the equation to determine the system frequency is given by

$$\frac{F_{\text{system}} = [4(\mathrm{Y}+1)(2^{2\mathrm{W}+\mathrm{X}})]F_{\text{reference}}}{128}$$

This equation holds for reference frequencies between 3.2 and 6.4 MHz. You can think of the operation as being the same with either range of frequencies, with the higher frequency being divided by 128 prior to the adjustment by the frequency synthesizer. The hardware determines automatically when division by 128 is needed. The development board used to test programs for this book is the MC68HC16Y1MPB. This board uses a 4.00-MHz crystal oscillator. Therefore, if the value of the X bit is set to 1, the system frequency is 16.00 MHz.

Also, the default timer clock prescaler is set to a value of 4. Thus the input to the GPT should be running at a frequency of 4.00 MHz when the reference frequency is 4.00 MHz, the X bit of the SYNCR register is set to 1, and the Y field in this register has its default value.

There are two popular development boards that you will find for the M68HC16 family of components. The one mentioned above supports the larger MC68HC16Y1 chip. Alternatively, the MC68HC16Z1EVB supports the MC68HC16Z1 chip. This chip has different on-board peripheral components. The board itself has a 32,768-Hz crystal to provide the reference frequency for the chip. In that case, with the same setup as discussed above, the input to the GPT will be 4.194304 MHz rather than 4.00 MHz. This difference in system frequency will cause significant differences in any delay or clock operation that you might program into the part.

The main program here is relatively simple once the various classes have been created properly. The first three instructions define pointers to a timer, a semaphore, and a delay object. A timer parameter block is also created. The SIM (system integration module) registers are set up. The clock speed is set to 16.00 MHz, the watchdog is disabled, and the built-in wait-state generator for the boot memory chip select is set to 0 wait states. The system interrupts are then enabled.

```
#include "hc16y1.h"
#include "semaphor.h"
#include "timer.h"
#include "delay.h"
#include "scim.h"
#include "defines.h"

#define TIMECOUNT 4000
#define DELAY_TIME 10000

main()
{
    Timer *t;
    Semaphore *sem;
    Delay *d;
    Timer_parameters tp;

    /* initialize the SIM registers */
    /* set the clock to 16.00 MHz, disable the watchdog, and 0
        wait state */
    SYNCR.X=ON;      /* double the clock speed—16.00 MHz */
    SYPCR.SWE=OFF;   /* disable the watchdog */
    CSORBT.DSACK=0;  /* use zero wait states for now */
    cli();           /* enable the system interrupts */

    tp.number=3;     /* set up the timer parameter structure */
    tp.tick=TIMECOUNT;   /* 1 ms interrupts */
    tp.action=0;         /* no output action */
    tp.OC1_connect=0;    /* OC1 not connected to another OC */
    tp.connect_data=0;
    tp.interrupt=YES;    /* need an interrupt here */
    t=timer_(&tp);
    sem=semaphore_();    /* make the semaphore */
    d=delay_(t,sem,DELAY_TIME);
    wait_for_semaphore(sem);
    semaphore__(sem);
    timer__(t);
}
```

Listing 5.4 Delay Test Program

The timer parameter block is properly filled. I arbitrarily chose output compare 3 to be the timer for this system. The tick count is set to provide 1-ms interrupts. There is no external action when these interrupts occur. Also, OC1 is not being used with this program. We will need an interrupt to occur. These appropriate values are placed in the timer parameter block, and a pointer to this block is sent to the timer constructor.

The program then gets an instance of a semaphore and creates an instance of the delay component. The delay constructor receives pointers to the timer, the semaphore and the delay time as arguments. The operation of this program returns the value from delay_(), but the semaphore is attached to delay. Therefore, the wait_for_semaphore() call will lock up operation of the program until the semaphore is released by the object d. When the semaphore is released by delay, it is destroyed, and the timer object is also destroyed. Recall that it is not necessary to destroy the delay because the exercise program contained within the delay takes care of this little piece of business.

The program in Listing 5.4 demonstrates operation of the timer, the semaphore, and the delay objects. Shown below is a series of programs. These programs will show the operation of a timer component in a slightly more complicated operation. The program is written is three phases. These phases, clock, clock1, and clock2, first build a simple time-of-day clock. There is only one piece of business processed with each timer interrupt. The time output is sent out of the computer through the serial port. There is no provision that allows setting the clock from the external system. In other words, the only way that the clock can be set to a specific time is to modify the time values in memory with a debug system. We start with this simple system and later add more features that will make our clock more useful.

CLOCK

The routine clock is a simple clock that cannot do much more than tell time. In clock1, this routine is expanded to allow two distinct operations to be executed during the interrupt service routine of the timer. These two operations are contained on a linked list, and if more items were needed, the linked list could be extended. Finally, in clock2, it is shown how to add the capability of setting the clock through the keyboard.

The header files for the program are listed below. The first four header files have to do with the chip. The MC68HC16Y1 chip contains, among other modules, the general-purpose timer (GPT), the multichannel communications interface (MCCI), and the single-chip integration module (SCIM). These headers are each included. We will also make use of the serial input/output object along with the timer object. These headers are included along with the usual defines.h header.

```
#include "HC16Y1.H"
#include "gpt.h"
```

```
#include "mcci.h"
#include "scim.h"
#include "serio.h"
#include "timer.h"
#include "defines.h"
```

Next follows a series of definitions needed by the program. You will remember that the hardware parameters for the serial i/o operation are all determined by the program. These parameters were locked into specific values in the timer object. There is no correct or incorrect approach to where the system parameters are delivered to the program. The parameters must be provided. In the case of the timer class, the programmer has no choice as to the location of the interrupt vector, the IARB, and the interrupt level. These parameters are established within the class definition. In the case of the serial i/o class, the interrupt parameters along with the serial i/o baud rate must be passed to the class as arguments to the class constructor. The set of defines that establish these values are shown below. Remember, it is always better to use a series of defines or an enumeration statement to create these values for the program rather than to use the actual numbers within the function calls. Such numbers, used as function arguments, are called *magic numbers*. When inserted as numbers, there is no connection to their real meaning. When defined, all numbers are inserted into the program as mnemonics with some program meaning.

```
#define SERIO_BAUD_19200 19200
#define SERIO_INT_VECTOR 0x40
#define SERIO_IARB 10
#define SERIO_INT_LEVEL 3
#define TIMECOUNT 4000
#define ONE_SECOND 1000
```

The next program items are the function prototypes. There are only four functions used for this program. The first, count_ticks(), is a simple function that merely increments the content of the address passed to the function as a parameter. This function is quite important because it is another example of use of the do_hook approach that we use to add a function to the interrupt service routine of an instance of the timer class. The remaining three functions are used to convert the integer type data stored in memory into a character form that can be sent to the serial port. This function is convert_itoa(). The function build_time() creates a complete message to be sent to the serial port and uses convert_itoa() and output_time() sends the message to the serial port.

```
/* function prototypes */

void count_ticks(WORD *);
void output_time(void);
```

```
void build_time(void);
void convert_itoa(WORD a,BYTE *p);
```

Next to follow in the program are the variable definition statements. The first is a string variable in which the message to be sent to the serial port is placed. This string is followed by parameter blocks and pointers to objects needed for the program. The variables hours, minutes, seconds, and count are defined as external variables to the program.

```
BYTE pszMessage[]="          \r"; /* a place to store the time */
io_command_block *oob1,ob1;       /* i/o command block */
Timer_parameters tp;              /* timer parameter block */
WORD hours, minutes, seconds;
WORD count;
Serial_io *sio;
Timer *t3;
```

The main() function starts with the usual initialization routines. The SIM is initialized to give a 16.00-MHz system clock frequency, the watchdog is disabled, and the memory wait states associated with the boot chip select are set to zero. Any other initialization needed within the SIM will use the default, reset value, values.

The serial input/output is then set up. The object sio is a pointer to a type Serial_io. This pointer is given a value by the call to the serial_io_() constructor. Note that the arguments passed to this constructor are all defined earlier, so that anybody who is reading the program should be able to understand which argument is given the specific value. The values assigned to these parameters are not really important to the program at this point. However, if it is necessary later to change any of these values, they should be changed within the #define statements shown earlier.

The input-output control block pointer is given a value, and the parameters call_complete and io_command are initialized. This component is used as an output only, so the command should never change during the program.

An instance of a timer is needed with this program. The timer parameter block is filled with the appropriate values. Timer 3 is used and the tick value of TIMECOUNT will provide 1-millisecond interrupts. There is no output compare 1 connection or action with this timer object, and we will need an interrupt. The timer is then instantiated as t3. We will then attach a pointer to the function count_ticks() to the hook_method and a pointer to the memory location count to the hook_object in the instance of timer t3.

In a final bit of initialization, the value of count is set to zero, and the system interrupts are enabled. After this initialization, the system should be operating properly with all interrupts enabled and occurring when called for.

```
main()
{
        /* initialize the program */
```

```
/* initialize the SIM registers */
SYNCR.X=ON;      /* double the clock speed—16.00 MHz */
SYPCR.SWE=OFF;   /* disable the watchdog */
CSORBT.DSACK=0;  /* use zero wait states for now */

/* set up the serial communications */
sio=serial_io_(SERIO_BAUD_19200,       /* set the baud rate */
                SERIO_INT_VECTOR,       /* interrupt vector
                                                        */
               SERIO_IARB,             /* iarb */
                SERIO_INT_LEVEL);       /* and interrupt
                                                   level */

/* set up the io block */
oob1=&ob1;
oob1->call_complete=TRUE;  /* start with no message in
                                                progress */
oob1->io_command=OUTPUT;   /* make this block for outputs */

/* set up the timer parameter structure */
tp.number=3;          /* use output compare number 3 */
tp.tick=TIMECOUNT;    /* 1 ms interrupts */
tp.action=0;          /* no output action */
tp.OC1_connect=0;     /* OC1 not connected to another OC */
tp.connect_data=0;
tp.interrupt=YES;     /* need an interrupt here */
t3=timer_(&tp);             /* instantiate the timer */
attach_object(t3,&count); /* attach object and method to
                             timer*/
attach_method(t3,count_ticks);

/* initialize application program details */
count=0;
cli();           /* enable the system interrupts */
```

The next program section is usually called the applications section. It is in this section that all continuing business that must be executed by the program is processed. In this case, the applications section is relatively simple. Note that, as usual, the applications section is comprised of a code loop that executes FOREVER. That is not to say that the code never exits this loop, but rather, the loop is executed and interrupts will remove control to the interrupt service routines within the program. Whenever no interrupt service is being handled, control will be returned to the FOREVER loop.

The code within the loop in this case will maintain a time-of-day clock. Whenever the value stored in count exceeds or equals the value ONE_SECOND, count is reset to zero and seconds is incremented. If the incremented value of seconds is greater than or equal to 60, seconds is reset to zero and minutes is incremented, and so on, for the minutes and the hours. You will note that hours, minutes, seconds, and count are each of the type WORD, which is an unsigned integer. Therefore, these parameters can never have a negative value. Also, the test to determine the value in each case is "greater than or equal to." We should expect that these values will never exceed the test values shown. However, if any should, by some accident, the "greater than or equal to," along with the use of the unsigned variable type, will guarantee that the values of these parameters will be kept within their acceptable range of values.

The range of minutes and seconds is from 0 to 59. If the value of either of these variables is ever found to be 60, it is reset to zero. The range of hours is from 1 to 12. Note that hours is reset to 1 whenever its incremented value becomes 13 or greater.

Note that the code to keep the time is executed only when the value of count becomes ONE_SECOND. Also, build_time() and output_time() are executed at this time. Therefore, a new time will be sent to the serial port once each second.

```
        /* end of initialization and beginning of the applications
           section of the program */
        FOREVER
        {
                if(count>=ONE_SECOND)
                {
                        count=0;
                        if(++seconds>=60)
                        {
                                seconds=0;
                                if(++minutes>=60)
                                {
                                        minutes=0;
                                        if(++hours>=13)
                                                hours=1;
                                }
                        }
                        build_time();
                        output_time();
                }
        }
}
```

The next portion of the program is the inclusion of the functions needed for the applications portion of the program. The three functions in this case, output_time(), build_time(), and convert_itoa(), are shown below. Let us examine build_time() first. This function receives no arguments, but it uses the values stored in the external variables hours, minutes, and seconds. These values are integer values that must be converted to character values before they can be sent to the serial port. A pointer to the message area pszMessage and the value of hours is sent to the function convert_itoa(). This function converts the integer value to two characters less than 100 and puts these characters in the memory area pointed to by the argument p. A character ':' is then put into the message area, and the value of minutes is converted to two characters and placed into the message area. Finally, this sequence is repeated for the seconds, and the data are then ready to be sent to the serial port.

The data are converted to character form by the function convert_itoa(). This function receives two parameters: the value to be converted and a pointer to the memory area where the result is to be stored. The conversion merely evaluates the number of tens in the value and adds a character zero to this value. It then evaluates the number of units in the number and adds a character zero to the number of units. These characters are put into the proper memory locations as they are calculated.

The final function needed to complete the applications portion of the program is called output_time(). This function first waits until there is no message being sent out the serial port. When the serial port is available, new values are placed in the io command block, and the output message is sent to the serial_io object. This object, in turn, sends the message contained in pszMessage[] to the serial port.

```
/* functions needed for the applications portion of the program
*/

/* send out the time message */

void output_time(void)
{
       while(!oob1->call_complete)
             ;                    /* wait until any other message
                                                        is out */
       oob1->buffer=pszMessage; /* clear out the background */
       oob1->buffer_length= sizeof pszMessage;
       serial_io(sio,oob1);     /* message to the i/o object */
}

/* This routine builds the time message to be sent out. */

void build_time(void)
{

     BYTE *p=pszMessage;

     convert_itoa(hours,p);
     p+=2;
     *p++=':';
     convert_itoa(minutes,p);
     p+=2;
```

```
        *p++=':';
        convert_itoa(seconds,p);
        p+=2;
        *p++='\r';
        *p='\0';
    }

    /* This routine converts an unsigned integer, a, into an ascii
       string of the value and puts the results into the string
       pointed to by p. */

    void convert_itoa(WORD a,BYTE *p)
    {
        *p++=(a/10)+'0';
        *p=(a%10)+'0';
    }
```

There is only one function left that is needed to complete this program. Recall that count_ticks() is attached to the hook of the timer object. In this case the hook method is very simple. All it must do is to increment count and return. In later cases, the hook method will be somewhat more complicated.

```
    /* function needed for the interrupt service routine */
    /* the timer is interrupted each millisecond.
       count_ticks keeps track of the number of
       interrupts that have occurred. */

    void count_ticks(WORD *a)
    {
          ++*a;
    }
```

Usually, when a program is shown in small pieces as was done above, the entire program is listed immediately following the description. In this case, this program will be expanded significantly in the next two programs. Therefore, the total listing of the program above will not be included here or anywhere, but will be replaced by a total listing of one of the following programs. The program above shows the insertion of a single function into the hook part of the timer object. The program that follows will expand a little on that idea. In this case, rather than a single function being put into the timer object, a linked list of several programs will be used. Each timer interrupt will cause the several functions in the link list to be executed. Again the program will be broken into small segments for descriptive purposes. The changes in this program are incremental changes in the above program. Therefore, only the changes will be examined. The changes will be highlighted so they can be seen easily.

CLOCK1

In this program we are going to make use of the linked list developed in Chapter 3. Recall that the linked list hooked link objects together into a list. Each link object contained a pointer to a single object. The linked list class contains a method called walk_list(). When walk_list() is executed, the object method named exercise() is executed for each object in the linked list. These capabilities can be used to advantage when it is needed to have more than one distinct function executed at each timer interrupt.

The #include files needed for this program are shown in the program segment below. The new files here are object1.h, link.h, and linklist.h. The class object1 differs from the class object in that it allows the routine exercise to be specified as a parameter to the constructor that creates the various instances of the type Object1. We saw applications of link.h and linklist.h in Chapter 3.

```
#include "HC16Y1.H"
#include "gpt.h"
#include "mcci.h"
#include "scim.h"
#include "serio.h"
#include "timer.h"
#include "defines.h"
#include "object1.h"
#include "link.h"
#include "linklist.h"
```

The same #define constants are needed with this program. One additional piece of business will be added to the program. Here we will have a timer function that will cause a transaction to take place each half second. We must, therefore, add a value named ONE_HALF_SECOND to our list of #defined constants as shown below. Also, a function that is used to determine the occurrence of 1/2-second periods is needed. The function prototype of this function is added to the function prototype list.

```
#define SERIO_BAUD_19200 19200
#define SERIO_INT_VECTOR 0x40
#define SERIO_IARB 10
#define SERIO_INT_LEVEL 3
#define TIMECOUNT 4000
#define ONE_SECOND 1000
#define ONE_HALF_SECOND 500

/* function prototypes */

void output_time(void);
void build_time(void);
```

```
void convert_itoa(WORD a,BYTE *p);
void count_half_second_ticks(void);
void count_second_ticks(void);
```

Some objects of the type Object1, Link, and Link_list are needed for this program. Pointers to variables of these types are defined in the external memory area below. Two Object1 types will be placed in the linked list. These objects are identified as l1 and l2. Also, the linked list must be preloaded with a null object. This object is called null. These objects are embedded in link objects named lnk1, lnk2, and lnknull. Finally, they will all be hooked together in a single linked list named list1.

```
BYTE pszMessage[]="         \r"; /* array to hold the time */
io_command_block *oob1,ob1;
WORD hours, minutes, seconds;
WORD count_half_seconds,count_seconds;
Boolean second_flag,one_half_second_flag;
Serial_io *sio;
Timer *t3;
Timer_parameters tp;
Object1 *l1,*l2,*null;
Link *lnk1,*lnk2,*lnknull;
Link_list *list1;

main()
{

      /* initialize the program */

    /* initialize the SIM registers */
    SYNCR.X=ON;      /* double the clock speed—16.00 MHz */
    SYPCR.SWE=OFF;   /* disable the watchdog */
    CSORBT.DSACK=0;  /* use zero wait states for now */

    /* set up the serial communications */
    sio=serial_io_(SERIO_BAUD_19200,  /* set the baud rate  */
                    SERIO_INT_VECTOR, /* interrupt vector */
                   SERIO_IARB,        /* iarb */
                    SERIO_INT_LEVEL); /* and interrupt level */

    /* set up the io blocks */
    oob1=&ob1;
    oob1->call_complete=TRUE;    /* make certain no message going
                                    out */
    oob1->io_command=OUTPUT;   /* make this block for outputs */
```

```
/* set up the timer parameter structure */
tp.number=3;            /* use output compare number 3 */
tp.tick=TIMECOUNT;  /* 1 ms interrupts */
tp.action=0;          /* no output action */
tp.OC1_connect=0;    /* OC1 not connected to another OC */
tp.connect_data=0;
tp.interrupt=YES;    /* need an interrupt here */
t3=timer_(&tp);          /* instantiate the timer */
```

The code above is the same code as that seen in the earlier program. The code that follows is the newly added code needed to implement the linked list. The first seven lines of code are object constructors that create the various objects needed. The first line creates the linked list named list1. The next two lines create the two type Object1s l1 and l2 that are to be executed during the interrupts. Note that the functions count_second_ticks and count_half_second_ticks are used as arguments to these constructors. Each linked list must be started with a null object. We create such an object when the constructor object1_() is executed with a NULL argument. Remember that NULL is

```
#define NULL (void *) 0
```

which is a pointer to a type void that happens to have a value of zero.

The next three lines of code create the three objects that will be placed into the linked list. Then follows three lines of code that place these link objects in the linked list. Note that the object lnknull is added to the list first. Finally, this list is placed into the hook object of the timer t3 and the hook method is given a pointer to the linked list method walk_list. The code then sets the count_half_second_flag to FALSE and sets the value of count_half_seconds to zero, and control is ready to pass into the applications portion of the program.

```
/* set up the linked list and the linked objects for the
   timer. */
list1=link_list_();
l1=object1_(count_second_ticks);
l2=object1_(count_half_second_ticks);
null=object1_(NULL);
lnknull=link_(null);          /* create a null object */
lnk1=link_(l1);               /* and the two real objects */
lnk2=link_(l2);
add_link(list1,lnknull);      /* put the null object on the
                                                     list */
add_link(list1,lnk1);         /* first and then the real ob-
                                                   jects */
add_link(list1,lnk2);
attach_method(t3,walk_list);/* attach a method to timer*/
```

```
attach_object(t3,list1);     /* and its argument */
second_flag=FALSE;                  /* the output now flag and
                                                            */
one_half_second_flag=FALSE; /* the do one-half second stuff
                                                        are */
                             /* reset to FALSE */
/* initialize application program details */
count_seconds=0;             /* initialize the time counts */
count_half_seconds=0;
cli();                       /* enable the system interrupts
                             */
```

Several significant modifications were made in the applications program. First, the code to keep the clock time was moved from the applications portion of the program to the routine count_second_ticks(). This code is executed during the timer interrupt service routine. Usually, it is wise to keep the code executed within the interrupt service routines as short as possible. Unless the program does something special, some interrupts are blocked during execution of any interrupt service routine. With the type of program we are running here, this delay in execution of any interrupt service routine is minimal. For example, if you examine the code for the routine shown below, you will see that this routine requires four comparisons, four increments, and five assignments maximum. This amount of code execution occurs only at the second of midnight and noon. Most of the time when this routine is executed, it requires one increment, one comparison, and one assignment. With a 16-MHz part, this total code should require less than 2 microseconds. Therefore, there is little danger in placing the keeping of the clock in the interrupt service routine.

Within the applications section of the program, there are two tests to determine what should be done. The first checks to see if the second_flag is TRUE. In that event, the second_flag is set to FALSE, and the time message is built and sent out the serial port. Then the one_half_second_flag is tested to see if it is TRUE. If it is, the one_half_second_flag is set to FALSE and any code needed on a 1/2-second period is executed. There is no code change from this point in the program until it reaches the two functions that are attached to the timer interrupt service routine.

```
/* end of initialization and beginning of the applications
   section of the program */
FOREVER
{

        if(second_flag==TRUE)  /* sendout time each second */
        {
                second_flag=FALSE;
                build_time();        /* set up the new time */
                output_time();       /* and send it to the screen
                                     */
```

```
                }
                if (one_half_second_flag==TRUE)
                {
                /* do one-half second things here */
                    one_half_second_flag=FALSE;
                }
        }
}

/* functions needed for the applications portion of the program
*/

/* send out the time message. */

void output_time(void)
{
    while(!oob1->call_complete)
            ;                   /* wait until any other message is
                                   out */
    oob1->buffer=pszMessage;  /* clear out the background */
    oob1->buffer_length= sizeof pszMessage;
    serial_io(sio,oob1);      /* message to the i/o object */
}

/* This routine builds the time message to be sent out. */

void build_time(void)
{

    BYTE *p=pszMessage;

     convert_itoa(hours,p);
      p+=2;
      *p++=':';
      convert_itoa(minutes,p);
      p+=2;
      *p++=':';
      convert_itoa(seconds,p);
      p+=2;
      *p++='\r';
      *p='\0';
}

/* This routine converts an unsigned integer, a, into an ascii
   string of the value and puts the results into the strint
   pointed to by p. */
```

```
void convert_itoa(WORD a,BYTE *p)
{
     *p++=(a/10)+'0';
     *p=(a%10)+'0';
}

/* functions needed for the interrupt service routines */
```

The two functions that are executed during each interrupt service routine for the timer are shown below. There is nothing really significant about these two functions. They are both placed into a type Object1 and then these Object1s are placed into Link types. These several links are then put into a linked list. The function walk_list() then executes these functions in order whenever it is called.

```
/* The following two routines, count_half_second_ticks() and
   count_second_ticks() are the methods to be attached to two
   instances of the type object1. These objects will be hooked
   into the link_list list1 which is in turn attached to the
   timer object. The method sent to the timer object is the
   walk_list() method of list1. Therefore, each timer interrupt
   will cause the following two routines to be executed as part
   of the timer interrupt service routine. */

/* This routine counts the timer interrupts and sets the
   one_half_second_flag to TRUE each half second. this flag is
   a notice to the main program to do the one-half second things
   needed */

void count_half_second_ticks(void)
{
     if(++count_half_seconds>=ONE_HALF_SECOND)
     {
          count_half_seconds=0;
          one_half_second_flag=TRUE;
     }
}

/* the timer is interrupted each millisecond. count_ticks keeps
   track of the number of interrupts that have occurred and also
   keeps a time of day clock. */

void count_second_ticks(void)
{
       if(++count_seconds>=ONE_SECOND)
       {
              count_seconds=0;
```

```
                if(++seconds>=60)
                {
                        seconds=0;
                        if(++minutes>=60)
                        {
                                minutes=0;
                                if(++hours>=13)
                                        hours=1;
                        }
                }
                second_flag=TRUE;
        }
}
```

The program above executes, and it takes little programming effort to determine that it executes as desired. There is yet one important capability that is missing from the program. There is no way to set the clock time. In the program that follows, this capability is added.

CLOCK2

The way that the time is set is to read in a time value from a keyboard. So far, we have been using the class Serial_io to meet our needs for asynchronous communications. Serial_io has one weakness that prevents its use directly in this application. Recall that each message terminator with this class is a null character. Therefore, an object of the type Serial_io can be used to send messages to a terminal or another computer set up to receive asynchronous communications. There is a difficulty if it is expected to receive asynchronous data from a keyboard. A keyboard has no capability to send a null character. This is not quite true: A ^@ character is a null, but one does not usually terminate messages with such a character. To use the Serial_io type comfortably, we will have to modify it to accept a different message termination character. This serial i/o system will be oriented strictly toward accessing the system through a terminal with a keyboard and a screen.

This time around, let us choose a carriage return as our message termination character. With this choice, we have a simple block-oriented transmission scheme. The block is the length of the line prior to the carriage return.

This choice leaves us with the unpleasant task of modifying an existing, fully tested class—a no-no if there ever was one. Our choice here must be to create an inherited class that meets our needs without modification of the base class. This class is relatively easy to create. Recall that the class Serial_io has a pair of virtual functions that execute as part of the interrupt service routine. These virtual functions contain the only reference to the block terminator. Our new inherited class will contain a new pair of functions with the newly defined message terminator character used rather than the null used earlier. Also, we will need a function such as the keyboard hit routine found in ANSI C. We will include this function as a method of the class Serkb_io.

It is not really necessary to change the block terminator character for the do_transmit() routine. As this whole program is set up, all transmitted blocks are terminated with an EOM character. The EOM character is a null or a character '\0'. The program will never change this output character because all the messages created to be sent out are C strings that automatically terminate in a null character. If we should change only the do_receive() routine and not the do_transmit() routine, we would have a nonsymmetric class that was designed to receive characters from a keyboard and to send messages to another device that is not necessarily the screen of a terminal. It is better to change both methods at the same time so that we will have a machine communications system with serial_io and a terminal communications system with serkb_io.

This inherited class should make maximum use of the methods, definitions, even the class itself that can be created from within the base class. The header file serkb.h is shown below. Note that it includes the header serio.h, which will include all of the base class definitions. Also notice that a constant EOL is defined for use in this version of the i/o driver. A new object constructor will be needed. It will create a type Serial_io * as did the base class; there will be some differences in the final class, though. The two interrupt function prototypes do_receive_kb() and do_transmit_kb() and the prototype for the function kbhit() are included in the header.

```
#ifndef SERKB_H
#define SERKB_H

#include "serio.h"

#define EOL      '\r' /* End Of Line */

/* Function prototypes */
Serial_io *serkb_io_(int baud_rate,int vector,int iarb,int
int_level);
void do_receive_kb(void);
void do_transmit_kb(void);
Boolean kbhit(void);

#endif
```

The implementation file for serkb is shown below. The header files included include serkb.h and two-chip oriented headers that are needed to determine register locations for the MCCI.

The item that follows is the kbhit() function. Any time that a key is hit, a character will arrive in the receiver data register. The RDRF bit in the serial communications status register is set whenever the data register is filled with a new character.

The kbhit() routine must do two things. First, if there are data in the data register, the register must be emptied to turn the RDRF bit off. Second, the fact that data were found in the register must be returned to the calling program as a TRUE return. The code in the routine below does exactly these things. First, the contents of the RDRF bit is saved in the Boolean variable *able,* and then the data register is read to both empty the register and turn the RDRF off. Then the status of the RDRF that was saved in *able* is returned to the calling program.

```
#include "serkb.h"
#include "hc16y1.h"
#include "mcci.h"
Boolean kbhit(void)
{
    Boolean able;
    BYTE a;

    able=SCSRA.RDRF; /* do those things needed to turn */
    a=SCDRA.DATA;    /* the RDRF flag off */
    return able;     /* return status of Receive Data Register */
}
```

A methods table was used in Serial_io to hold the methods executed during processing of the interrupt services. This table was of the type Serio_Methods, and it was defined in the serio implementation file. This same table will be used with serkb, so it must be declared as external in this file. We also have a serkb_flag, which is Boolean, that is used to indicate that the serio_methods table has been modified.

The serkb_io_() constructor is relatively simple. First an instance of a Serial_io is created when serial_io_() is executed. After this instance is created, the serio_methods entries are given new values if they have not been changed earlier, and both the receiver and transmitter of the UART are turned ON. Finally, a pointer to the newly created instance of a Serial_io is returned to the calling program.

```
extern Serio_Methods serio_methods;
Boolean serkb_flag=FALSE;

Serial_io *serkb_io_(int baud_rate,int vector,int iarb,int
int_level)
{
    Serial_io *this =serial_io_(baud_rate,vector,iarb,int_
    level);
    if(!serkb_flag) /* fix up the virtual method table */
    {
        serkb_flag=TRUE;
        serio_methods.do_rec=do_receive_kb;
```

```
        serio_methods.do_trans=do_transmit_kb;
    }
    SCCR1A.RE=ON;     /* enable both the receiver and */
    SCCR1A.TE=ON;     /* the transmitter */
    return this;
}
```

The little code sequence

```
if(!serkb_flag)
{
      serkb_flag=TRUE;
      .
      .
      .
```

might seem a bit unusual. This particular sequence is chosen because serkb_flag is initialized to FALSE when it is defined. We could have initialized serkb_flag to TRUE and reversed the logic in the code sequence above. Such an initialization would have complicated the initialization routine of the entire program. Global variables are initialized to zero when the program is started. If there are any variables initialized to other values, special code must be created to accomplish this initialization. Therefore, whenever you have a choice, you should use an initialized value of zero for any external or global variable. If you can allow all such variables to be zero, you can simplify the program code significantly.

The code processed in the interrupt service routine will be changed slightly. The message is terminated by an EOM character rather than an EOL character. These values are defined in the header files of the two serial drivers. The io_command_blocks giob and goob from the Serial_io system will be used here and must be declared external. In the do_receive_kb(), there are three minor changes. The input message termination test uses an EOL, any character entered is echoed back to the terminal, and finally, the receiver is left on even though the receiver interrupt is disabled. Otherwise, the code that follows is exactly the same as that described in Chapter 4.

```
extern io_command_block *giob;
extern io_command_block *goob;

/* almost the same as earlier. the main change is to terminate on
   an EOL rather than an EOM, and this routine echos the received
   character. also, these routines leave both the transmitter and
   the receiver enabled. */

void do_receive_kb(void)
{
```

```
    BYTE cr;
    if((cr=getch())!= EOL && giob->characters_transferred++ <
                    giob->buffer_length)
    {
        putch(cr);    /* echo the received character */
        *giob->buffer++=cr;
    }
    else
    {
        if(cr==EOL)
        {
            giob->characters_transferred++;
            *giob->buffer=cr;
        }
        giob->call_complete=TRUE;
        SCCR1A.RIE=OFF;     /* turn the receiver interrupt off */
        if(giob->characters_transferred >=giob->buffer_length)
            giob->error=BUFFER_OVERFLOW;
        else
            giob->error=NO_ERROR;
        giob=NULL; /* get rid or iocb */
    }
}
```

Modifications of the do_transmit_kb() routine are even fewer than shown above. Here the message is terminated with an EOL and the transmitter is left ON when the transmit interrupt is disabled.

```
void do_transmit_kb(void)
{
    BYTE ct;
    putch(ct=*goob->buffer++); /* send out the character */
    goob->characters_transferred++;
    if(goob->characters_transferred<goob->buffer_length &&
    ct!=EOL)
        ; /* go back if more data to be sent */
    else
    {
        SCCR1A.TIE=OFF;  /* disable the transmitter interrupt */
        goob->call_complete=TRUE;
        if(goob->characters_transferred>goob->buffer_length)
            goob->error=BUFFER_OVERFLOW;
        else
            goob->error=NO_ERROR;
        goob=NULL;          /* delete iocb */
    }
}
```

Recall what our program is to do now. First, it is to do everything the earlier programs did, which is to maintain a time-of-day clock and execute at the proper time the things needed every 1/2 second. We now want to add the capability of setting the clock from the keyboard. The earlier programs were not able to adjust the time. The numbers displayed on the screen were the values of the data stored in the variables hours, minutes, and seconds. These variables, being external variables, were always initialized to zero when the program is started. So there was no connection between the time shown and the real time of day. With a keyboard input capability, it is possible at any time to input the time. The display value will then reflect the time entered from the keyboard. This additional capability requires some modification of the test program, which is shown below.

In the header file list, two new headers are added. The first is the serkb.h header shown above. This header is needed to allow us to create a keyboard-based serial input output system. A second header file, ctype.h, is also added. In the added program it is necessary to determine if a character read in from the keyboard is a digit. The function isdigit() is prototyped in the header file ctype.h. A point of interest here. We can write a function that will return a TRUE if a character is a digit and a FALSE if it is not. We can easily write this function as a function or a macro function. For example, the macro version of such a function is

```
#define isdigit(c)   (c)>='0'&&(c)<='9'
```

This program is so simple. You cannot see it, but I made two errors when I typed the foregoing macro into the manuscript. I got the “less than” and “greater than” symbols reversed. I caught these errors in editing, but there was no reason for me to have to see such errors. The function isdigit() is a part of the C library, and any attempt to rewrite it is an ego thing for the programmer that subjects your code to needless, but normal, programming errors. Whenever possible, use the features and functions provided by the language and do not bother trying to reinvent working code.

```
#include "HC16Y1.H"
#include "gpt.h"
#include "mcci.h"
#include "scim.h"
#include "timer.h"
#include "defines.h"
#include "object1.h"
#include "link.h"
#include "linklist.h"
#include "serkb.h"
#include "ctype.h"

#define SERIO_BAUD_19200 19200
#define SERIO_INT_VECTOR 0x40
#define SERIO_IARB 10
```

```
#define SERIO_INT_LEVEL 3
#define TIMECOUNT 4000
#define ONE_SECOND 1000
#define ONE_HALF_SECOND 500
```

A few changes will be needed in the messages handled by this program. You will note below that three new character array constants are added to the list of external variables. The message pszMessage2[] is used to overwrite the line created by the concatenation of pszMessage1[] and pszMessage3[] after the new time has been placed into pszMessage3[]. Because we will be doing inputs from the keyboard, we need an io_command_block that is dedicated to inputs. This block is ib1, and a pointer to this block will be saved in iob1.

```
/* function prototypes */
void output_time(void);
void build_time(void);
void convert_itoa(WORD a,BYTE *p);
void count_half_second_ticks(void);
void count_second_ticks(void);
BYTE pszMessage[]="          \r"; /* array to hold the output time
                                                                 */
BYTE pszMessage1[]="Enter the new time HH:MM > ";
BYTE pszMessage2[]="                                 \r";
BYTE pszMessage3[]="          \r"; /* array to hold the time
                                                            input*/
io_command_block *oob1,ob1,*iob1,ib1;
WORD hours, minutes, seconds;
WORD count_half_seconds,count_seconds;
Boolean second_flag,one_half_second_flag,new_time_flag;
Serial_io *sio;
Timer *t3;
Timer_parameters tp;
Object1 *l1,*l2,*null;
Link *lnk1,*lnk2,*lnknull;
Link_list *list1;
main()
{
    /* initialize the program */


    /* initialize the SIM registers */
    SYNCR.X=ON;      /* double the clock speed--16.00 MHz */
    SYPCR.SWE=OFF;   /* disable the watchdog */
    CSORBT.DSACK=0; /* use zero wait states for now */
```

In setting up the serial input/output operations, the program must use the constructor serkb_io_() rather than the serial_io_() used in the earlier example. Otherwise, the instantiation of sio is no different from that shown in the earlier example. We will now be doing both input and output. The earlier example set up output the same, as shown below. Rather than use only one io_command_block for both inputs and outputs, a separate block will be created for each. The input command block is initialized at this time. This block is filled with an INPUT command, and the call_complete flag is set to FALSE to facilitate initialization of the program. No other modifications are needed in the initialization portion of the program.

```
/* set up the serial communications */
sio=serkb_io_(SERIO_BAUD_19200,      /* set the baud rate   */
               SERIO_INT_VECTOR,     /* interrupt vector */
               SERIO_IARB,           /* iarb   */
                SERIO_INT_LEVEL);    /* and interrupt level */

/* set up the io blocks */
oob1=&ob1;                      /* output block */
oob1->call_complete=TRUE;       /* have no message going out */
oob1->io_command=OUTPUT;        /* oob1 is always output */
iob1=&ib1;                      /* a block for inputs */
iob1->io_command=INPUT;         /* iob1 is always input */
iob1->call_complete=FALSE;      /* need to have no message in
                                   progress */

/* set up the timer parameter structure and instantiate a
   timer */
tp.number=3;          /* use output compare number 3 */
tp.tick=TIMECOUNT;    /* 1 ms interrupts */
tp.action=0;          /* no output action */
tp.OC1_connect=0;     /* OC1 not connected to another OC */
tp.connect_data=0;    /* therefore no connect data needed */
tp.interrupt=YES;     /* need an interrupt here */
t3=timer_(&tp);             /* instantiate the timer */

/* set up the linked list and the linked objects for the
   timer. */
list1=link_list_();   /* create list and the objects to be
                         linked */
l1=object1_(count_second_ticks);
l2=object1_(count_half_second_ticks);
null=object1_(NULL);
lnknull=link_(null);            /* create the link objects */
lnk1=link_(l1);
lnk2=link_(l2);
add_link(list1,lnknull);        /* put the null object on the
                                   list */
add_link(list1,lnk1);           /* first and then the real ob-
                                   jects */
```

```
add_link(list1,lnk2);
attach_method(t3,walk_list);/* attach a method to timer*/
attach_object(t3,list1);    /* and its argument */

/* initialize application program details */
second_flag=FALSE;              /* the output now flag and */
one_half_second_flag=FALSE;     /* the one-half second flags
                                   are reset */
new_time_flag=FALSE;            /* not receiving a new time
                                                          */
count_seconds=0;                /* initialize the time counts
                                                          */
count_half_seconds=0;
cli();                          /* enable the system inter-
                                   rupts */
```

Recall that kbhit() returns a TRUE if the keyboard has been touched. The code shown below tests the state returned from kbhit(), and if it is FALSE, the code that follows is skipped. Otherwise, when the program detects a depressed key on the keyboard, it executes the code in the block following the if statement below. Some variables are needed to implement the keyboard input routine. These variables are defined at the beginning of the block. The main loop is a do/while loop because it is imperative that the code inside the block be executed at least once. This form of the loop provides this guarantee. Inside the loop, the first four lines of code send a message to the screen requesting that the operator enter a new time. In response to this message, the input object is executed and the input message is put into the memory area pszMessage3[]. The serial input is one of those routines that can lock up the computer for a long time—at best the time required to input the time from the keyboard, and at worst, there is no requirement that there ever be a keyboard response after the first keyboard entry causes program control to pass to this code. The operator could go off to get coffee and go to bed. The 1/2 second code must be executed routinely each 1/2 second regardless of what the program or the operator is doing. Otherwise, the system will not perform its necessary duties. When the serial_io() method is executed, control is always returned to the calling program as soon as the input is set up. There is a flag in the io command block that indicated when the input is completed. It is usual to follow the serial_io() call with a test loop that holds the program execution at that point until the io is complete as determined by the state of the call_complete flag. We can extend the use of this loop to observe other program items. In this case, a test of the one_half_second_flag will show during service of the 1/2 second part of the program while the keyboard input is proceeding at its own slow pace.

It is expected that the input in pszMessage3[] will be of the form HH:MM. The range for the hours is from 1 to 12 and the range of the minutes is from 0 to 59. Two tests are needed to determine if the input message is in the correct format. The first uses isdigit() to make certain that the proper characters in the input array pszMessage3[] are digits and that the two two-digit fields are separated by a ':'. If these characters are correct, the flag message_ok is set to TRUE and then the second test is completed. In the second test, the first two digits are converted from characters to integer form and stored in the memory location temphours. The value of temphours is checked to determine if it lies within the acceptable range 1 to 12. Then characters 3 and 4 are converted to an integer type and stored in tempminutes. This variable can have a range of 0 to 59. It is only necessary to check to determine that tempminutes is less than 60 because it is an unsigned variable that cannot be less than 0. If tempminutes has a proper range, the flag time_ok is set to TRUE and we do have good input from the keyboard. In that case, the value of temphours is put into hours and tempminutes is put into minutes, and a series of spaces is sent to the screen to clear the messages that were written there in requesting the new clock time.

If the code above results in a TRUE value for both message_ok and time_ok, the new time to be sent to the screen is in place and control is passed out of this routine. Otherwise, control is passed back to the beginning of the do loop, where the time message is reentered through the keyboard until it is done correctly.

```
/* end of initialization and beginning of the applications
   section of the program */
  FOREVER
  {
    /* reset the time clock from the keyboard whenever any
         key on the keyboard is hit */
    if(kbhit())
    {
        BYTE *p; /* need a pointer here */
        Boolean message_ok, time_ok; /* and a couple of flags
                                       */
        BYTE temphours,tempminutes;


        do
        {
            putch('\r');  /* put cursor in correct location */
             oob1->buffer=pszMessage1; /* clear out the back
                                         ground */
             oob1->buffer_length= sizeof pszMessage1;
             serial_io(sio,oob1);      /* message to the i/o
                                         object */
             iob1->buffer=pszMessage3;
             iob1->buffer_length= sizeof pszMessage3;
             serial_io(sio,iob1);      /* get input message */
             /* must keep one-half second business going */
             while(!iob1->call_complete)
                     if(one_half_second_flag==TRUE)
                     {
```

```
                        one_half_second_flag=FALSE;
                      /* do one-half second stuff here too */
                  }   /* wait until input is in */
              message_ok=FALSE;
              time_ok=FALSE;
              p=pszMessage3;
              if(isdigit(*p) && isdigit(*(p+1)) && *(p+2)==':'
              &&
                   isdigit(*(p+3)) && isdigit(*(p+4)))
              {   /* got a good message, are numbers sensible?
                  */
                  message_ok=TRUE;
                  if((temphours=(*p-'0')*10+*(p+1)-'0')<13 &&
                       temphours >0 &&
                           (tempminutes=(*(p+3)-'0')*10+*
                           (p+4)-'0')<60 )
                  { /* yes! set up a new time */
                      time_ok=TRUE;
                      hours=temphours;
                      minutes=tempminutes;
                      seconds=0;/* reset seconds to 0 when time
                      is reset*/
                       putch('\r'); /* do a carriage return and
                                   */
                      oob1->buffer=pszMessage2; /* clear the
                                                 screen */
                      oob1->buffer_length= sizeof pszMessage2;
                      serial_io(sio,oob1);
                  }
              }
          }while(!(time_ok && message_ok));
      }


      /* sendout time each second */
      if(second_flag==TRUE)
      {
          second_flag=FALSE;
           build_time();      /* set up the new time */
           output_time();     /* and send it to the screen */
      }


     /* do one-half second things here */
      if (one_half_second_flag==TRUE)
      {
              one_half_second_flag=FALSE;
      }
  }
}
```

```
/* functions needed for the applications portion of the program
*/

/* send out the time message. */
void output_time(void)
{
    if(!new_time_flag) /* don't send out time while reading new
                          time */
    {
            while(!oob1->call_complete)
                  ;                  /* wait until any other mes-
                                        sage is out */
            oob1->buffer=pszMessage; /* clear out the background
                                        */
            oob1->buffer_length= sizeof pszMessage;
            serial_io(sio,oob1);      /* message to the i/o ob-
                                         ject */
    }
}

/* This routine builds the time message to be sent out. */
void build_time(void)
{
    BYTE *p=pszMessage;
      convert_itoa(hours,p);
      p+=2;
      *p++=':';
      convert_itoa(minutes,p);
      p+=2;
      *p++=':';
      convert_itoa(seconds,p);
      p+=2;
      *p++='\r';
      *p='\0';
}

/* This routine converts an unsigned integer, a, into an ascii
   string of the value <100 and puts the results into the string
   pointed to by p. */
void convert_itoa(WORD a,BYTE *p)
{
     *p++=(a/10)+'0';
     *p=(a%10)+'0';
}

/* functions needed for the interrupt service routines */
/* The following two routines, count_half_second_ticks() and
   count_second_ticks(), are the methods to be attached to two
```

```
   instances of the type object1. These objects will be hooked
   into the link_list list1 which is in turn attached to the
   timer object. The method sent to the timer object is the
   walk_list() method of list1. Therefore, each timer interrupt
   will cause the following two routines to be executed as part
   of the timer interrupt service routine. */


/* This routine counts the timer interrupts and sets the
   one_half_second_flag to TRUE each half second. this flag is
   a notice to the main program to do the one-half second things
   needed */
void count_half_second_ticks(void)
{
    if(++count_half_seconds>=ONE_HALF_SECOND)
    {
        count_half_seconds=0;
        one_half_second_flag=TRUE;
    }
}


/* the timer is interrupted each millisecond. count_ticks keeps
   track of the number of interrupts that have occurred and also
   keeps a time-of-day clock. */


void count_second_ticks(void)
{
      if(++count_seconds>=ONE_SECOND)
      {
            count_seconds=0;
            if(++seconds>=60)
            {
                  seconds=0;
                  if(++minutes>=60)
                  {
                        minutes=0;
                        if(++hours>=13)
                              hours=1;
                  }
            }
            second_flag=TRUE;
      }
}
```

We reach the end of this program. The entire program is presented again in Listing 5.5 to allow you to see it in one piece.

```
#include "HC16Y1.H"
#include "gpt.h"
#include "mcci.h"
#include "scim.h"
#include "serkb.h"
#include "timer.h"
#include "defines.h"
#include "object1.h"
#include "link.h"
#include "linklist.h"
#include "ctype.h"

#define SERIO_BAUD_19200 19200
#define SERIO_INT_VECTOR 0x40
#define SERIO_IARB 10
#define SERIO_INT_LEVEL 3
#define TIMECOUNT 4000
#define ONE_SECOND 1000
#define ONE_HALF_SECOND 500

/* function prototypes */
void output_time(void);
void build_time(void);
void convert_itoa(WORD a,BYTE *p);
void count_half_second_ticks(void);
void count_second_ticks(void);

BYTE pszMessage[]="         \r"; /* array to hold the output
                                                           time */
BYTE pszMessage1[]="Enter the new time HH:MM > ";
BYTE pszMessage2[]="                                  \r";
BYTE pszMessage3[]="        \r"; /* array to hold the time
                                                           input*/
io_command_block *oob1,ob1,*iob1,ib1;
WORD hours, minutes, seconds;
WORD count_half_seconds,count_seconds;
Boolean second_flag,one_half_second_flag,new_time_flag;
Serial_io *sio;
Timer *t3;
Timer_parameters tp;
Object1 *l1,*l2,*null;
Link *lnk1,*lnk2,*lnknull;
Link_list *list1;

main()
{
```

Listing 5.5 Clock2 Timer Test Program

```
      /* initialize the program */

    /* initialize the SIM registers */
    SYNCR.X=ON;      /* double the clock speed—16.00 mHz */
    SYPCR.SWE=OFF;   /* disable the watchdog */
    CSORBT.DSACK=0;  /* use zero wait states for now */

/* set up the serial communications */
sio=serkb_io_(SERIO_BAUD_19200,      /* set the baud rate   */
              SERIO_INT_VECTOR,       /* interrupt vector */
              SERIO_IARB,             /* iarb  */
              SERIO_INT_LEVEL);        /* and interrupt level */

/* set up the io blocks */
oob1=&ob1;                    /* output block */
oob1->call_complete=TRUE;     /* have no message going out */
oob1->io_command=OUTPUT;      /* oob1 is always output */
iob1=&ib1;                    /* a block for inputs */
iob1->io_command=INPUT;       /* iob1 is always input */
iob1->call_complete=FALSE;    /* need to have no message in
                                 progress */

/* set up the timer parameter structure and instantiate a timer
*/
tp.number=3;          /* use output compare number 3 */
tp.tick=TIMECOUNT;    /* 1 ms interrupts */
tp.action=0;          /* no output action */
tp.OC1_connect=0;     /* OC1 not connected to another OC */
tp.connect_data=0;    /* therefore no connect data needed */
tp.interrupt=YES;     /* need an interrupt here */
t3=timer_(&tp);             /* instantiate the timer */

/* set up the linked list and the linked objects for the
   timer. */
list1=link_list_();   /* create list and the objects to be linked
                       */
l1=object1_(count_second_ticks);
l2=object1_(count_half_second_ticks);
null=object1_(NULL);
lnknull=link_(null);         /* create the link objects */
lnk1=link_(l1);
lnk2=link_(l2);
add_link(list1,lnknull);     /* put the null object on the list */
add_link(list1,lnk1);        /* first and then the real objects */
add_link(list1,lnk2);
```

Listing 5.5 (continued)

```
ttach_method(t3,walk_list);/* attach a method to timer*/
attach_object(t3,list1);    /* and its argument */

/* initialize application program details */
second_flag=FALSE;                /* the output now flag and */
one_half_second_flag=FALSE; /* the one-half second flags are
                                                      reset */
new_time_flag=FALSE;        /* not receiving a new time */
count_seconds=0;            /* initialize the time counts */
count_half_seconds=0;
cli();                      /* enable the system interrupts */

/* end of initialization and beginning of the applications
   section of the program */
  FOREVER
  {
    /* reset the time clock from the keyboard whenever any key
       on the keyboard is hit */
    if(kbhit())
    {
        BYTE *p; /* need a pointer here */
        Boolean message_ok, time_ok; /* and a couple of flags */
        BYTE temphours,tempminutes;

        do
        {
            putch('\r');     /* put cursor in correct location */
             oob1->buffer=pszMessage1; /* clear out the back-
                                          ground */
             oob1->buffer_length= sizeof pszMessage1;
             serial_io(sio,oob1);       /* message to the i/o ob-
                                           ject */
             iob1->buffer=pszMessage3;
             iob1->buffer_length= sizeof pszMessage3;
             serial_io(sio,iob1);       /* get input message */
             /* must keep one-half second business going */
             while(!iob1->call_complete)
                     if(one_half_second_flag==TRUE)
                     {
                           one_half_second_flag=FALSE;
                        /* do one-half second stuff here too */
                        } /* wait until input is in */
             message_ok=FALSE;
             time_ok=FALSE;
             p=pszMessage3;
```

Listing 5.5 (continued)

```
            if(isdigit(*p) && isdigit(*(p+1)) && *(p+2)==':' &&
                 isdigit(*(p+3)) && isdigit(*(p+4)))
            {   /* got a good message, are numbers sensible? */
                message_ok=TRUE;
                if((temphours=(*p-'0')*10+*(p+1)-'0')<13 &&
                   (tempminutes=(*(p+3)-'0')*10+*(p+4)-'0')<60 )
                { /* yes! set up a new time */
                    time_ok=TRUE;
                    hours=temphours;
                    minutes=tempminutes;
                    seconds=0;/* reset seconds to 0 when time is
                                 reset*/
                      putch('\r'); /* do a carriage return and
                                     */
                     oob1->buffer=pszMessage2; /* clear the
                                                  screen */
                     oob1->buffer_length= sizeof pszMessage2;
                     serial_io(sio,oob1);
                }
            }
        }while(!(time_ok && message_ok));
    }

    /* sendout time each second */
    if(second_flag==TRUE)
    {
            second_flag=FALSE;
           build_time(); /* set up the new time */
           output_time(); /* and send it to the screen */
       }

      /* do one-half second things here */
       if (one_half_second_flag==TRUE)
       {
        one_half_second_flag=FALSE;
       }
   }
}

/* functions needed for the applications portion of the program */
/* send out the time message. */
void output_time(void)
{
    if(!new_time_flag) /* don't send out time while reading new
                          time */
```

Listing 5.5 (continued)

```
    {
            while(!oob1->call_complete)
                 ;                   /* wait until any other mes-
                                                sage is out */
            oob1->buffer=pszMessage; /* clear out the background
                                                            */
            oob1->buffer_length= sizeof pszMessage;
            serial_io(sio,oob1); /* message to the i/o object */
    }
}

/* This routine builds the time message to be sent out. */
void build_time(void)
{
    BYTE *p=pszMessage;

      convert_itoa(hours,p);
      p+=2;
      *p++=':';
      convert_itoa(minutes,p);
      p+=2;
      *p++=':';
      convert_itoa(seconds,p);
      p+=2;
      *p++='\r';
      *p='\0';
}

/* This routine converts an unsigned integer, a, into an ascii
   string of the value <100 and puts the results into the string
   pointed to by p. */
void convert_itoa(WORD a,BYTE *p)
{
    *p++=(a/10)+'0';
    *p=(a%10)+'0';
}

/* functions needed for the interrupt service routines */
/* The following two routines, count_half_second_ticks() and
   count_second_ticks(), are the methods to be attached to two
   instances of the type object1. These objects will be hooked
   into the link_list list1 which is in turn attached to the
   timer object. The method sent to the timer object is the
   walk_list() method of list1. Therefore, each timer interrupt
   will cause the following two routines to be executed as part
   of the timer interrupt service routine. */
```

Listing 5.5 (continued)

```
/* This routine counts the timer interrupts and sets the
   one_half_second_flag to TRUE each half second. this flag is
   a notice to the main program to do the one-half second things
   needed */
void count_half_second_ticks(void)
{
     if(++count_half_seconds>=ONE_HALF_SECOND)
     {
          count_half_seconds=0;
          one_half_second_flag=TRUE;
     }
}


/* the timer is interrupted each millisecond. count_ticks keeps
   track of the number of interrupts that have occurred and also
   keeps a time-of-day clock. */


void count_second_ticks(void)
{
       if(++count_seconds>=ONE_SECOND)
       {
              count_seconds=0;
              if(++seconds>=60)
              {
                     seconds=0;
                     if(++minutes>=60)
                     {
                            minutes=0;
                            if(++hours>=13)
                                   hours=1;
                     }
              }
              second_flag=TRUE;
       }
}
```

Listing 5.5 (continued)

PULSE-WIDTH MODULATOR

We must look at one more example of the use of a timer class before we leave this chapter. The pulse-width modulation system is one of the basic digital-to-analog conversion devices, and a PWM can easily be implemented with two timers. The general-purpose timer system on the MC68HC16Y1 has two built-in PWM devices.

These devices are relatively slow and have eight-bit resolution only. The speed is quite flexible, but the fastest sample rate is 32 kHz. The system outlined below is not always as fast, but it is easily possible to generate analog signals with up to 16-bit resolution. You will see that the speed of the converter and its resolution are interrelated.

We will start with the assumption that the timer system prescaler is set to the fastest speed. With the system we are using, this speed is 4 MHz or the clock time is 250 nanoseconds. The time needed to complete a sample is the time required to count the number of resolution bits. If the resolution is to be eight bits, a count of 256 will require 64 microseconds. With 10-bit resoultion, the count will be 256 microseconds. The sample time is, in this case, fixed to the resolution of the DAC. The built-in PWM devices have a fixed resoultion and merely change the clock rate when the time is adjusted.

The class definition file is shown in Listing 5.6. This system will use two Output Compare channels to construct the PWM. The class must, therefore, provide access to the timer subsystem, so the header files hc16y1.h, gpt.h and timer.h are included. The class definition includes the error handler, so this class is derived from the error handler, as are the several other classes shown earlier. Three attributes, time_on, period, and on_timer, are needed. The attribute time_on is the count during which the output is to be turned on, the period is the rate at which the on-time is repeated, and the on_timer is the output compare subsystem that will control the turn-off time.

The PWM base period will be established by OC1. Remember that OC1 output can be coupled to any other output compare, and the output at that output compare output pin can be programmed to do anything possible when the OC1 event occurs. In this case we program coupled output compare to turn on whenever OC1 happens. The program will have the output turn off when the coupled output compare event occurs. We will describe this operation further when the program for the pwm is discussed.

The usual form for definition files is followed here. The class Pwm is generated. The function prototypes for the constructor, pwm_(), and the destructor, pwm__(), are included here. A macro definition for the method set_on() is also included. This function is used to adjust the time the output pulse is turned on.

The implementation file follows. Because this subsystem uses OC1 in its coupled mode, it is dangerous to plan to make more than one PWM at a time with this class.

Let us return to the workings of this PWM. OC1 will be coupled to a second output compare, say OCx. The OCx output pin will be programmed to turn on whenever OC1 occurs. There will be no interrupt for OC1, but an interrupt will be requested whenever OCx occurs. Also, when OCx occurs, the OCx output pin will be turned off. Within this interrupt service routine, the base period needed for OC1 will be programmed, and the time after the next OC1 event that the next OCx must occur is calculated and programmed. This approach means that OC1 turns the output on and OCx turns it off. The design of the output compare sub-

```
#ifndef PWM_H
#define PWM_H

#include "hc16y1.h"
#include "gpt.h"
#include "timer.h"
#include "defines.h"

#define PWM_CLASS \
            ERROR_HANDLER \
            WORD time_on, period; \
            BYTE on_timer;

typedef struct
{
      PWM_CLASS
} Pwm;

#define set_on(a,b) ((a)->time_on=(b))

Pwm *pwm_(WORD period,WORD time_on,BYTE on_timer);
void pwm__(Pwm *);
#endif
```

Listing 5.6 Pulse-Width Modulator Definition File

system is such that it is possible to have OCx occur as soon as one clock cycle after OC1. Therefore, the shortest output pulse is one clock cycle wide. Unfortunately, the operation is not so smooth at the other end of the pulse. If we want the pulse to be on essentially all the time, there will be problems that cannot be overcome with the approach we take here. The time that the next OC1 event will occur is established within the interrupt service routine of the OCx. Therefore, if the on-time is very long compared to the period, it is possible that OCx will occur so late in the cycle that it will not be possible to insert the next OC1 time before that time has expired. As it turns out, the maximum on-time is about 30 clock cycles short of 100%. This error is not serious for very long periods, but 30 clocks out of 256 is quite a limitation.

It is possible to overcome this problem. In the case above, we set the base period by OC1 and the on-time by OCx. Suppose that we used OCx to set the base period and OC1 to determine the on-time. In this case, the problem would reverse. It would be possible to have an on-time that is one cycle less than the base, but the system would not be able to generate short periods. It is possible to make a system that will have a one cycle minimum on-time and a one cycle minimum off-time. Here, the relative on-time must be tested to determine which approach to take, and the functions of OC1 and OCx must be interchanged to meet the program needs.

A PWM is a hardware function. It is set into operation and whenever the output needs to be changed, a message is sent to the object informing it of the new on-time. Otherwise, there is no other interaction with the program. You will note below that there is one function needed, one instance of a Timer_parameter, and pointers to two Timers. The function ocxint() is attached to the second timer interrupt service routine. Two timers, pwm_timer1 and pwm_timerx, are used as described above, and the single Timer_parameter block is used to initialize both timers.

The approach used here to construct the pwm object is similar to that used earlier. A temporary instance of the error handler is created and the memory space for the new PWM is allocated with the malloc() call. The error handler is moved into the newly allocated memory and then the error handler is deleted when error__() is executed. The three parameters passed into the constructor as arguments are then stored in the proper locations in the newly created object.

```
#include "pwm.h"

/* WARNING Only one pwm can be instantiated from this class at
   a time. Each pwm would use OC1 and the program could request
   different base periods of OC1. */

void ocxint(Pwm *this);

Timer_parameters tp;
Timer *pwm_timer1,*pwm_timerx;

Pwm *pwm_(WORD period, WORD time_on ,BYTE on_timer)
{
     Pwm *this;
     Error_handler *temp = error_();

     this=(Pwm*) malloc(sizeof(Pwm));
     if(this==NULL)
     error_handler(temp,TYPE_1,PWM);
     memmove(this, temp, sizeof(Error_handler));
     error__(temp);

     this->time_on=time_on;
     this->period=period;
     this->on_timer=on_timer;
```

The two timers needed to create the PWM are instantiated next. To create a timer, we must fill a timer parameter block properly and send a pointer to this block as an argument to the timer constructor. The first timer to be instantiated will be for

OC1. The parameter tp.number is therefore set to 1. The period of this timer was passed into the constructor as the parameter period. There will be no action on the OC1 output pin when an OC1 event occurs, but OC1 will be connected to the timer passed in as on_timer. The connect data indicate that the on_timer output will be turned on when the OC1 event occurs. Finally, there is no interrupt to occur on the OC1 event. Timer1 is instantiated by a call to the timer_() constructor.

```
/* set up the timer parameter structure and instantiate
    the base period timer which must be output compare 1 */
tp.number=1;                     /* use output compare 1 */
tp.tick=period;                 /* OC1 period */
tp.action=0;                    /* no OC1 output action */
tp.OC1_connect=on_timer;        /* connect OC1 to on_timer */
tp.connect_data=1;              /* Turn OC2 ON at OC1 */
tp.interrupt=NO;                /* need no interrupt here */
pwm_timer1=timer_(&tp);         /* instantiate the timer */
```

The second timer is set up. This timer setup differs little from that above. The timer number is now the value passed in as the on_timer parameter when the constructor is called. The time-on value passed in is stored in the tick entry of the parameter block. In this case the action that is to occur at the OCx output pin is that it is to be turned off when the OCx event occurs. A value of 2 placed in the tp.action parameter will cause this to happen. There can be no connect data for any output compare but 1, and we will need an interrupt to occur at the OCx event. This timer is instantiated and the method ocxint() along with the object *this* is placed in the pwm_timerx object. The function ocxint(this) will be executed during the process of each pwm_timerx interrupt. Finally, a pointer to the newly created object, *this*, is returned to the calling program.

```
    /* set up the timer parameter structure and instantiate the
        time on timer */
    tp.number=on_timer;            /* use output compare */
    tp.tick=time_on;
    tp.action=2;                   /* output action - turn timer
                                                         OFF */
    tp.OC1_connect=0;
    tp.connect_data=0;             /* no connect data */
    tp.interrupt=YES;              /* need an interrupt here */
    pwm_timerx=timer_(&tp);            /* instantiate the timer */
    attach_method(pwm_timerx,ocxint); /* need a modification to
                                                      the isr */
    attach_object(pwm_timerx,this);
    return this;
}
```

The PWM destructor pwm__() must delete not only the object created in the pwm constructor but also both timers created for use by the pwm object. Therefore, the destructor will contain two timer destructor calls, timer__(pwm_timer1) and timer__(pwm_timerx), followed by a free call to reallocate the memory assigned to hold the pwm object.

```
void pwm__(Pwm *this)
{
    timer__(pwm_timer1);  /* get rid of the timers */
    timer__(pwm_timerx);
    free(this);           /* and delete the Pwm */
}
```

The function attached to the interrupt service routine of timerx is listed below. A pointer to the specific PWM is passed in as an argument. First, it is necessary to update the period value for OC1. The value this->period is added to the contents of the output compare register for OC1. This register is TOC1. Second, the time on the second timer must be updated. This timer was chosen by the programmer, and the particular timer is stored in this->on_timer. The switch/case statement places the proper on-time in the output compare register.

```
void ocxint(Pwm *this)
{
    TOC1+=this->period;
    switch(this->on_timer)
    {
        case 2 : TOC2=TOC1+this->time_on;
                 break;
        case 3 : TOC3=TOC1+this->time_on;
                 break;
        case 4 : TOC4=TOC1+this->time_on;
    }
}
```

The code snippets above are collected together in Listing 5.7, which completes implementation of the PWM.

The program shown in Listing 5.8 is a simple test that demonstrates the performance of the PWM. This program creates a 15-bit PWM. This value is selected by the choice of 0x8000 for the maximum on-time. This number is the count of the maximum on-time. The pwm.h header and the defines.h header are included in the program. Also, there is a pointer to a single instance of a type Pwm defined. Inside the main program, the SIM is initialized as usual, and an instance of a PWM named pw is created. Then the system interrupts are turned on. The test code is very simple. A FOREVER loop that contains a pair of nested for loops is executed. The outer for loop steps the on-time of the PWM through its range of values. The inner loop merely delays operation slightly so that it is easy to see the result of the test on an oscilloscope.

```
#include "pwm.h"

/* WARNING Only one pwm can be instantiated from this class at
   a time. Each pwm would use OC1 and the program could request
   different base periods of OC1. */

static void ocxint(Pwm *this);

static Timer_parameters tp;
static Timer *pwm_timer1,*pwm_timerx;
Pwm *pwm_(WORD period, WORD time_on ,BYTE on_timer)
{
    Pwm *this;
      Error_handler *temp = error_();

      this=(Pwm*) malloc(sizeof(Pwm));
      if(this==NULL)
            error_handler(temp,TYPE_1,PWM);
      memmove(this, temp, sizeof(Error_handler));
      error__(temp);

    this->time_on=time_on;
    this->period=period;
    this->on_timer=on_timer;

      /* set up the timer parameter structure and instantiate
         the base period timer which must be output compare 1 */
    tp.number=1;                 /* use output compare 1 */
    tp.tick=period;              /* OC1 period */
    tp.action=0;                 /* no OC1 output action */
    tp.OC1_connect=on_timer;     /* connect OC1 to on_timer */
    tp.connect_data=1;           /* Turn OC2 ON at OC1 */
    tp.interrupt=NO;             /* need no interrupt here */
    pwm_timer1=timer_(&tp);          /* instantiate the timer */

      /* set up the timer parameter structure and instantiate
         the time on timer */
    tp.number=on_timer;           /* use output compare */
    tp.tick=time_on;
    tp.action=2; /* output action - turn timer OFF */
    tp.OC1_connect=0;
    tp.connect_data=0; /* no connect data */
    tp.interrupt=YES; /* need an interrupt here */
    pwm_timerx=timer_(&tp); /* instantiate the timer */
    attach_method(pwm_timerx,ocxint); /* need a modification to
                                         the  isr */
```

Listing 5.7 Pulse-Width Modulator Implementation File

```
        attach_object(pwm_timerx,this);
      return this;
}

void pwm__(Pwm *this)
{
      timer__(pwm_timer1);  /* get rid of the timers */
      timer__(pwm_timerx);
      free(this);           /* and delete the Pwm */
}

void ocxint(Pwm *this)
{
        TOC1+=this->period;
      switch(this->on_timer)
      {
          case 2 : TOC2=TOC1+this->time_on;
                   break;
          case 3 : TOC3=TOC1+this->time_on;
                   break;
          case 4 : TOC4=TOC1+this->time_on;
      }
}
```

Listing 5.7 (continued)

SUMMARY

All the programs shown in this chapter were compiled and tested on the MC68HC16Y1 evaluation module. The clock runs accurately and each program works as desired. There are some other capabilities that we will add to this program later in the book. This summary must note several important items that have been obtained through the use of a component, or object-oriented approach to these programs. Code written to interface with the internal peripherals of the chip is all contained within a set of classes. If you look over the code above, you will see minimal reference to chip-oriented things in the programs, and the details of running these peripherals is hidden from the main program within the component code. Such an approach provides the program management team with an excellent mechanism for the use of both senior and less experienced programmers on the same team. The applications code, or main program, although it does require some knowledge of the microcontroller chip during initialization, needs no direct reference to the microcontroller or its peripherals in the applications code. With this approach we have succeeded in creating an abstract machine that has the capabilities of the microcontroller, but we have succeeded in hiding the exact nature of the machine from the applications programmer. Even the parts where the initialization program access registers in the system integration module could easily be combined into a class that

```
#include "pwm.h"
#include "defines.h"

#define MAX_ON 0x8000

Pwm *pw;

main()
{

    /* initialize the program */

    /* initialize the SIM registers */

    SYNCR.X=ON;       /* double the clock speed—16.00 mHz */
    SYPCR.SWE=OFF;    /* disable the watchdog */
    CSORBT.DSACK=0;   /* use zero wait states for now */

    pw=pwm_(MAX_ON,0,2);
    cli();                /* enable the system interrupts */

    FOREVER
    {
        WORD i;
        BYTE j;

            for(i=0;i<MAX_ON;i++)
            {
                set_on(pw,i);
                for(j=0;j<0xff;j++);
            }
    }
}
```

Listing 5.8 Pulse-Width Modulator Test Program

instantiates the SIM. Then the initialization code would merely have to send messages to the SIM object to set up the registers for the desired operation.

Recall that we saw a difference between the serial_io and the timer classes. The serial_io required that such features as the IARB and the interrupt level be passed to the serial_io constructor. When the timer class was designed, it was decided to choose appropriate values for these types of parameters within the timer class and not give the applications programmer a chance to select these values. The timer class approach improves the abstraction, but it also decreases the flexibility of the programmer to do the needed job.

In the last three examples, we started with a rather simple clock program. This program required the use of only two classes and the objects instantiated from them. The second program added the linked list to the timer interrupt service routine. To implement this list, we added three additional classes, object1, link, and linklist. We instantiated three Object1 types, three Link types, and only one Linklist type. The code combined these several types into a working linked list that was attached to the timer, and the linked list executed each routine exercise () for every object when the routine walklist () executed with each timer interrupt. Of course, more items could be added to the list if needed. Also, all of this work was under control of only one output compare. We will see more output compare subsystems being used simultaneously later.

Finally, in the last example, it was decided to add a keyboard input to the system that allows entry of the correct time from the keyboard. In this case, the earlier version of the serial io system would not work quite correctly. Rather than modify the older code or rewrite a whole new system, it was shown how to create a new class that inherits the characteristics of the older class and make the necessary modifications to the newly inherited class. This approach allows use of the older, debugged code and does not require that the working code be changed at all.

In the last program, the serial io was used as both an input and an output at the same time. In this instance, there was no great pressure on the system to perform full-duplex or simultaneous input and output, but it was used, and there was no difficulty with the implementation developed.

It seemed interesting that the addition of capability to the basic program required the addition of new objects needed to implement the new functions, followed by a little new code to create and process messages to and from these new objects. We saw essentially no code added to the applications portion of the program when we added the second interrupt service through the link list for the timer. A block of code was added to process the keyboard input.

If you look back over the last several listings you will observe that modifications needed to add the new features to the clock programs were always rather self-contained. There were no modifications to the existing code, only additions needed to implement the new features. This result is one that you should expect from object-oriented code. The code is in self-sufficient blocks. There is little interaction between the various code modules that make up the program. Therefore, addition or deletion of features is relatively easy and debugging the code is almost always easier than you would find with conventional coding techniques.

Another point should be noted. In both the Delay and Pwm code, new classes were created that were based on the Timer class. In other words, Timer is a building block upon which both Delay and Pwm were predicated. If new classes need to be based on these classes, they can also be used as building blocks. A collection of components is being put together to create new components. The limit to the depth of such code construction for microcontrollers is limited by the amount of RAM available in which the various components must be stored.

6

ADDITIONAL TIMER APPLICATIONS: INPUT CAPTURE AND INTERNAL PWM

In Chapter 5 we saw extensive use of the output compare subsystem of the general purpose timer. In this chapter, use of other features of this timer system is explored. We have not yet seen the use of built-in PWM subsystems and the input capture portions of the GPT. These devices are examined in this chapter. The pulse accumulator subsystem is not discussed nor is use made of the single timer that can be programmed as either an output compare or an input capture.

INPUT CAPTURE SUBSYSTEM

The input capture subsystem is a means of measuring time. The same free-running counter that was used to drive the output compare system is used with the input capture subsystem. This counter is clocked as some fraction of the system clock frequency determined by the system prescaler. Through the setup of this prescaler, the programmer can select any power-of-2 fraction between 4 and 256 of the system clock frequency to drive the timer counter register (TCNT). The content of this register can also be clocked from an external source if desired. The default prescaler value is 4, the value used throughout this book.

Each input capture has a register named ICx, where x has the range 1 to 3. There are three input capture subsystems. Associated with each input capture is an input pin connected to the circuitry outside the chip. Signals to this pin control operation of the input capture. An event at this pin will cause the content of the TCNT to be captured and held in the corresponding ICx register. The next event that occurs at the input pin will cause a new value to be saved in ICx. An event can be defined as a rising edge, a falling edge, or either a rising or falling edge. The bits fields that control the choice of an event are named EDGEx, where x has the range 1 to 3. These bit fields are found in TCTL2 (timer control register 2), and the control that they establish is shown in Table 6.1.

There is a bit field named EDGE4 in the TCTL2 register. This bit field controls the timer subsystem that can be programmed as either an input capture or an output compare, and it is not used in this book. These values are enumerated in the timer1 class definition file so that the programmer will be able to use mnemonic calls rather than trying to remember the numerical values.

When an input event occurs, the contents of the TCNT register is captured in the corresponding input capture register. At that time the corresponding ICxF bit in the timer interrupt flag register (TFLG1) is set. If the corresponding bit, ICxI, in the timer interrupt mask register (TMSK1) is set, an interrupt is requested. In programming an input capture system, it is important to remember that any event on the input pin will cause the ICxF bit to be set. This bit must be reset by the program before an interrupt for that channel is enabled by setting the ICxI bit. Otherwise, when this bit is set, an immediate interrupt would be requested. You might note that when these inputs are not being used as input captures, they can be interrupts from outside the chip or used as binary input signals.

We shall implement a class called Timer1 that controls the three input captures. The class definition file, timer1.h, is shown in Listing 6.1. Recall that we decided to place all the timer interrupt controls at a level specified by the class and not give the programmer the flexibility to set these parameters at program time. These three parameters—the IARB or the interrupt arbitration level; the VBA, which is the most significant nibble of the interrupt vector; and the LEVEL, the CPU interrupt level—are set by the #defines below. The timer system is given high priorities in the interrupt system. The maximum interrupt level is 7, and this level of interrupt is nonmaskable. The timer should be assigned a level that is maskable. The IARB arbitrates multiple internal interrupts that occur at the same interrupt level and also at the same time. The range of this parameter is from 0 to 15. The requesting interrupting device with the largest IARB will be processed first.

As we go through the development of the input capture system, you will note that it is similar to the output compare system. This should not surprise you because they are both timers, and even though the features that they each implement are different, the basic function that each performs is still that of a timer.

Table 6.1 Configuration Bits in TCTL2

EDGEx	Configuration
00	Capture disabled
01	Capture rising edge only
10	Capture falling edge only
11	Capture any (rising or falling) edge

```
#ifndef TIMER1_H
#define TIMER1_H

#include "defines.h"
#include "error.h"

#ifndef GPT_IARB
      #define GPT_IARB 12    /* iarb value of 12 for the GPT */
      #define GPT_VBA 5      /* GPT vectors start at 0x50 */
      #define GPT_LEVEL 6    /* use interrupt level 6 */
#endif

typedef enum BYTE
{
      DISABLE,
      RISING,
      FALLING,
      ANY
}Edges;

enum input_captures{IC1=1,IC2,IC3};

#define TIMER1_CLASS \
            ERROR_HANDLER \
            WORD who_am_I; \
            Edges edge; \
            void *hook_object;\
            void (*hook_method)(void*);

typedef struct
{
      TIMER1_CLASS
}Timer1;
#ifndef ATTACH

#define ATTACH
      #define attach_object(a,b) ((a)->hook_object=(b))
      #define attach_method(a,b) ((a)->hook_method=(b))
#endif

#define last_time(a) ((a)->capture_time((a)))

WORD capture_time(Timer1 *);
void set_edge(BYTE number, Edges edge);
void new_edge(Timer1 *,BYTE );
Timer1* timer1_(BYTE number, Edges edge, Boolean interrupt);
void timer1__(Timer1 *);
Boolean get_status(Timer1 *);

#endif
```

Listing 6.1 Timer1 Class Definition File

The TIMER1_CLASS contains the entries that will be found in the Timer1 structure. This device will inherit the features of the ERROR_HANDLER. It needs two attributes, who_am_I and edge. Also, in this case, we will use hook_object and hook_method, as was done with Timer. These parameters will allow the programmer to attach any function that is desired to the interrupt service routine. The hook_object and hook_method parameters are attached to an instance of Timer1 exactly the same as they were for Timer. Therefore, the macro functions to attach these parameters to the object will be the same for both classes. However, there is no guarantee that both Timer1 and Timer will be used together in any program. These macros must be defined in both Timer1 and Timer, and their inclusion must be excluded if they are already defined in another part of the program. The #ifndef ATTACH ... code will exclude multiple definitions of the macros.

There are six function prototypes describing access to methods of this class. Each of these methods is described below at their implementation.

The implementation file for Timer1 is described below. The first nine lines of the program follow the usual programming style. Three header files are needed to connect this class to a particular microcontroller. The first header file is HC16Y1.H. This file contains the definitions of all peripheral addresses for the MC68HC16Y1 microcontroller. Also, some registers with specific bitfield contents are defined. The header GPT.H contains all of the register and bit-field definitions for the general-purpose timer. If you should want to switch this class to another part that has a multichannel communications interface, say the MC68331, you would replace the header HC16Y1.H with a 68331 header file, and the class would compile and work as desired.

Three interrupts can be implemented with this class. The vectors are contiguous in the vector space, and the first vector is offset by one from the timer vector base address. These offsets are defined to make the code more easily understood. There are also three interrupt service routines, whose prototypes are included next.

Within the interrupt service routines, a function do_hook must be executed. This function prototype is included next.

```
#include "hc16y1.h"
#include "gpt.h"
#include "timer1.h"

#define IC1_offset 1    /* output compare vector offsets */
#define IC2_offset 2
#define IC3_offset 3

@port void IC1Isr(void);
@port void IC2Isr(void);
@port void IC3Isr(void);

static void do_hook(Timer1 *);
```

The method capture_time() shown below simply returns the value contained in the input capture register of the specified timer. Here is a case where you can see the need to define the value who_am_I. This attribute contains the number of the input capture, which will be merely a value from 1 to 3. This parameter is used here as a switch to select the correct input capture register value to return to the calling program.

```
WORD capture_time(Timer1 *this)
{
     switch( this->who_am_I)
     {
          case 1: return TIC1;
          case 2: return TIC2;
          case 3: return TIC3;
     }
}
```

The next two functions appear to be very similar. They each allow you to set the parameter EDGEx in TCTL2. This parameter controls the edge, rising, falling, or any, that comprises an event of the input pin. There are occasions where it is desirable to be able to set these values based on the input capture number. Also, in most programs it is best to control these parameters based on the specific instance of a Timer1 where the programmer knows nothing of which input capture number is being executed. The method set_edge() sets the edge parameter based on the input capture number; new_edge() is called with a Timer1 as a parameter, and it, in turn, calls *set edge* with the correct input capture number as a parameter.

There is also a need to be able to poll the status of each input capture. The method get_status() returns the value of the corresponding input capture flag bit. These bits are found in the TCTL2 register.

```
void set_edge(BYTE number,Edges edge)
{
     switch(number)
     {
          case 1 : TCTL2.EDGE1= edge;
                   break;
          case 2 : TCTL2.EDGE2= edge;
                   break;
          case 3 : TCTL2.EDGE3= edge;
     }
}
void new_edge(Timer1 *this,Edges edge)
{
      this->edge=edge;
      set_edge(this->who_am_I,edge);
}
```

```
Boolean get_status(Timer1 *this)
{
        switch (this->who_am_I)
    {
               case 1 : return TFLG1.IC1F;
               case 2 : return TFLG1.IC2F;
               case 3 : return TFLG1.IC3F
    }
}
```

The constructor for Timer1 follows the outline shown with the constructor for Timer in Chapter 5. Pointers to the open timers are needed in the various interrupt service routines. These values are stored in the external static locations identified as IC1_T through IC3_T. Two variables are needed in the constructor. A pointer to a type Timer1 is identified as this, and a temporary pointer to an error handler is saved in temp. The construct in the line

```
Error_handler *temp =error_();
```

causes the creation of a storage location in which to save temp and also executes the constructor error_(), which provides a value with which to initialize temp.

The next two if statements are error tests to make certain that the parameter values provided by the method call are within the correct range. When an error is detected here, a value FALSE is returned to the calling program, where the error must be corrected before a timer can be constructed.

```
/* Timer1 constructor */

Timer1 *IC1_T,*IC2_T,*IC3_T;

Timer1* timer1_(BYTE number, Edges edge, Boolean interrupt)
{
      Timer1* this;
      Error_handler *temp = error_();
      if(number >3)        /* error, must be between 1 and 3 */
            return FALSE;
      if(edge>ANY)
        return FALSE;         /* got a bad edge */
```

The next sequence of operations creates a proper object of the class Timer1. Memory is first allocated to hold the object. A test is made to determine if the memory was allocated properly. If not, the error handler is executed. Otherwise, the instance of the error handler that was created earlier is moved into the memory space allocated for the new instance of Timer1, and then the instance of temp is deleted by execution of the destructor error__().

```
this=(Timer1*) malloc(sizeof(Timer1));
if(this==NULL)
      error_handler(temp,TYPE_1,TIMER);
memmove(this, temp, sizeof(Error_handler));
error__(temp);
```

Once the memory is allocated for this instance of Timer1, the system is initialized and the initial values are placed into the attributes of the new object. Notice that the IARB, interrupt level, and vector base address are set each time an object is instantiated. Since all the timer objects use these same values, these three lines of code are probably duplicated if other instances of timers exist. A test could be made to determine if these values were set by another call to a timer constructor. It would probably require more code to do the test than is needed to reinitialize these parameters.

The value of number is stored in who_am_I, and the initial edge control bitfield is placed in edge. Both hook_object and hook_method are given pointer values of zero. These values will be changed by the program that creates an instance of Timer1.

```
/* initialize the GPT */
GPT_MCR.IARB=GPT_IARB; /* pick an IARB for the timers */
ICR.IRL=GPT_LEVEL;     /* interrupt level 6 */
ICR.VBA=GPT_VBA;       /* vectors start at 0x50 */
set_edge(number,edge); /* set the edge control bits */
this->who_am_I=number; /* save the number of the timer */
this->edge=edge;
this->hook_object=NULL;
this->hook_method=NULL;
```

The last item needed in execution of the constructor is to set the proper value into the interrupt vector and initialize the interrupt control bits. Let us look at the initialization of the interrupt for input capture 1 and recognize that the initialization is the same for the other input captures. Recall that any input event will cause the corresponding ICxF flag to be set regardless of the state of the various input masks. Therefore, it is important that this flag be reset before any interrupts are enabled. The first line of code resets the IC1F bit in TFLG1. The next line of code,

```
vector(IC1Isr,VAL*(GPT_VBA*0x10+IC1_offset));
```

creates a vector address and places the address of the input capture 1 interrupt service routine into this address. In the M68HC16, the first 512 bytes of the memory space, addressed from 0 to 0x1fe, comprise the vector table. The vectors are each two bytes long and they hold the least significant 16 bits of the isr address. As a matter of fact, the chip has no mechanism for direct access to an isr with an address outside the page zero range, where the extension bits of the address are all zero. The

VBA value defined by GPT_VBA is the upper nibble of a hexidecimal value of the vector. This value is multiplied by 0x10, and calculation of the vector value is completed by adding the value of the specific offset. Finally, this value must be multiplied by a value 2 or 4 because the vector number is not the address of the vector. The address of the vector is exactly twice the number of the vector in the M68HC16. The macro vector() places the value IC1Isr into this location. In the MC68331, the vector is four bytes long, and the vector address is four times the vector number. The constant VAL is defined in the chip header file—hc16y1.h or m332.h—so that this code can be used on either of these chips.

If the interrupt is requested, the interrupt enable bit IC1I in the register TMSK1 is turned ON and finally the address of the new object is saved in the location IC1_T.

The remainder of the setup for the interrupt service routines is essentially the same as that described above. With the completion of the interrupt service routine setup, the new version of the Timer1 object is completed. The pointer to the object, *this*, is returned to the calling program.

```
switch(number)
      {
            case 1: TFLG1.IC1F=OFF; /* reset event flag */
                    vector(IC1Isr,VAL*(GPT_VBA*0x10+IC1_offset));
                                        /* put vector in place */
                    if(interrupt) /* do we need an interrupt? */
                            TMSK1.IC1I=ON; /* enable the inter-
                                                          rupt*/
                    IC1_T=this; /* keep Timer1 pointer */
                    break;
            case 2: TFLG1.IC2F=OFF;
                    vector(IC2Isr,VAL*(GPT_VBA*0x10-IC2_offset));
                    if(interrupt)
                            TMSK1.IC2I=ON;
                    IC2_T=this;
                    break;
            case 3: TFLG1.IC3F=OFF;
                    vector(IC3Isr,VAL*(GPT_VBA*0x10+IC3_offset));
                    if(interrupt)
                            TMSK1.IC3I=ON;
                    IC3_T=this;
                    break;
      }
        return this;
}
```

The destructor for a Timer1 object should disable the interrupt for the corresponding input capture. The code needed to disable this interrupt is shown below. The parameter who_am_I contains the input capture number. The switch statement will direct the program to the proper line of code to turn the ICxI bit in TMSK1 off. Then the memory allocated for the instance of the object is freed.

```
/* Timer1 destructors */

void timer1__(Timer1* this)
{
        switch(this->who_am_I)
        {
                case 1 : TMSK1.IC1I=OFF; /* turn off the timer inter-
                                                                rupt */
                         break;
                case 2 : TMSK1.IC2I=OFF;
                         break;
                case 3 : TMSK1.IC3I=OFF;
                         break;
        }
        free(this);
}
```

The interrupt service routines shown below are quite simple. The first business of the interrupt service routine is to disable the cause of the interrupt. The line of code

```
TFLG1.ICxF=OFF;
```

performs this operation. Then the function do_hook() is executed. This function is shown below and requires a parameter that is a pointer to the specific object that is responsible for the interrupt. These values were stored in ICx_T when the interrupts were enabled by the constructor. The function do_hook() is shown below also. This function is called from each interrupt service routine. When an application wants to use a Timer1, it has the option of changing the two parameters hook_object and hook_method saved as Timer1 attributes. Then during the interrupt service routine, the function (*hook_method)() can be called with hook_object as an argument. Therefore, the application can have complete control over the code executed during the service of an interrupt.

```
/* interrupt service routines */

@port void IC1Isr(void)
{
        TFLG1.IC1F=OFF;
        do_hook(IC1_T);
}
```

```
@port void IC2Isr(void)
{
        TFLG1.IC2F=OFF;
        do_hook(IC2_T);
}

@port void IC3Isr(void)
{
        TFLG1.IC3F=OFF;
        do_hook(IC3_T);

}/* function that allows external access to the isr */

static void do_hook(Timer1 *time)
{
        if(time->hook_method !=NULL)
           (*time->hook_method)(time->hook_object);
}
```

As is our normal practice, the code for the implementation file for Timer1 was broken into several small pieces when it was described. A complete version of the file is shown in Listing 6.2 so that you can easily see the entire program.

```
#include <hc16y1.h>
#include <gpt.h>
#include <timer1.h>

#define IC1_offset 1  /* output compare vector offsets */
#define IC2_offset 2
#define IC3_offset 3

@port void IC1Isr(void);
@port void IC2Isr(void);
@port void IC3Isr(void);

static void do_hook(Timer1 *);

WORD capture_time(Timer1 *this)
{
    switch( this->who_am_I)
    {
      case 1: return TIC1;
```

Listing 6.2 Timer1 Class Implementation File

```
        case 2: return TIC2;
        case 3: return TIC3;
    }
}

void set_edge(BYTE number,Edges edge)
{
        switch(number)
        {
                case 1 : TCTL2.EDGE1=edge;
                         break;
                case 2 : TCTL2.EDGE2=edge;
                         break;
                case 3 : TCTL2.EDGE3=edge;
        }
}
void new_edge(Timer1 *this,Edges edge)
{
        this->edge=edge;
        set_edge(this->who_am_I,edge);
}

Boolean get_status(Timer1 *this)
{
        switch (this->who_am_I)
    {
        case 1 : return TFLG1.IC1F;
        case 2 : return TFLG1.IC2F;
        case 3 : return TFLG1.IC3F;
    }
}

/* Timer1 constructor */

Timer1 *IC1_T,*IC2_T,*IC3_T;

Timer1* timer1_(BYTE number, Edges edge, Boolean interrupt)
{
        Timer1* this;
        Error_handler *temp = error_();

        if(number >3)         /* error must be between 1 and 4 */
                return FALSE;
        if(edge>3)
        return FALSE;         /* got a bad OC1_connect */
```

Listing 6.2 (continued)

```
    set_edge(number,edge);
    this=(Timer1*) malloc(sizeof(Timer1));
    if(this==NULL)
          error_handler(temp,TYPE_1,TIMER);
    memmove(this, temp, sizeof(Error_handler));
    error__(temp);
    /* initialize the GPT  */
    GPT_MCR.IARB=GPT_IARB; /* pick an IARB for the timers */
    ICR.IRL=GPT_LEVEL;     /* interrupt level 6 */
    ICR.VBA=GPT_VBA;       /* vectors start at 0x50 */
    this->who_am_I=number; /* save the number of the timer */
    this->edge=edge;
    this->hook_object=NULL;
    this->hook_method=NULL;
    switch(number)
    {
    case 1: TFLG1.IC1F=OFF;       /* reset event flag */
                  vector(IC1Isr,VAL*(GPT_VBA*0x10+IC1_off-
                                                   set));
                        /* put vector in place */
                  if(interrupt)        /* do we need an
                                             interrupt? */
                        TMSK1.IC1I=ON;   /* enable the
                                              interrupt*/
                  IC1_T=this;          /* keep Timer1
                                              pointer */
                  break;
    case 2: TFLG1.IC2F=OFF;
                  vector(IC2Isr,VAL*(GPT_VBA*0x10+IC2_off-
                                                   set));
                  if(interrupt)
                        TMSK1.IC2I=ON;
                  IC2_T=this;
                  break
    case 3: TFLG1.IC3F=OFF;
                  vector(IC3Isr,VAL*(GPT_VBA*0x10+IC3_off-
                                                   set));
                  if(interrupt)
                        TMSK1.IC3I=ON;
                  IC3_T=this;
                  break;
   }
    return this;
}
```

Listing 6.2 (continued)

```
/* Timer1 destructors */

void timer1__(Timer1* this)
{
        switch(this->who_am_I)
        {
                case 1 : TMSK1.IC1I=OFF; /* turn off the timer in-
                                                                 terrupt */
                         break;
                case 2 : TMSK1.IC2I=OFF;
                         break;
                case 3 : TMSK1.IC3I=OFF;
                         break;
        }
        free(this);
}

/* interrupt service routines */

@port void IC1Isr(void)
{
        TFLG1.IC1F=OFF;
        do_hook(IC1_T);
}

@port vcid IC2Isr(void)
{
        TFLG1.IC2F=OFF;
        do_hook(IC2_T);
}

@port void IC3Isr(void)
{
        TFLG1.IC3F=OFF;
        do_hook(IC3_T);
}

/* function that allows external access to the isr */

static void do_hook(Timer1 *time)
{
        if(time->hook_method !=NULL)
         (*time->hook_method)(time->hook_object);
}
```

Listing 6.2 (continued)

TIMER1 TEST PROGRAM

Demonstration programs that show the use of simple features of a microcontroller present a serious challange. Most such programs are large and complicated, and if they are carefully chosen to be simple, they are usually meaningless and have little application in the real world. Fortunately, there is an excellent application need that can be used to demonstrate the practical use of an input capture subsystem. This application is the automatic measurement of baud rate on an asynchronous serial port. We usually specify the baud rate of a serial port, and that is the value that it must be. With the program we develop here, the baud rate is measured with an input capture.

This program will measure the baud rate, set the serial port to the proper baud rate and send a message to the screen. We have a little problem here. Both of the serial i/o classes that have been developed require that the baud rate be specified as a numerical number of bits per second, and this number is converted to a divisor to be placed in the baud rate control bit field. As it turns out, this divisor can be calculated easily from the measured time of a single character. The difficult part at this point is to convert this value to a bit rate just to be converted back to a divisor. This problem can be resolved if we modify the serial class to take the divisor as an argument when the class constructor is executed rather than the bit rate. Such a change is quite simple, and we will create a new class named serial1 that is inherited from the class serkb.

The definition file for this class is simple. The class inherits serkb, and it has only a constructor and a destructor. The definition file is shown in Listing 6.3. This class definition includes the header file serkb.h. The type created by this class is still a Serial_io, but we use a different constructor to generate this type.

The code in Listing 6.4 is the implementation file for our new Serial_io. The constructor takes as its first argument the baud_value, which could be measured or taken from a table in a data manual. The remaining parameters, vector, iarb, and

```
#ifndef SERIO1_H
#define SERIO1_H

#include "serkb.h"
Serial_io *serial1_io_(WORD baud_value,
                         int vector,
                            int iarb,
                            int int_level);
void serial1_io__(Serial_io *this);

#endif
```

Listing 6.3 Definition File for the Class Serial1_io

int_level, are the same as earlier. The constructor executes the constructor for serkb_io_() with a value of 9600 for the baud rate. This value is changed to the selected value by the line of code

```
SCCR0A.BR=baud_value;
```

A pointer to the newly created object is returned to the calling program. The destructor simply deallocates the memory space allocated by the constructor where the object was stored.

Let us first write a function named get_baud() that will do everything that we want in this case. Such a function will be shown later. This function is given two parameters. The first, number, is the input capture number to be used in the measurement and the second, t3, is a pointer to a Timer that interrupts each millisecond. Within get_baud() an instance of Timer1 will be created. The input capture associated with Timer1 is assumed to be connected to the serial line. The serial data format is shown in Figure 6.1. The default serial definition is usually n, meaning no parity; 8, meaning eight data bits; and 1, meaning 1 stop bit. The serial line in its idle condition is high. The first bit transmitted is called the *start bit* and is labeled S in Figure 6.1. There follows a series of eight data bits, each labeled 0, 1, ..., 7. These data are transmitted least significant bit first. After the last data bit there is one

```
#include <hc16y1.h>
#include <seriol.h>
#include <mcci.h>

Serial_io *serial1_io_(WORD baud_value,
                       int vector,
                       int iarb,
                       int int_level)
{
    Serial_io *this;

    this=serkb_io_(9600,vector,iarb,int_level);
    SCCR0A.BR=baud_value;
    return temp;
}

void serial1_io__(Serial_io *this)
{
     free(this);
}
```

Listing 6.4 Serial1_io Implementation File

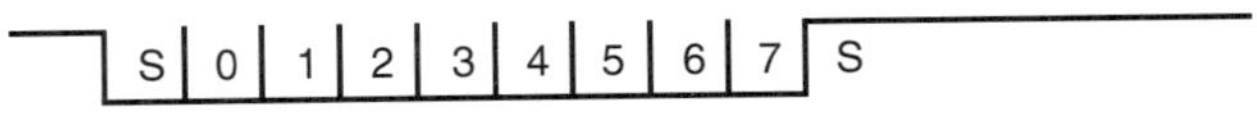

Figure 6.1 Serial Data Character Format

additional bit that is held high for one bit time. This bit is also labeled S and is called the *stop bit*. There can be either 1 or 2 stop bits, depending on the system setup.

The beginning of the start bit is sensed when the input falls from an idle or high state to a low state. After the eighth bit, the signal is set to high for at least one bit time, corresponding to the stop bit. In high-speed transmission, a new start bit can occur immediately after completion of the stop bit.

A character is surrounded by start and stop bits. The beginning of the character can be sensed by the high-to-low transition that marks the beginning of the start bit. The end of the character can be sensed by a low-to-high transition that signals the beginning of the stop bit. In total, the time from the first falling edge to the beginning of the stop bit is nine bit times. Of course, the data bits will have changing values, but it is the last transition that is necessary to see. All printable characters and standard control characters that can be sent from the keyboard have a value of zero for bit seven. Therefore, the transition from bit seven to the stop bit will always be a low-to-high transition and will always be seen.

Let us now examine the operation of the input capture timer and the MCCI subsystems. In the MCCI, the baud rate is set by placing a 13-bit value in SCCR0A.BR field. This value is found by the equation

$$\text{BR} = \frac{f_s}{32\ \text{baud}} \tag{1}$$

where BR is the bit-field value and the baud rate is in bits per second. The value f_s is the system clock frequency. With the input capture subsystem, the total time for a single character can be measured. This time is actually the time for nine bits. The time is expressed in counts of the system clock, which has been prescaled. The default prescale value that is used in this example is 4. Therefore, the measured time is

$$\text{baud} = \frac{9}{\text{count}} \times \frac{f_s}{4}$$

When this value is substituted into the first expression and cleaned up, it is found that

$$\text{BR} = \frac{\text{count}}{72}$$

which is somewhat surprisingly independent of the system clock frequency.

Our code must measure the count time from the beginning of the start bit to the beginning of the stop bit and divide this value by 72 to find the value needed to be placed in the SCCR0A.BR field. The code shown in Listing 6.5 will accomplish this task. The first task is to instantiate a semaphore that will be used with a delay.

Then input capture timer is instantiated. This timer will be the number specified by the calling program, its event will be a falling edge, and no interrupt will be used. The program is then stalled until an event occurs by the statement

```
while(!get_status(t))
      ;                        /* wait until an event occurs */
```

This statement will hang on itself until a falling edge is sensed. At that time control is returned to the next statement in which the measured start time is saved. The edge sensitivity of Timer1 is then changed to rising, to sense the transition to the stop bit, and an 11-millisecond delay is implemented. Eleven milliseconds was chosen to be longer than one would expect with a 1200-baud system. The program then waits until Delay releases the specified semaphore. At that time, the value stored in the output compare register should be the time, relative to the TCNT register, of the be-

```
/* This routine returns the value to be placed in SCCR0A.BR to
   make the baud rate match that measured by an input capture.
   The measured value may not match the book value exactly. */

WORD get_baud(BYTE number, Timer *t3)
{
    WORD start_time;
    Delay *d;
    Semaphore *s;
    Timer1 *t;

    s=semaphore_();
    t=timer1_(number,        /* Build input capture--number */
             FALLING,        /* capture falling edge */
             NO);            /* no interrupt */
    while(!get_status(t))
      ;                     /* wait until an event occurs */
    start_time=capture_time(t); /* get event time immediately */
    new_edge(t,RISING);      /* set the sensitivity to rising
                                                        edge */
    d=delay_(t3,s,11);       /* t3 must be 1 ms timer to delay 11
                                                          ms */
    wait_for_semaphore(s);  /* wait out the delay */
    start_time=capture_time(t)-start_time;
    timer1__(t);             /* get rid of this timer */
    return start_time%72>36?start_time/72+1: start_time/72;
}
```

Listing 6.5 get_baud() Bit-Rate Measuring Function

ginning of the stop bit. The difference between the time of the start bit and the time measured is saved and the instance of Timer1 is deleted. The measured value is then divided by 72 and returned to the calling program. At high baud rates, the value returned becomes relatively small. When the value calculated by the division is rounded down, a noticeable error can occur, so the code that calculates the return value rounds the result to the nearest integer value.

The function described above uses several software components. The semaphore, delay, timer, and timer1 components are used together to measure the bit rate of the serial port. These components all work together smoothly. You should never expect any bad interaction between the components because they have each been encapsulated as tightly as the C language will allow.

The final portion of the program is to build code that calls the get_baud() function to determine the speed of the serial port. This program is shown in Listing 6.6. The function listed above is to be compiled with this program, so all of the necessary header files are #included here. Recall that in the case of the serial input/output subsystem components, the various interrupt parameters are specified by the calling program rather than being specified within the component itself. Either approach is useful. All the necessary parameters are defined by the calling program for the serial input/output, as shown below. In this way the programmer has complete flexibility to choose these parameters when the system is designed. The approach used with Timer and with Timer1 components was to specify these parameters within the class itself, and then the programmer did not have to worry about the choice of values.

Is one approach better than the other? Probably, but it depends more on the shop standards set up by the organization where the coding is being done. Many groups will deplore the arbitrary choice by the code of things such as interrupt vectors and levels. This approach takes away the flexibility of programmers to do their job. On the other hand, many programmers really dislike the need to get into the nature of the microcontroller being programmed. We can hide this nature inside the components that are developed for the system, as was done with the timer.

```
#include <HC16Y1.H>
#include <scim.h>
#include <mcci.h>
#include <timer.h>
#include <timer1.h>
#include <delay.h>
#include <serio1.h>
#include <semaphor.h>
#include <defines.h>

/* serial port parameters */

#define SERIO_BAUD_19200 19200
#define SERIO_INT_VECTOR 0x40
```

```
#define SERIO_IARB 10
#define SERIO_INT_LEVEL 3
#define TIMECOUNT 4000

/* function prototypes */
void printd(unsigned long);
WORD get_baud(BYTE number, Timer *t3);
```

While discussing philosophy, there is another styling item that is shown in the following code. A parameter block has been used to pass data to the Timer constructor. This block is a structure and you will note that it is filled with tp.tick=xxx; type statements. In this case we use the structure name. A little farther down, a similar parameter block, called an io_command_block, is filled for use with the serial1 component. In that case the pointer assignment mechanism, oob1->call_complete=xxx;, was used. In both cases, pointers to the parameter blocks were sent to the object when needed. Which approach is better? Here is another case where both approaches work equally well. There is no clear winner with regard to code space or execution speed, and both are equally easy to read and understand. Within a programming team or group standard, one and only one of these approaches should be chosen and used. Regardless of the approach, the idea of object-oriented programming is to make the interface between the various components uniform and easy to follow. The coding approach shown below works well, but it is in no way a uniform approach to the problem.

```
void main(void)
{
    Timer *t3;
    Timer_parameters tp;
    Serial_io *sio;
    io_command_block *oob1,ob1;
    BYTE pszMessage[]="The selected baud rate is ";
    BYTE pszMessage1[]=" bits per second\n\r";
    WORD baud;
    unsigned long baud_rate;

      /* initialize the program */

    /* initialize the SIM registers */
    SYNCR.X=ON;           /* double the clock speed--16.00 MHz */
    SYPCR.SWE=OFF;        /* disable the watchdog */
    CSORBT.DSACK=0;       /* use zero wait states for now */
    cli();                /* enable system interrupts */

      /* set up the timer parameter structure and instantiate a
                                                        timer */
    tp.number=3;          /* use output compare number 3 */
    tp.tick=TIMECOUNT;    /* 1 ms interrupts */
    tp.action=0;          /* no output action */
```

```
tp.OC1_connect=0;    /* OC1 not connected to another OC */
tp.connect_data=0;   /* therefore no connect data needed */
tp.interrupt=YES;    /* need an interrupt here */
t3=timer_(&tp);            /* instantiate the timer */
baud=get_baud(1,t3);/* measure the baud rate */
timer__(t3);         /*don't need timer any more */
```

After the system is set up, the timer is programmed to provide a 1-millisecond interrupt and then started. The function shown above, get_baud(), is then executed. Upon return from the get_baud() routine, the timer is no longer needed, so it is destroyed. The serial port is then instantiated with serial1_io_() and the baud value returned by get_baud() is used. The message "The selected baud rate is" is sent to the screen. The baud rate is then claculated using Equation (1) above. Here we need to know that the system frequency, f_s, is 16-MHz. This value divided by 32 provides the numerator of 500,000 used to calculate the baud_rate. The value calculated is sent to the screen and then the message "bits per second\r\n" is sent to the screen. This program was executed many times at many standard baud rates between 1200 and 57,600. The chip is incapable of providing a 57,600-bits /second rate. Return to Equation (1) and observe that

$$\frac{16{,}000{,}000}{32 \times 57{,}600} = 8.68$$

This value will be rounded to 9. In that case the baud rate will be

$$\frac{16{,}000{,}000}{32 \times 9} = 55{,}555.555$$

If you execute the program, this is the baud-rate value printed out when requesting a 57,600-bits/second rate.

```
/* set up the serial communications */
  sio=serial1_io_(baud,                /* set the baud rate */
                  SERIO_INT_VECTOR,   /* interrupt vector */
                 SERIO_IARB,          /* iarb */
                  SERIO_INT_LEVEL);   /* and interrupt level
                                                         */

/* set up the io blocks */
oob1=&ob1;                    /* output block */
oob1->call_complete=TRUE;     /* have no message going out */
oob1->io_command=OUTPUT;      /* oob1 is always output */
oob1->buffer=pszMessage;      /* select the message */
oob1->buffer_length= sizeof pszMessage;
serial_io(sio,oob1);          /* message to the i/o object */
while(!oob1->call_complete)
```

```
            ;                       /* wait until transmission is
                                                              done */
        baud_rate=500000ul/baud;
        printd(baud_rate);          /* send baud rate to screen */
        oob1->buffer=pszMessage1;
        oob1->buffer_length= sizeof pszMessage1;
        serial_io(sio,oob1);        /* send out rest of message */
        while(!oob1->call_complete)
            ;
    }
```

The standard printd() function is used to print the numerical value to the screen. This function, shown below, is probably the simplest integer-to-ASCII conversion available for microcontrollers. The controller as well as the compiler used with this function must support recursion.

```
    void printd(unsigned long x)
    {
        if(x/10)
            printd(x/10);
        putch(x%10+'0');
    }
```

The program above was not only broken into pieces for description, but the order of functions was switched around. Therefore, the entire program is shown in Listing 6.6.

```
#include <HC16Y1.H>
#include <scim.h>
#include <mcci.h>
#include <timer.h>
#include <timer1.h>
#include <delay.h>
#include <serio1.h>
#include <semaphor.h>
#include <defines.h>

/* serial port parameters */

#define SERIO_BAUD_19200 19200
#define SERIO_INT_VECTOR 0x40
#define SERIO_IARB 10
#define SERIO_INT_LEVEL 3
#define TIMECOUNT 4000

/* function prototypes */
```

Listing 6.6 Baud Rate Measuring Program

```
void printd(unsigned long);
WORD get_baud(BYTE number, Timer *t3);

void main(void)
{
    Timer *t3;
    Timer_parameters tp;
    Serial_io *sio;
    io_command_block *oob1,ob1;
    BYTE pszMessage[]="The selected baud rate is ";
    BYTE pszMessage1[]=" bits per second\n\r";
    WORD baud;
    unsigned long baud_rate;

      /* initialize the program */

    /* initialize the SIM registers */
    SYNCR.X=ON;           /* double the clock speed--16.00 MHz */
    SYPCR.SWE=OFF;        /* disable the watchdog */
    CSORBT.DSACK=0;       /* use zero wait states for now */
    cli();                /* enable system interrupts */

    /* set up the timer parameter structure and instantiate a
                                                       timer */
    tp.number=3;          /* use output compare number 3 */
    tp.tick=TIMECOUNT;    /* 1 ms interrupts */
    tp.action=0;          /* no output action */
    tp.OC1_connect=0;     /* OC1 not connected to another OC */
    tp.connect_data=0;    /* therefore no connect data needed */
    tp.interrupt=YES;     /* need an interrupt here */
    t3=timer_(&tp);              /* instantiate the timer */
    baud=get_baud(1,t3);/* measure the baud rate */
    timer__(t3);          /*don't need timer any more */

    /* set up the serial communications */
      sio=serial1_io_(baud,              /* set the baud rate */
                       SERIO_INT_VECTOR,  /* interrupt vector
                                                          */
                     SERIO_IARB,         /* iarb */
                       SERIO_INT_LEVEL);  /* and interrupt level
*/

    /* set up the io blocks */
    oob1=&ob1;                  /* output block */
    oob1->call_complete=TRUE;   /* have no message going out */
    oob1->io_command=OUTPUT;    /* oob1 is always output */
    oob1->buffer=pszMessage;    /* select the message */
```

Listing 6.6 (continued)

```
    oob1->buffer_length= sizeof pszMessage;
    serial_io(sio,oob1);        /* message to the i/o object */
    while(!oob1->call_complete)
          ;                           /* wait until transmission
                                                   is done */
    baud_rate=500000ul/baud;
    printd(baud_rate);          /* send baud rate to screen */
    oob1->buffer=pszMessage1;
    oob1->buffer_length= sizeof pszMessage1;
    serial_io(sio,oob1);        /* send out rest of message */
    while(!oob1->call_complete)
        ;
}

void printd(unsigned long x)
{
      if(x/10)
      printd(x/10);
    putch(x%10+'0');
}

/* This routine returns the value to be placed in SCCR0A.BR to
   make the baud rate match that measured by an input capture.
   The measured value may not match the book value exactly. */

WORD get_baud(BYTE number, Timer *t3)
{
    WORD start_time;
    Delay *d;
    Semaphore *s;
    Timer1 *t;

    s=semaphore_();
    t=timer1_(number,          /* Build input capture--number */
              FALLING,         /* capture falling edge */
              NO);             /* no interrupt */
    while(!get_status(t))
      ;                      /* wait until an event occurs */
    start_time=capture_time(t); /* get event time immediately */
    new_edge(t,RISING);        /* set the sensitivity to rising
                                                   edge */
    d=delay_(t3,s,11);         /* t3 must be 1 ms timer to delay 11
                                                     ms */
    wait_for_semaphore(s);    /* wait out the delay */
    start_time=capture_time(t)-start_time;
    timer1__(t);               /* get rid of this timer */
    semaphore__(s);            /* don't need semaphore any more */
    return start_time%72>36?start_time/72+1: start_time/72;
}
```

Listing 6.6 (continued)

INTERNAL PULSE-WIDTH MODULATORS

In Chapter 5 we developed a pulse-width modulation system that made use of two input capture subsystems. One input capture was used to set the period of the signal and the other controlled the on-time. This scheme can be used efficiently and offers some flexibility beyond that available from the two built-in pulse-width modulators (PWMs), found in the GPT. Specifically, these two PWMs are both eight-bit devices and the PWM developed in Chapter 5 provided at least 15-bit accuracy and resolution if needed. On the other hand, the Chapter 5 PWM was very slow and the internal PWMs can run considerably faster. But this value is also flexible because a prescaler can be applied to the PWM counter that will allow very precise PWM rates, down to as slow as 4 Hz.

This PWM system performs the same type of operation as that described in Chapter 5. There is one major difference, however; these two different approaches use completely different internal portions of the microcontroller. Therefore, if we should decide to make this PWM system inherit the attributes and methods of the system described in Chapter 5, we would be causing peripheral components to be tied up that would never be used. For example, the Chapter 5 system uses Output Compare 1 timer and another timer specified by the programmer. This system does not employ any timer functions other than the built-in PWM subsystems.

The internal PWM systems are driven by the system clock through the PWM prescaler. In the PWMC (PWM control register), are three bits that control the level of the prescaler and a pair of bits called SFA and SFB. These bits set the speed mode of the PWM to either slow or fast. Table 6.2 contains a summary of the operation of the prescaler along with the slow/fast bits for each of the PWM devices. There is only one prescaler for both PWMs, so the two PWMs must run at the same basic clock speed. However, the slow/fast bit can be set for each PWM.

The header file, shown in Listing 6.7, has some new items for a header file. The first is the enumeration of some values to be used labeled static. The mnemonics A and B can be used in this program and any file where pwmi.h is included, but these names are hidden from the rest of the program. Several times a bit-field defin-

Table 6.2 PWM Frequency Range Using 16.78-MHz System Clock

PPR[2:0]	Prescaler Tap	Fast Mode	Slow Mode
000	Div 2 = 8.39 MHz	32.8 kHz	256 Hz
001	Div 4 = 4.19 MHz	16.4 kHz	128 Hz
010	Div 8 = 2.10 MHz	8.19 kHz	64.0 Hz
011	Div 16 = 1.08 Mhz	4.09 kHz	32.0 Hz
100	Div 32 = 524 kHz	2.05 kHz	16.0 Hz
101	Div 64 = 262 kHz	1.02 kHz	8.0 Hz
110	Div 128 = 131 kHz	512 Hz	4.0 Hz
111	PCLK	PCLK/256	PCLK/32768

Source: Motorola Microcontroller Family General Purpose Timer, Motorola Document GPTRM/AD.

ition contained within a general header file is not quite that needed for a specific program. For example the register PWMC is defined as a type Register, 16-individual bits, in the header file gpt.h. In this case it will make the code simpler if a bit field that is three bits wide and contains bits 9 through 11 in this memory location were available. Shown below is an example of how such a modification is made. A

```
#ifndef PWMI_H
#define PWMI_H

#include <defines.h>
#include <hc16y1.h>
#include <gpt.h>
#include <timer.h>

static enum {A,B};

typedef struct
{
    unsigned PWM_NULL0 : 9;
    unsigned PR02 :3;
    unsigned PWM_NULL1 : 4;
}  Pwmcspec;

#define PWMCSPEC (*(@far Pwmcspec*)(GPT_Register+0x24))

#define PWMI_CLASS    \
            ERROR_HANDLER \
            WORD time_on; \
            BYTE channel;

typedef struct
{
      PWMI_CLASS
} Pwmi;

#define ON_TIME(a,b) ((a)->channel==A)?(PWMA.PWA=(b)) :
(PWMB.PWB=(b))

Pwmi *pwmi_(BYTE channel,BYTE time_on,
                  BYTE prescale,Boolean speed);
void pwmi__(Pwmi *);

#endif
```

Listing 6.7 Internal PWM Object Header File

structure that has the desired bit-field arrangement is typedefed and then the desired address is cast onto a pointer to this new type. Then, in the program, this new pointer can be used the same as the one defined in the header file.

The remainder of this header file is about the same as usual. The parameter on_time in the object must be set by the program. Therefore, a macro function to set the proper value in the object is included. The parameter, a, above is a pointer to an instance of the specific pwmi to be changed, and b is the new value for the on_time.

The warning shown in Listing 6.8 bears mentioning again. Each PWM within the system is turned on and running whenever an object that contains it is instantiated. If more than one instance of the PWM were created, the hardware would have no mechanism for sorting out which values to use. The tests upon entering the constructor returns an error to the calling program when an improper PWM is instantiated. You should note that this error is a program error, not a system error. Therefore, the error handler will not be needed to take care of this type of error. A simple return to the calling program with an error flag set is superior to our using the error handler in cases such as these. The calling program can test the pointer that is returned by the constructor, and if there is an error, the pointer will have a NULL value.

The remainder of this constructor follows the usual approach for the creation of an object. A Pwmi is derived from the error_handler class. An instance of the error handler is created when the variable temp is defined, and this variable is initialized by the call to the error constructor following the initial tests to determine if there is a calling error. It is important that the instance of error be created after these tests because if it were called prior to the tests, program control would be returned to the calling program with an unused error handler object that would never be destroyed.

After the object has been created, its parameters are initialized with the values time on and channel that are passed into the constructor as arguments. The value of the prescale is put into the bit field defined in the header file, and the switch statement selects the proper internal channel and provides them with values. In addition to the usual job of destroying the memory allocated for the instance of the component, the destructor in this case must also turn the static memory flag ach or bch off whenever an instance of a PWMI is destroyed.

```
#include <pwmi.h>

/* WARNING Only one pwm per channel can be instantiated
   from this class at a time. The system has two channels.
   Also, the prescaler must have the same value for both. */
```

Listing 6.8 PWMI Object Implementation File

```
static Boolean ach,bch;
Pwmi *pwmi_(BYTE channel,BYTE time_on ,
                  BYTE prescale,Boolean speed)
{
    Pwmi *this;
    Error_handler *temp;

    if(channel==A && ach==ON)
        return NULL;
    if(channel==B && bch==ON)
        return NULL;
    temp=error_();
    this=(Pwmi*) malloc(sizeof(Pwmi));
    if(this==NULL)
        error_handler(temp,TYPE_1,PWM);
    memmove(this, temp, sizeof(Error_handler));
    error__(temp);
    this->time_on=(WORD)time_on;
    this->channel=channel;
    PWMCSPEC.PR02=prescale;
    switch (channel)
    {
        case A : PWMC.SFA=speed;
                 PWMC.FPWMA=0; /* normal pwm output */
                 PWMC.PPROUT=0; /* normal pwm output */
                 PWMA.PWA=time_on; /* start with correct time-on*/
                 ach=ON;
                 break;
        case B : PWMC.SFB=speed;
                 PWMC.FPWMB=0;
                 PWMB.PWB=time_on;
                 bch=ON;
    }
    return this;
}

void pwmi__(Pwmi * this)
{
    if(this->channel==A)
        ach=OFF;
    else
        bch=OFF;
    free(this);
}
```

Listing 6.8 (continued)

A very simple test program is shown in Listing 6.9. This program implements both of the internal pulse-width modulators. This program will implement a serial port and read data from this port to obtain the PWM value. A range of value 0 to 500 can be input into the serial port. This value is 100 times the voltage that will be output from the PWM system. In an attempt to make this program simple, the passing in of data is rather clumsy. The data are read into a buffer, and the buffer contents, which are assumed to be a series of digits, is converted into an integer. Only three characters are converted. If any character converted is not a digit, the conversion is terminated and the value already created is used. The voltage value read in is converted to the range 0 to 255, where 255 corresponds to 5.0 volts, and this PWM on-time value is sent to both PWM outputs.

```
#include <HC16Y1.h>
#include <scim.h>
#include <pwmi.h>
#include <serkb.h>
#include <defines.h>
#include <ctype.h>

#define SERIO_BAUD_19200 19200
#define SERIO_INT_VECTOR 0x40
#define SERIO_IARB 10
#define SERIO_INT_LEVEL 3
#define MAX_ON 0xff

io_command_block *iob1,ib1;
BYTE pszMessage[]=" ";
Pwmi *pwa, *pwb;
Serial_io *sio;
BYTE *msg;

main()
{
    WORD value;
    /* initialize the program */

    /* initialize the SIM registers */
    SYNCR.X=ON;      /* double the clock speed-16.00 MHz */
    SYPCR.SWE=OFF;   /* disable the watchdog */
    CSORBT.DSACK=0;  /* use zero wait states for now */
    cli();           /* enable system interrupts */
```

Listing 6.9 PWMI Test Program

```
    /* set up the serial communications */
    sio=serkb_io_(SERIO_BAUD_19200,      /* set the baud rate */
                  SERIO_INT_VECTOR,      /* interrupt vector */
                  SERIO_IARB,            /* iarb */
                  SERIO_INT_LEVEL);      /* and interrupt level */

    /* set up the io block */
    iob1=&ib1;                    /* a block for inputs */
    iob1->io_command=INPUT;       /* iob1 is always input */
    iob1->call_complete=FALSE;/* need to have no message in
                                                  progress */
    iob1->buffer_length=sizeof pszMessage;
    pwa=pwmi_(A,0x80,2,FAST);
    pwb=pwmi_(B,0x80,2,SLOW);

    FOREVER
    {
        while(kbhit())     /* execute this code after a key is */
        {                          /* depressed */
            int i;
            putch('\r');                  /* do a carriage return
                                                       and */
            putch('\n');                           /* line feed */
            iob1->buffer=pszMessage;      /* must reset the
                                                    buffer */
            serial_io(sio,iob1);
            while(!iob1->call_complete)   /* read in volts */
                ;                         /* wait until data are
                                                        in */
            i=0;
            value=0;
            while(isdigit(pszMessage[i])&&i<3) /* convert to
                                                    binary */
                value=pszMessage[i++]-'0'+10*value;
            if(value>500)                 /* 5 volts(*100)
                                                   maximum */
                break;
            value=value*255/500;          /* convert volts to
                                                    binary */
            ON_TIME(pwa,(BYTE)value);     /* send data to the
                                                      pwms */
            ON_TIME(pwb,(BYTE)value);
        }
    }
}
```

Listing 6.9 (continued)

Pwma is set to high speed, and pwmb is set to slow speed. Both of these devices are set at a prescale division value of 2. Of course, they must both be set at the same prescale value, but one can run at high speed and the other at low speed. For this demonstration, we will run pwma at high speed and pwmb at low speed. The clocking speeds, as shown in Table 6.2, are 8.19 kHz and 64.0 Hz, respectively.

Here again we have an example of the ease of use of a software component. The serial input/output program used in this case is the serkb_io system designed to send messages to and receive messages from a terminal. The code needed to implement this interface is simply the serkb_io constructor followed by the construction of an input/output parameter block. When the actual serial port access is executed, the method serial_io() is executed with pointers to the object and the parameter block as arguments.

SUMMARY

This chapter contains descriptions of components that make use of the imput capture system and the built-in pulse-width modulation system in the general-purpose timer system. This timer is used on the M68HC11, M68HC16, and M68300 families of components.

7

DATA MANUAL

We have seen the development of several important components all associated with the MC68CH16Y1 microcontroller. Some important items to remember: All essential knowledge of a component is contained in the class definition or header file. To use or understand the operation of the component, there is no need to see the class implementation file. In fact, the component, or class programmers, should feel free to alter or improve the content of the class implementation files as they are moved from project to project. There is a contract, however, between the class programmer and the applications programmer. When viewed from an external program, the operation of any component will never change as the component is upgraded. As such, a Delay will always be a Delay, it will always have the same class constructor prototype, and its operation in the program will always be the same. Otherwise, the class programmer can change the implementation code at will.

The function of the components developed here have been gathered into a series of data sheets. You will find that each component is described completely on its data sheet along with the constructor arguments and a simple coding example that show use of the component in a program.

DELAY

Device Name and Description

Delay Delay causes a delay by a specified number of output compare interrupts. A semaphore is created by the calling program and this semaphore is attached to the delay component. This semaphore is released when the delay has expired. This component is used to delay execution of a program by an accurate time.

Super Classes

Delay inherits the features of the **error handler.** The error handler inherits the features of the class **object.**

Attributes

None.

Methods

```
void error_hand(void *, int, int)     /* from Error_handler */
arguments                            /* see Error_handler */
void exercise( Object * )            /* from Object */
arguments                            /* See Object */
```

Constructor

```
struct delay *delay_(struct time*, /* Timer causing output
                                   compare interrupts */
                    Semaphore*,     /* Semaphore to control
                                    program continution */
                     WORD);         /* number of output com-
                                      pare interrupts to
                                      delay */
```

Destructor

```
void delay__(Delay *);
```

Macro Methods

None.

Header *File*

```
#include "error.h"
#include "timer.h"
#include "semaphor.h"
#include "defines.h"

#define DELAY_CLASS \
                  ERROR_HANDLER \
                  unsigned int delay_time; \
                  struct time *Time;\
                  Semaphore *semaphore;


typedef struct delay
{
      DELAY_CLASS
}Delay;

struct delay *delay_(struct time*, Semaphore*,unsigned int);
void delay__(struct delay *);
#endif
```

Other Features and Special Calling Procedures

The delay destructor is executed automatically at the end of the delay and prior to the release of the semaphore. This component alters the hook_method and the hook_object attributes of the timer that is passed into the delay constructor, and these parameters are both restored to a NULL value at the completion of the delay. The timer used here should be dedicated completely to the delay operation.

Coding Examples

```
/* delay the execution of a program by 2000 ms */
       .
       .
       .
#include <timer.h>
#include <delay.h>
#include <semaphor.h>
       .
       .
       .
main()
{
    Semaphore *S1=semaphore_();
    Timer *T1; /* 1 ms interrupt */
    Timer_parameters tp;
    Semaphore *S1=semaphore_();
             .
             .
             .
/* set up the timer parameter structure and instantiate a
timer */
    tp.number=OC3;        /* use output compare number 3 */
    tp.tick=MS_PERIOD;    /* 1 ms interrupts */
    tp.action=0;          /* no output action */
    tp.OC1_connect=0;     /* OC1 not connected to another OC */
    tp.connect_data=0;   /* therefore no connect data needed */
    tp.interrupt=YES;     /* need an interrupt here */
    T1=timer_(&tp);       /* instantiate the timer */
             .
             .
             .
    delay_(T1,S1,2000); /* 2000 ms delay */
    wait_for_semaphore(S1);
    timer__(T1); /* delete the timer */
    semaphore__(S1); /* delete the semaphore */
             .
             .
             .
```

ERROR HANDLER

Device Name and Description

Error Handler The error handler provides a uniform mechanism for handling errors within components. This class is usually a super class, for classes need error handling capability. It is often used to detect errors that can occur when an object is being instantiated.

Super Classes

The **error handler** inherits the features of the class object.

Attributes

None.

Methods

```
void error_hand(void *, int, int)          /* from Error_handler */
arguments                                 /* see Error_handler */
void exercise( Object * )                 /* from Object */
arguments                                 /* See Object */
```

Constructor

```
    Error_handler *error_(void);
```

Destructor

```
    void error__(Error_handler *);
```

Macro Methods

None.

Header File

```
#ifndef ERROR_H
#define ERROR_H


#include "defines.h"
#include "object.h"


enum {TYPE_1,TYPE_2};
#define ERROR_HANDLER   \
```

```
        OBJECT                  \
        void (*error_hand)(void*,int,Error_source);

typedef struct err
{
      ERROR_HANDLER
} Error_handler;

#define error_handler(a,b,c) (*a->error_hand)(a,b,c)
Error_handler *error_(void);
void error__(Error_handler *);

#endif
```

Other Features and Special Calling Procedures

The following enumeration is used to determine the error sources for the error handler.

```
typedef enum BYTE
{
      SEMAPHORE,
      SERIAL,
      TIMER,
      DELAY,
      PWM,
      PWMI
}Error_source;
```

This enum is contained in the header file defines.h. It is placed there because these values are subject to change, and it is better to place changeable values outside the class definition file.

The enum seen in the error header file

```
enum {TYPE_1, TYPE_2};
```

identifies the type of error to the error handler. A type 1 error is a nonrecoverable error that implies that the program is unable to continue operation, and a type 2 error occurs when there is an easily recoverable error that usually needs no additional code to repair the situation. There is yet another error that can occur when the program encounters an erroneous parameter. With the third type of error, the return to the calling program will be a value of 0. A test for a NULL pointer return will show this type of error. The type 1 error is an error that cannot easily be corrected. An example of a type 1 error is that a malloc() call returns a NULL value. In such a case, the system cannot be repaired by local code and a special initialization will be executed. An error of type 2 is an error, but it will be an error that can be fixed by the calling program. In this case, the error occurrence is logged and the program is continued with the expectation that the error will be corrected. An example of a type 2 error will occur when a serial port detects a parity error or perhaps a framing error.

Coding Examples

The coding example is taken from the constructor for the serial i/o class.

```
Serial_io *serial_io_(...)
{
    Error_handler *temp;  /* the object from which inheritance
                            takes place */
    Serial_io *this; /* this object */
            .
            .
            .
    temp=error_(); /* create error object */
    this=(Serial_io*)malloc(sizeof(Serial_io)); /* make new ob
                                                  ject */
    if(this==NULL) /* a malloc() error */
            error_handler(this,TYPE_1,SERIAL);
    memmove(this,temp,sizeof(Error_handler));/* move in inherited
                                                        object */
    error__(temp); /* get rid of the error object */
            .
            .
            .
```

LINK

Device Name and Description

Link A link is a container that holds a single object. It is intended for use in some type of linked list. The class link contains a pointer to the object and two pointers to the type Link. One is the previous link and the other is the next link. These two pointers provide the capability of creation of single linked lists, double linked lists, binary trees, stacks, queues, and so on.

Super Classes

None.

Attributes

```
struct object *current_object;
struct link *previous_link;
struct link *next_link;
```

Methods

None.

Constructor

```
Link * link_(void *object);
```

Destructor

```
void link__( Link *);
```

Macro Methods

None.

Header File

```
#ifndef LINK_H
#define LINK_H


#include "defines.h"
#include "object.h"
#define LINK_CLASS \
                struct object *current_object; \
                struct link *previous_link; \
                struct link *next_link;


typedef struct link
{
      LINK_CLASS
} Link;


Link * link_(void *object);
void link__( Link *);


#endif
```

Other Features and Special Calling Procedures

A link receives a pointer to an object and places this pointer into a structure along with pointers designated previous_link and next_link. The previous_link and next_link values are initialized to a NULL value.

Coding Examples

```
#include <link.h>
#include <object.h>
       .
       .
       .
Object *l1,*l2,*null;        /* define some objects */
Link *lnk1,*lnk2,*lnknull;   /* and links */
       .
       .
       .
       l1=object_(count_second_ticks);/* create two real objects */
       l2=object_(count_half_second_ticks);
       null=object_(NULL); /* and a null object */
              .
              .
              .
       lnk1=link_(l1); /* and put these objects */
       lnk2=link_(l2); /* into links */
       lnknull=link_(null);
              .
              .
              .
```

LINK LIST

Device Name and Description

Link List A link list is a doubly linked list of objects. Each object is contained in a type Link that contains a pointer to the object and pointers to the previous link and the next link.

Super Classes

None.

Attributes

```
void *head;
```

Methods

```
void walk_list(Link_list *list);  /* the list to be walked */
int add_link(Link_list *list,     /* the list to receive */
Link *new_link);                  /* the new link */
int delete_link(Link_list *list,  /* the list from which */
Link *old_link);                  /* old_link is to be deleted */
```

Constructor

```
    Link_list *link_list_(void);
```

Destructor

```
    void link_list__(Link_list *);
```

Macro Methods

None.

Header File

```
#ifndef LINKLIST_H
#define LINKLIST_H


#include "defines.h"
#include "object.h"
#include "link.h"


#define LINK_LIST void *head;
typedef struct
{
      LINK_LIST
}     Link_list;


Link_list *link_list_(void);
void link_list__(Link_list *);
void walk_list(Link_list *list);
int add_link(Link_list *list,Link *new_link);
int delete_link(Link_list *list, Link *old_link);


#endif
```

Other Features and Special Calling Procedures

Each object contained in a link has a method called exercise(). The method walk_list() executes the method exercise for each object in the list. Add link receives a pointer to a new link as a parameter and a pointer to the list to which it is to be added. The method add_link() places this new link at the head of the list. Links contained in the list can be removed by delete_link(). This method has two parameters, the linked list containing the link and a pointer to the link to be deleted. The location of the head of the linked list is saved in the attribute head, but there is no tail saved. The end of the list is designated by a "null" link. A null link is a link with all three of its attributes equal to NULL. A null link must be placed on the list before any other links are added.

In the coding example shown below, the method walk_list() will be executed from the Timer component. The Timer methods attach_method() and attach_object() place the method walk list into the interrupt service routine of the timer t3, and the argument of the method when it is executed is list1.

Coding Examples

```
#include <object.h>
#include <link.h>
#include <linklist.h>
          .
          .
          .
Object *l1,*l2,*null;
Link *lnk1,*lnk2,*lnknull;
Link_list *list1;
          .
          .
          .
          l1=object_(count_second_ticks); /* create the objects */
          l2=object_(count_half_second_ticks);
          null=object_(NULL);
                    .
                    .
                    .
          list1=link_list_(); /* and the linked list */
                    .
                    .
                    .
          lnknull=link_(null); /* create a null link */
          lnk1=link_(l1); /* and the two real links */
          lnk2=link_(l2);
```

```
        .
        .
        .
 add_link(list1,lnknull);   /* add null object to list */
add_link(list1,lnk1);       /* first,then real objects */
add_link(list1,lnk2);
        .
        .
        .
attach_method(t3,walk_list);/* attach a method to timer*/
attach_object(t3,list1);    /* and its argument */
        .
        .
        .
```

LOOK-UP TABLE

Device Name and Description

Look_up The class Look_up defines a look-up table. This component provides a means of searching a table for the closest value and then returning a linear interpolated value between the two points in the table between which the value lies. This look-up table operation is called two-dimensional because it receives a single input and returns a single value.

Super Classes

None.

Attributes

```
int x_length;
Entry *table;
```

Methods

```
BYTE (*get_val)(struct LU *this, BYTE value);
```

Constructor

```
Look_up *look_up_(int x_length, Entry *table);
```

Destructor

```
void look_up__(Look_up * this);
```

Macro Methods

```
#define get_value_2d(a,b) (*a->get_val)(a,b)
```

Parameter a is a pointer to a look-up table component, and b is the BYTE value to be calculated.

Header File

```
#ifndef LUTOBJ_H
#define LUTOBJ_H

#include "defines.h"

/* table used below is a pointer to an array of the type Entry.
   The number of entries in the array must be equal to x_length.
   Of course, each entry contains two values which are of the
   type BYTE */

typedef struct
{
   BYTE x,y;
}Entry;

#define LOOK_UP_CLASS \
            int x_length; \
            Entry *table; \
            BYTE (*get_val)(struct LU *this, BYTE value);

typedef struct LU
{
      LOOK_UP_CLASS
} Look_up;

#define get_value_2d(a,b) (*a->get_val)(a,b)

Look_up *look_up_(int x_length, Entry *table);
void look_up__(Look_up * this);
int find_index(Look_up *this, BYTE value);
BYTE interpolate(BYTE value,BYTE x0,BYTE y0,BYTE x1,BYTE y1);

#endif
```

Other Features and Special Calling Procedures

One of the parameters sent to the constructor is a pointer to a table of the type Entry. Entry contains two BYTE members, the first being the ordinate and the second being the abscissa of the input data points. There can be as many input data points as needed. The range of values for both the x and y values is that of an unsigned character, 0 to 255. The number of points contained in the table is passed in as the parameter length.

Coding Examples

```
#include <lutslope.h>

const Entry taba[]={
        0,0,
        96,40,
        144,68,
        166,128,
        221,160,
        255,160 };

void main(void)
{
    int i;

   Look_up *a=look_up_(6,taba), /* create three look-up tables */

   get_value(b,i),get_value(c,i));
   look_up__(a);       /* destroy all objects when no longer
                                                        needed*/
```

OBJECT

Device Name and Description

Object The class Object is the base class of many of the other classes. It is, however, not an abstract class and it can be instantiated by itself whenever needed.

Super Classes

None.

Attributes

None.

Methods

```
void (*exercise)(struct object*);
```

Constructor

```
Object *object_(void (*exercise)());
```

Destructor

```
void object__(Object *);
```

Macro Methods

None.

Header File

```
#ifndef OBJECT_H
#define OBJECT_H

#include "defines.h"

#define OBJECT \
      void (*exercise)(struct object*);

typedef struct object
{
      OBJECT
} Object;

Object *object_(void (*exercise)());
void object__(Object *);

#endif
```

Other Features and Special Calling Procedures

When instantiated, Object receives a parameter that is a pointer to a function in the calling program. This function is convenient in operations such as linked lists, where the program might need to execute a method, not necessarily the same method, in several objects contained within the list.

Coding Examples

See the Linked List class shown above for a coding example that uses the component Object.

PULSE-WIDTH MODULATOR 1

Device Name and Description

Pwm The class Pwm creates a pulse-width modulator type of digital-to-analog converter. Such a component is quite useful in the implementation of control systems. Pwm makes use of two output compare timer subsystem devices. One of these output compares controls the period of the output signal, and the other controls the on-time.

Super Classes

Pwm inherits the features of the **error handler.** The error handler inherits the features of the class **object.**

Attributes

```
WORD time_on,        /* unsigned integer time on */
WORD period;         /* unsigned integer period */
BYTE on_timer;       /* timer that controls on time, 2 through 4 */
```

Methods

```
void error_hand(void *, int, int)       /* from Error_handler */
arguments                              /* see Error_handler */
void exercise( Object * )              /* from Object */
arguments                              /* See Object */
```

Constructor

```
Pwm *pwm_( WORD period,      /* Period of the output signal */
           WORD time_on,     /* initial on time of the output */
           BYTE on_timer);   /* timer, 2-4, that controls on time
                                                              */
```

Destructor

```
void pwm__(Pwm *);
```

Macro Methods

```
#define set_on(a,b) ((a)->time_on=(b))
```

Parameter a is a pointer to the Pwm being controlled, and b is the unsigned integer value of the new time on.

Header File

```
#ifndef PWM_H
#define PWM_H

#include "hc16y1.h"
#include "gpt.h"
#include "timer.h"
#include "defines.h"

#define PWM_CLASS \
            ERROR_HANDLER \
            WORD time_on, period; \
            BYTE on_timer;

typedef struct
{
      PWM_CLASS
} Pwm;

#define set_on(a,b) ((a)->time_on=(b))
Pwm *pwm_(WORD period,WORD time_on,BYTE on_timer);
void pwm__(Pwm *);
#endif
```

Other Features and Special Calling Procedures

The component Pwm instantiates two output compare timer subsystems. Output compare 1 is always used as the timer to control the period. This timer event can be coupled to any other output compare, and the code couples it to the timer specified as a parameter in the Pwm constructor call. The Pwm system takes control of the two timers without testing to see if they are in use. The timer clock speed is set by the prescaler in the calling program. Numbers—period and time_on—are unsigned integer values and they are counts applied to the output compare timers when they are initialized or set up. Therefore, the programmer has complete control over the period of the Pwm as well as the on-time of the signal. The on-time can be changed at any time by use of the macro method set_on(). This new on-time becomes effective at the completion of the current on-time. The system interrupts must be enabled whenever a Pwm is being used.

The resolution of this Pwm is the number of bits required to specify the period. If the period is a 10-bit number, resolution of the Pwm will also be 10 bits. The Pwm will provide a minimum on-time of 1 timer clock period. It does not work well at nearly 100% on-times. If it is necessary to work at on-times greater than 90%, it will be necessary to modify the code and reverse the role to the two output compare timers. In this mode the Pwm system works well near 100% on-time, but its performance fails at small on-times. Of course, if the full range of operation is needed, a new Pwm can be defined that will choose its control strategy to suit the specified on-time.

Coding Examples

```
#include <pwm.h>
       .
       .
       .
Pwm *pw;
       .
       .
       .
    pw=pwm_(MAX_ON,0,2);
    cli();                /* enable the system interrupts */
       .
       .
       .
          set_on(pw,value);
             .
             .
             .
```

PULSE-WIDTH MODULATOR 2

Device Name and Description

Pwmi Pwmi is a class that implements a pulse-width modulator that uses either of the internal pulse-width modulators in the general-purpose timer. These PWMs are both eight-bit timers and the resolution cannot be adjusted. The speed of the timers is set by a special prescaler that has two modes, fast and slow.

Super Classes

Pwmi inherits the features of the **error handler.** The error handler inherits the features of the class **object.**

Attributes

```
BYTE channel;  /* channel is either A or B corresponding to the
                  specific internal pwm channel */
```

Methods

```
void error_hand(void *, int, int)       /* from Error_handler */
arguments                             /* see Error_handler */
void exercise( Object * )             /* from Object */
arguments                             /* See Object */
```

Constructor

```
Pwmi *pwmi_(BYTE channel,      /* Specific channel A or B */
            BYTE time_on,      /* on time from 0 to 255 */
            BYTE prescale,     /* Prescaler value 0 to 6 */
            Boolean speed);    /* FAST or SLOW */
```

Destructor

```
void pwmi__(Pwmi *);
```

Macro Methods

```
#define ON_TIME(a,b) ((a)->channel==A)?(PWMA.PWA=(b)) :
(PWMB.PWB=(b))
```

Parameter a is a pointer to the controlled Pwmi, either A or B, and b is a BYTE with a range of 0 to 255, which is the requested on-time.

Header File

```
#ifndef PWMI_H
#define PWMI_H

#include <hc16y1.h>
#include <gpt.h>
#include <timer.h>
#include <defines.h>
#include <error.h>
```

```
enum channels{A,B};

typedef struct
{
    unsigned PWM_NULL0 : 9;
    unsigned PR02 :3;
    unsigned PWM_NULL1 : 4;
} Pwmcspec;

#define PWMCSPEC (*(@far Pwmcspec*)(GPT_Register+0x24))

#define PWMI_CLASS \
            ERROR_HANDLER \
            BYTE channel;

typedef struct
{
      PWMI_CLASS
} Pwmi;

#define ON_TIME(a,b) ((a)->channel==A)?(PWMA.PWA=(b)) :
(PWMB.PWB=(b))

Pwmi *pwmi_(BYTE channel,BYTE time_on,
                  BYTE prescale,Boolean speed);
void pwmi__(Pwmi *);

#endif
```

Other Features and Special Calling Procedures

Both PWM devices must run at the same PWM clock frequency; however, each may be run in either the slow or fast mode, which will give the two PWM outputs widely different frequencies. Table 7.1 provides a summary of the PWM clock speeds with different PWM prescaler values when operated in the slow or fast modes. Of course, the digital-to-analog output range with these PWMs is eight bits or 0 to 255.

Coding Examples

```
#include <scim.h>
#include <pwmi.h>
#include <defines.h>
      .
      .
      .
Pwmi *pwa, *pwb;      /* define pwmi pointers */
```

Table 7.1 Clock Speeds

PPR[2:0]	Prescaler Tap	Fast Mode	Slow Mode
000	Div 2=8.39 MHz	32.8 kHz	256 Hz
001	Div 4=4.19 MHz	16.4 kHz	128 Hz
010	Div 8=2.10 MHz	8.19 kHz	64.0 Hz
011	Div 16=1.08 Mhz	4.09 kHz	32.0 Hz
100	Div 32=524 kHz	2.05 kHz	16.0 Hz
101	Div 64=262 kHz	1.02 kHz	8.0 Hz
110	Div 128=131 kHz	512 Hz	4.0 Hz
111	PCLK	PCLK/256	PCLK/32768

```
   .
   .
   .
pwa=pwmi_(A,0x80,2,FAST);    /* instantiate two pwmis */
pwb=pwmi_(B,0x80,2,SLOW);
   .
   .
   .
ON_TIME(pwa,(BYTE)value); /* send data to the pwms */
ON_TIME(pwb,(BYTE)value);
```

SEMAPHORE

Device Name and Description

Semaphore Semaphore is a flag that is used to grant exclusive access of a resource to a process.

Super Classes

None.

Attributes

```
sem; /* the Boolean status of the semaphore */
```

Methods

```
Boolean attach_semaphore(struct semaphor *);
void release_semaphore(struct semaphor *);
Boolean semaphore_status(struct semaphor*);
void wait_for_semaphore(struct semaphor*);
```

Constructor

```
Semaphore* semaphore_(void);
```

Destructor

```
void semaphore__(Semaphore *);
```

Macro Methods

None.

Header File

```
#ifndef SEMAPHORE_H
#define SEMAPHORE_H

#include "defines.h"

typedef struct semaphor
{
    Boolean sem;
}Semaphore;

Boolean attach_semaphore(struct semaphor *);
void release_semaphore(struct semaphor *);
Boolean semaphore_status(struct semaphor*);
void wait_for_semaphore(struct semaphor*);

Semaphore* semaphore_(void);
void semaphore__(Semaphore *);

#endif
```

Other Features and Special Calling Procedures

The semaphore component is used to exclude simultaneous access by different processes to a resource. The semaphore is usually created at an operating-system level in a program, and when a task or process needs exclusive access to a resource, it first tests to determine if the semaphore is available and then attaches the semaphore to itself and proceeds to use the resource. When the process is done with the resource, it releases the semaphore so that other processes can access the resource.

Coding Examples

```
#include <semaphor.h>
#include <timer.h>
```

```
#include <delay.h>
      .
      .
      .
   Semaphore *S1=semaphore_(); /* create the semaphore */
      .
      .
      .
   delay_(T1,S1,2000); /* execute 2000 ms delay */
      .
      .
      .
wait_for_semaphore(S1); /* wait here for the semaphore to be
                         released by the delay component */
      .
      .
```

SERIAL INPUT/OUTPUT BASIC

Device Name and Description

Serial The class Serial implements a serial input/output system through serial port A on the multichannel communications interface. This asynchronous serial interface is block oriented and all blocks are terminated with a NULL character. A NULL character is a pointer to a type BYTE with a zero address. This component works asynchronous serial port A only.

Super Classes

Serial inherits the features of the **error handler.** The error handler inherits the features of the class **object.**

Attributes

```
BYTE (*i_o)(struct serio *,io_command_block *); /* i/o function
                                                             */
```

Methods

```
void error_hand(void *, int, int)             /* from Error_handler
                                                             */
arguments                                   /* see Error_handler */
void exercise( Object * )                   /* from Object */
arguments                                   /* See Object */
```

```
static BYTE i_o(Serial_io * this,      /* a pointer to the Ser-
                                              ial_io object */
               io_command_block *block); /* i/o command block */
BYTE getch(void);                       /* standard byte input
                                                    routine */
void putch(BYTE ) ;                     /* standard byte output
                                                    routine */
void do_receive(void);                  /* block receive routine
                                                          */
void do_transmit(void);                 /* block transmit routine
                                                          */
```

Constructor

```
Serial_io *serial_io_(int baud_rate,        /* baud rate in
                                              bits/second */
                   int vector,          /* serial io interrupt
                                                   vector */
                   int iarb,            /* interrupt arbitration
                                                    level */
                   int int_level);      /* interrupt level */
```

Destructor

```
void serial_io__(Serial_io *);
```

Macro Methods

```
#define serial_io(a,b) (*a->i_o)(a,b)
```

Parameter a is a pointer to an instantiated Serial_io and argument b is a pointer to an io_command_block with instructions to execute on this i/o transaction.

Header File

```
#ifndef SERIO_H
#define SERIO_H

#include "error.h"
#include "iodefs.h"
#include "defines.h"

#define EOM               0          /* End Of Message */

#define SERIO_METHODS \
            void (*do_rec)(void); \
            void (*do_trans)(void);
```

```
typedef struct
{
      SERIO_METHODS
} Serio_Methods;

enum io_commands{INPUT,OUTPUT };

enum io_errors{NO_ERROR,
               BUFFER_OVERFLOW,
               COMMAND_ERROR};

/* i/o command block */

typedef struct /* See enumerates above for commands and error
returns */
{
    int io_command;                 /* input parameters */
    BYTE *buffer;
    int buffer_length;
    int characters_transferred;     /* output parameters */
    Boolean call_complete;
    int error;
} io_command_block;

#define SERIAL_IO\
      ERROR_HANDLER\
    BYTE (*i_o)(struct serio *,io_command_block *);

typedef struct serio
{
      SERIAL_IO
} Serial_io;

#define serial_io(a,b) (*a->i_o)(a,b)
/* Function prototypes */
Serial_io *serial_io_(int baud_rate,int vector,int iarb,int
                        int_level);
void serial_io__(Serial_io *);
static BYTE i_o(Serial_io * this, io_command_block *block);
BYTE getch(void);
void putch(BYTE ) ;
void do_receive(void);
void do_transmit(void);

#endif
```

Other Features and Special Calling Procedures

Observe in the header file that there is a definition of an i/o parameter block. The contents of this block is needed for successful completion of every input or output transaction. In operation, the i/o will be established by execution of the constructor. Whenever an i/o operation is needed, the function serial_io(a,b) is executed, with a pointer to a properly instantiated Serial_io and b a pointer to an io_parameter_block. This class uses virtual functions in the case of the block receive and transmit commands.

Coding Examples

```
#include <serio.h>
       .
       .
       .
#define SERIO_BAUD_19200 19200  /* baud rate value with */
#define SERIO_INT_VECTOR 0x40   /* interrupt vector, */
#define SERIO_IARB 10           /* interrupt arbitration level, */
#define SERIO_INT_LEVEL 3       /* interrupt level */
       .
       .
       .
/* function prototype */
void output_time(void);
       .
       .
       .
BYTE pszMessage[]="         \r"; /* array to hold the time */
io_command_block *oob1,ob1;     /* an io command block */
Serial_io *sio;                 /* and a Serial_io pointer */
       .
       .
       .
    /* initialization portion of the program */


    /* set up the serial communications */
      sio=serial_io_(SERIO_BAUD_19200,     /* set the baud rate */
                     SERIO_INT_VECTOR,    /* interrupt vector */
                     SERIO_IARB,           /* iarb */
                     SERIO_INT_LEVEL);    /* and interrupt level */


       /* set up the io blocks */
       oob1=&ob1;
```

```
        .
        .
        .
    cli(); /* enable the system interrupts */
        .
        .
        .
/* applications portion of the program */
/* a function here prepares the message to go out and puts it
   into pszMessage[]. it also executes the function output_time()
   */

void output_time(void)
{
      while(!oob1->call_complete)
            ;                     /* wait until any other message
                                                      is out */
      oob1->io_command=OUTPUT;    /* prepare the io command block
                                                          */
      oob1->buffer=pszMessage;    /* message to go out */
      oob1->buffer_length= sizeof pszMessage;
      serial_io(sio,oob1);        /* message to the i/o object */
}
```

SERIAL INPUT/OUTPUT: KEYBOARD-SPECIFIC

Device Name and Description

Serkb The class Serkb is a serial input/output system. This class is derived from the class Serial_io. It works the same as Serial_io, with two exceptions. The first is that both the input and output buffer is terminated with an '\r' character rather than a NULL as was seen earlier. Also, with this class, a keyboard hit routine is included. This component works asynchronous serial port A only.

Super Classes

Serkb inherits the attributes and methods of the class **Serial_io. Serial_io** inherits the features of the **error_handler,** which in turn inherits the features of the class **object.**

Attributes

```
BYTE (*i_o)(struct serio *,io_command_block *);
```

Methods

```
void error_hand(void *, int, int)           /* from Error_handler
                                                              */
arguments                                  /* see Error_handler */
void exercise( Object * )                  /* from Object */
arguments                                  /* See Object */
static BYTE i_o(Serial_io * this,             /* From Serial_io—see
                                                     Serial_io */
                io_command_block *block);
BYTE getch(void);
void putch(BYTE ) ;
void do_receive_kb(void);                   /* special block
                                                      receive */
void do_transmit_kb(void);                  /* and transmit
                                                     routines */
Boolean kbhit(void);                       /* tests for a keyboard
                                                          hit */
```

Constructor

```
Serial_io *serkb_io_(int baud_rate,              /* baud rate in
                                                   bits/second */
                     int vector,                /* serial io
                                                interrupt vector */
                     int iarb,                  /* interrupt
                                               arbitration level */
                     int int_level);            /* interrupt level
                                                              */
```

Destructor

```
void serial_io__(Serial_io *this);
```

This component uses its super class destructor.

Macro Methods

```
#define serial_io(a,b) (*a->i_o)(a,b)
```

Parameter a is a pointer to an instantiated Serial_io, and argument b is a pointer to an io_command_block with instructions to execute on this i/o transaction.

Header File

```
#ifndef SERKB_H
#define SERKB_H
```

```
#include "serio.h"

#define EOL     '\r'      /* End Of Line */

/* Function prototypes */
Serial_io *serkb_io_(int baud_rate,int vector,int iarb,int
int_level);
void do_receive_kb(void);
void do_transmit_kb(void);
Boolean kbhit(void);

#endif
```

Other Features and Special Calling Procedures

This component works exactly the same as Serial_io, with the exception that the buffer terminator is an '\r' rather than a NULL character and the Boolean function kbhit() has been added.

Coding Examples

```
#include <serkb.h>
       .
       .
       .
#define SERIO_BAUD_19200 19200
#define SERIO_INT_VECTOR 0x40
#define SERIO_IARB 10
#define SERIO_INT_LEVEL 3
       .
       .
       .
/* function prototypes */
void output_time(void);
.
.
.
BYTE pszMessage[]="         \r"; /* array to hold the output time
                                                                */
BYTE pszMessage1[]="Enter the new time HH:MM > ";
BYTE pszMessage2[]="                             \r"; /*
                                                  empty array */
BYTE pszMessage3[]="         \r"; /* array to hold the time
                                                         input*/
io_command_block *oob1,ob1,*iob1,ib1;
Serial_io *sio;
```

```
    .
    .
    .
/* in the initialization portion of the program */


/* set up the serial communications */
  sio=serkb_io_(SERIO_BAUD_19200,      /* set the baud rate */
              SERIO_INT_VECTOR,      /* interrupt vector */
               SERIO_IARB,            /* iarb */
              SERIO_INT_LEVEL);      /* and interrupt level
                                                            */


/* set up the io blocks */
oob1=&ob1;                   /* output block */
oob1->call_complete=FALSE;   /* have no message going out */
oob1->io_command=OUTPUT;     /* oob1 is always output */
iob1=&ib1;                   /* a block for inputs */
iob1->io_command=INPUT;      /* iob1 is always input */
iob1->call_complete=FALSE;   /* need to have no message in
                                                  progress */
    .
    .
    .
   /* in the applications portion of the program */


    /* reset the time clock from the keyboard whenever any
       key on the keyboard is hit */
    if(kbhit())
    {
        BYTE *p;     /* need a pointer here */
        Boolean message_ok, time_ok; /* and a couple of flags
                                                            */
        BYTE temphours,tempminutes;


        do
        {
            putch('\r');     /* put cursor in correct location
                                                            */
           oob1->buffer=pszMessage1; /* send out message */
           oob1->buffer_length= sizeof pszMessage1;
           serial_io(sio,oob1);    /* message to the i/o ob-
                                                       ject */
            iob1->buffer=pszMessage3;
            iob1->buffer_length= sizeof pszMessage3;
            serial_io(sio,iob1);      /* get input message */
```

```
            .
            .
            .
                putch('\r');  /* do a carriage return
                                                   and */
                 oob1->buffer=pszMessage2; /* clear the
                                                screen */
                 oob1->buffer_length= sizeof psz-
                                             Message2;
               serial_io(sio,oob1);
         .
         .
         .
```

SERIAL INPUT/OUTPUT: SPECIAL BAUD-RATE HANDLING

Device Name and Description

Serial1 The component Serial1 is identical to Serkb except that it takes a baud-rate count value rather than the actual baud rate of the port as a constructor argument. This component works asynchronous serial port A only.

Super Classes

Serial1 inherits the features of the **error handler.** The error handler inherits the features of the class **object.** It also inherits the features of **Serkb** and **Serial_io.**

Attributes

```
BYTE (*i_o)(struct serio *,io_command_block *);
```

Methods

```
void error_hand(void *, int, int)       /* from Error_handler */
arguments                             /* see Error_handler */
void exercise( Object * )             /* from Object */
arguments                             /* See Object */
static BYTE i_o(Serial_io * this,       /* From Serial_io—see
                                                  Serial_io */
               io_command_block *block);
BYTE getch(void);
void putch(BYTE ) ;
void do_receive_kb(void);               /* special block receive
                                                          */
void do_transmit_kb(void);              /* and transmit routines
```

```
                                                          */
Boolean kbhit(void);                   /* tests for a keyboard hit
                                                          */
```

Constructor

```
Serial_io *serial1_io_(WORD baud_value,      /* baud-rate internal
                                                     divisor */
                   int vector,             /* serial io interrupt
                                                      vector */
                   int iarb,               /* interrupt
                                              arbitration level */
                   int int_level);         /* interrupt level */
```

Destructor

```
void serial1_io__(Serial_io *this);
```

This component uses its super class destructor.

Macro Methods

```
#define serial_io(a,b) (*a->i_o)(a,b)
```

Parameter a is a pointer to an instantiated Serial_io, and argument b is a pointer to an io_command_block with instructions to execute on this i/o transaction.

Header File

```
#ifndef SERIO1_H
#define SERIO1_H


#include "serkb.h"


Serial_io *serial1_io_(WORD baud_value,int vector,int iarb,int
int_level);
void serial1_io__(Serial_io *this);


#endif
```

Other Features and Special Calling Procedures

This component was developed for use with the baud-rate measurement program. The argument baud_value in the constructor is the divisor by which the clock rate is divided to determine the baud rate of the serial port.

Coding Examples

```
#include <seriol.h>
       .
       .
       .
#define SERIO_BAUD_19200 19200      /* serial port parameters */
#define SERIO_INT_VECTOR 0x40
#define SERIO_IARB 10
#define SERIO_INT_LEVEL 3
       .
       .
       .
/* function prototypes */

void printd(unsigned long);
WORD get_baud(BYTE number, Timer *t3);
       .
       .
       .
       Serial_io *sio;
       io_command_block *oob1,ob1;
       BYTE pszMessage[]="The selected baud rate is ";
       BYTE pszMessage1[]=" bits per second\n\r";
       WORD baud;
       unsigned long baud_rate;
              .
              .
              .
       cli();             /* enable system interrupts */
       baud=get_baud(1,t3);/* measure the baud rate */
              .
              .
              .
        /* set up the serial communications */
       sio=serial1_io_(baud, /* value returned from get_baud() */
                  SERIO_INT_VECTOR, /* interrupt vector */
                   SERIO_IARB,       /* iarb */
                   SERIO_INT_LEVEL); /* and interrupt level */

     /* set up the io blocks */
     oob1=&ob1;                   /* output block */
     oob1->call_complete=TRUE;    /* have no message going out */
     oob1->io_command=OUTPUT;     /* oob1 is always output */
     oob1->buffer=pszMessage;     /* select the message */
     oob1->buffer_length= sizeof pszMessage;
     serial_io(sio,oob1);         /* message to the i/o object */
       while(!oob1->call_complete)
```

```
        ;                   /* wait until transmission is done
                                                            */
    baud_rate=500000ul/baud;
    printd(baud_rate);          /* send baud rate to screen */
    oob1->buffer=pszMessage1;
    oob1->buffer_length= sizeof pszMessage1;
    serial_io(sio,oob1);        /* send out rest of message */
    while(!oob1->call_complete)
        ;
```

OUTPUT COMPARE TIMER SUBSYSTEM

Device Name and Description

Timer Timer is a component that implements the four output compare subsystems in the general purpose timer. These timers can be used to create events in time.

Super Classes

Timer inherits the features of the **error handler.** The error handler inherits the features of the class **object.**

Attributes

```
WORD who_am_I;                     /* output compare number */
WORD ms_tick;                      /* Timer clock cycles */
                                   /* between interrupts */
void (*reset)(struct time *);         /* see Methods below */
void *hook_object;                 /* external function argument */
void (*hook_method)(void*);        /* see Methods below */
```

Methods

```
void error_hand(void *, int, int)  /* from Error_handler */
arguments                          /* see Error_handler */
void exercise( Object * )          /* from Object */
arguments                          /* See Object */
void (*reset)(struct time *);         /* reset specific timer */
void (*hook_method)(void*);        /* external function to */
                                   /* be executed during each */
                                   /* Output Compare interrupt */
                                   /* the argument of this */
                                   /* function is the value */
                                   /* pointed to by hook_object */
```

Constructor

```
Timer* timer_(Timer_parameters *); /* Timer_parameters is a */
                                   /* timer parameter block */
                                   /* described below in the */
                                   /* Other Features and Special */
                                   /* Calling Procedures section */
```

Destructor

```
void timer__(Timer*);
```

Macro Methods

```
#define attach_object(a,b) ((a)->hook_object=(b))
#define attach_method(a,b) ((a)->hook_method=(b))
```

Here parameter a is a pointer to a properly instantiated Timer. Parameter b in attach_method() is a pointer to a function that will be executed during the interrupt service routine of the timer identified in the parameter a. In the attach_object() method, parameter b is a pointer to the argument of the function identified by hook_method().

Header File

```
#ifndef TIMER_H
#define TIMER_H

#include "defines.h"
#include "error.h"

#ifndef GPT_IARB
      #define GPT_IARB 12    /* iarb value of 12 for the GPT */
      #define GPT_VBA 5      /* GPT vectors start at 0x50 */
      #define GPT_LEVEL 6    /* use interrupt level 6 */
#endif

typedef enum BYTE
{
      DISCONNECT,
      TOGGLE,
      CLEAR,
      SET
}Output;

typedef struct
{
```

```
        WORD    number,
                tick;
        Output action;
        BYTE    OC1_connect,
                connect_data;
        Boolean  interrupt;
} Timer_parameters;

#define TIMER_CLASS \
            ERROR_HANDLER \
            WORD  who_am_I;\
            WORD  ms_tick; \
            void  (*reset)(struct time *); \
            void  *hook_object;\
            void  (*hook_method)(void*);

typedef struct time
{
    TIMER_CLASS
}Timer;
#ifndef ATTACH
#define ATTACH
      #define attach_object(a,b) ((a)->hook_object=(b))
      #define attach_method(a,b) ((a)->hook_method=(b))

#endif

Timer* timer_(Timer_parameters *);
void timer__(Timer*);
#endif
```

Other Features and Special Calling Procedures

Almost all operations involving output compare timers require interrupts. Timer interrupts can be quite important. Therefore, it was decided in the design of the Timer component to "hardwire" the interrupt setup in the constructor of the class. Therefore, as is done here, the programmer has no say in things such as interrupt level. The specific values for these parameters are defined in the header file as shown below.

```
#define GPT_IARB 12     /* iarb value of 12 for the GPT */
#define GPT_VBA 5       /* GPT vectors start at 0x50 */
#define GPT_LEVEL 6     /* use interrupt level 6 */
```

The interrupt level of 6 is used because the Timer interrupt service routines are quick and the operations that must be executed during timer interrupts can be of very high priority. The IARB, interrupt arbitration level, is used when two interrupts at the same level request an interrupt at the same time. The IARB range is from 0 to 15, with 15 being the highest priority. When two, or more, interrupts occur at the same time and at the same level, the module with the largest IARB will be processed first. There is no important reason, but it was decided to place all the timer interrupt vectors in the vector table starting at 0x50. These parameters can be changed by the programmer if needed.

Six parameters are required to specify an output compare timer. These parameters are gathered into a timer_parameters structure and a pointer to this structure is passed to the timer constructor. A copy of this structure is as follows:

```
typedef struct
{
      WORD    number,
              tick;
      Output  action;
      BYTE    OC1_connect,
              connect_data;
      Boolean   interrupt;
} Timer_parameters;
```

The parameter number is the specific output compare time being set up. During execution of the interrupt service routine, the value tick is added to the specific TOCx register. When the timer counter register reaches this value later, the next event for this output compare will occur. The parameter action contains one of the values found in the typedef of Output. This value describes the action that will take place on the specified output compare pin. Output compare 1 can be coupled to any other output compare. OC1_connect indicates that the output pin of this output compare will be connected to OC1, and connect_data describes the output that will occur at the OCx pin when OC1 occurs. Finally, the parameter interrupt can have values YES or NO to indicate whether an interrupt service routine should be created for this timer and the interrupt should be enabled.

Coding Examples

```
#include <timer.h>
      .
      .
      .
#define TIMECOUNT 4000
#define ONE_SECOND 1000
      .
      .
      .
```

```
/* function prototype */
void count_ticks(WORD *);
      .
      .
      .
Timer_parameters tp; /* timer parameter block */

WORD seconds,minutes,...;
WORD count;
Timer *t3;
      .
      .
      .
main()
{
      .
      .
      .
    /* set up the timer parameter structure */
    tp.number=3;          /* use output compare number 3 */
    tp.tick=TIMECOUNT;    /* 1 ms interrupts */
    tp.action=0;          /* no output action */
    tp.OC1_connect=0;     /* OC1 not connected to another OC */
    tp.connect_data=0;
    tp.interrupt=YES;     /* need an interrupt here */
    t3=timer_(&tp);       /* instantiate the timer */
    attach_object(t3,&count); /* attach object and method to
                                                         timer*/
    attach_method(t3,count_ticks);
      .
      .
      .
    count=0;          /* initialize count */
    cli();            /* enable the system interrupts */
      .
      .
      .
    /* applications portion of the program */
    FOREVER
    {
        if(count>=ONE_SECOND)  /* count is incremented in the isr
                                                                */
        {
            count=0;
           if(++seconds>=60)
            {
                seconds=0;
               if(++minutes>=60)
```

```
                    {
                              .
                              .
                              .

/* function to be executed in the isr */
void count_ticks(WORD *a)
{
      ++*a;
}
```

INPUT CAPTURE TIMER SUBSYSTEM

Device Name and Description

Timer1 Timer1 implements the three input capture subsystems in the general-purpose timer. These devices are able to measure the time between events.

Super Classes

Timer1 inherits the features of the **error handler.** The error handler inherits the features of the class **object.**

Attributes

```
WORD who_am_I;               /* number of the Input Capture 1-3 */
Edges edge;                 /* definition of input event See
                              typedef of Edges in the header file*/
void (*hook_method)(void*);   /* function to be executed by isr */
void *hook_object;          /* argument of function executed by isr
                                                                 */
```

Methods

```
void error_hand(void *, int, int)        /* from Error_handler */
arguments                             /* see Error_handler */
void exercise( Object * )             /* from Object */
arguments                             /* See Object */
WORD capture_time(Timer1 *);
void set_edge(BYTE number, Edges edge); /* sets a new event to a
                                        specific numbered timer */
void new_edge(Timer1 *,Edges );         /* sets a new event to a
                                   specific instantiated Timer1 */
```

```
Boolean get_status(Timer1 *);            /* returns the state of
                                 the input capture interrupt flag */
```

Constructor

```
Timer1* timer1_(BYTE number,          /* Input Capture number */
                Edges edge,           /* definition of edge event */
                Boolean interrupt); /* interrupt?— YES or NO */
```

Destructor

```
void timer1__(Timer1 *);
```

Macro Methods

```
#define attach_object(a,b)  ((a)->hook_object=(b))
#define attach_method(a,b)  ((a)->hook_method=(b))
```

Here parameter a is a pointer to a properly instantiated Timer1. Parameter b in attach_method() is a pointer to a function that will be executed during the interrupt service routine of the timer identified in parameter a. In the attach_object() method, parameter b is a pointer to the argument of the function identified by hook_method().

Header File

```
#ifndef TIMER1_H
#define TIMER1_H

#include "defines.h"
#include "error.h"

#ifndef GPT_IARB
      #define GPT_IARB 12    /* iarb value of 12 for the GPT */
      #define GPT_VBA 5      /* GPT vectors start at 0x50 */
      #define GPT_LEVEL 6    /* use interrupt level 6 */
#endif

typedef enum BYTE
{
      DISABLE,
      RISING,
      FALLING,
      ANY
}Edges;

#define TIMER1_CLASS \
            ERROR_HANDLER \
```

```
            WORD who_am_I; \
            Edges edge; \
            void *hook_object;\
            void (*hook_method)(void*);


typedef struct
{
      TIMER1_CLASS
}Timer1;


#ifndef ATTACH
#define ATTACH
      #define attach_object(a,b) ((a)->hook_object=(b))
      #define attach_method(a,b) ((a)->hook_method=(b))
#endif


WORD capture_time(Timer1 *);
void set_edge(BYTE number, Edges edge);
void new_edge(Timer1 *,Edges );
Boolean get_status(Timer1 *);
Timer1* timer1_(BYTE number, Edges edge, Boolean interrupt);
void timer1__(Timer1 *);
#endif
```

Other Features and Special Calling Procedures

This component is set up by execution of the constructor. There is no need to prepare a parameter block to operate this function. There are four methods that give insight into the operation of the input captures. One, set_edge(), will set the event for any timer without regard to whether it is a part of an instantiated Timer1. This method should not be used externally. The function capture_time() returns the last value captured by the specified input capture subsystem. The method new_edge() changes the event edge event definition for the specified Timer1, and get_status() returns the specified input capture interrupt flag, whether or not an interrupt is requested.

Coding Examples

```
#include <timer.h>
#include <timer1.h>
#include <delay.h>
#include <semaphor.h>
      .
      .
      .
```

```
/* function to measure the time of 1 serial character to deter-
mine its baud rate */

WORD get_baud(BYTE number, Timer *t3)
{
     WORD start_time;
     Semaphore *s;
     Timer1 *t;
     Delay *d;

     s=semaphore_();           /* create semaphore */
     t=timer1_(number,FALLING,NO); /* build an Input Capture
                                                        timer */
                               /* number is Input Capture
                                                      number, */
                               /* event is FALLING edge and NO
                                                     interrupt */
     while(!get_status(t))
        ;                     /* wait until an event occurs */
     start_time=capture_time(t); /* get time immediately */
     new_edge(t,RISING);      /* set the event to a rising edge */
     d=delay_(t3,s,11);       /* t3 must be 1 ms timer to delay 11
                                                           ms */
     wait_for_semaphore(s); /* wait out the delay */
     start_time=capture_time(t)-start_time  /* character time */
     timer1__(t);             /* get rid of this timer */
     semaphore__(s);          /* don't need semaphore any more */
                            /* delay destroys itself */
     return start_time/80;
}
```

APPENDIX A: THE C COMPILER

In programming microcontrollers, one of the major tasks of the programmer is to make use of the peripheral components found on the chip. Most chips have components such as timers, serial communications ports, serial peripheral ports, analog-to-digital converters, even electrically erasable programmable read-only memory (EEPROM). We will find it very convenient to treat these components as objects and access them merely by sending instruction messages to an appropriate object. We have seen before that most treatment of objects in published material has to do with data structures treated as objects. We cannot avoid this important use of objects.

In Chapter 2, all the objects treated were designed to operate on a large computer. In later chapters, none of the objects will work with a large computer. These objects are all designed to operate on a microcontroller, the M68HC16, to be exact. The processors considered for use in this book included the M68HC11, the M68HC16, and the M68300 chips. The M68300 family has one major advantage when it comes to OOP for a microcontroller. It is a large enough computer that you can buy C++ compilers for it. The other chips are significantly smaller in internal CPU structure, but they have peripheral components that are similar, and in the case of the M68HC16, are exactly the same as those found on the M68300 parts. These chips are so small that there will probably never be a C++ compiler written for them, but in today's market, these chips are much more popular than even the M68300 chips. The internal structure of the M68HC16 is quite similar to that of the M68300 family. They both have an intermodule bus that interconnects the CPU with the chip peripherals. The peripherals are all memory mapped and placed in the highest memory page in both sets of chips. The peripheral components are exactly the same on the M68HC16 and M68300 chips. We can, therefore, create header files to access the registers and bits within the registers for these chips, and with the exception of an offset to the beginning of each module, the header files for both the M68HC16 and the M68300 family of chips will be the same.

The Cosmic Compiler. The compiler used for this book is the Cosmic M68HC16.* This compiler creates excellent code for the M68HC16. Cosmic sells compatible compilers for the M68HC11 and M68300 chips. It is not the intent of this book to teach you the ins and outs of any compiler, but enough of the compiler will be discussed to allow you to work with it. The operation of the compiler is complicated by the nature of the M68HC16 chip. This chip was designed to be compatible with the M68HC11. The major additions to the M68HC16 include an intermodule bus, bus peripherals, a truly 16-bit CPU, and expanded memory access. The M68HC16 can access up to 1 megabyte of data memory and 1 megabyte of program memory. This memory is broken into 16 blocks of 65 kilobytes each. Such a memory organization requires that the compiler handle these blocks or pages of memory. The data are addressed either directly (called extended addressing on this chip) or indexed. In either case, a 20-bit address is needed to access any byte in memory. The basic computer has three index registers, a program counter, and a stack pointer that are each 16 bits wide. To give these registers the necessary width to access the total memory range, the chip designers provided each register with a four-bit extension register. These registers are known as the XK, YK, ZK, PK, and SK, respectively. Additionally, for extended memory addressing, there is a four-bit extension register called the EK. These four bits are appended to the address of any direct data access. The contents of the extension registers are always the most significant four bits of any address.

Depending on the program, the size of the data memory used, the program memory used, and so on, these extension registers are usually set to some value at initialization of the program and then changed only when necessary while the program executes. It is possible in some instances to set the extension registers for all data accesses and never change them during execution. For example, if all the data storage can be contained within a single 65-kilobyte page, the extensions probably need never be changed. On the other hand, if the data storage spreads over several pages, the program will contain many changes to the respective extension registers during normal execution.

The compiler needs a means of identification of data that potentially will require extension register modification when being accessed by the program. If a variable is to be placed in a memory location that requires a full 20-bit address, the variable is identified by the flag @far when it is declared.

Extensive use is made of header files created specifically for each chip. A complete set of header files for the M68HC16 can be found in Appendix B. A portion of the file gpt.h is shown in Listing A.1. This file allows access to the general

*Cosmic Software, 100 Tower Office Park, Suite C, Woburn, MA 01801-2127; tel. (617) 932-2556.

purpose timer on the M68HC16. Quite a bit of the file is not shown here because it is repetition of bit definitions similar to those shown below. Note that this header begins with the usual conditional compile directives to prevent its inclusion in the code stream more than one time. Two type definitions of structures create two new types that will be used later. Note that these types contain individual bit fields, and these fields are named. The names of the fields are taken directly from the GPT manual.* The names of the registers are also given in the manual. Therefore, the GPT manual is the documentation upon which all code for operation of the general purpose timer in the M68HC16 is based.

There are some unused bits in the bit fields defined by the structures. It is necessary to name these unused fields with unique names. Here, we use the name Nul1gpt or Nul2gpt to create names that will probably not be used elsewhere in any program.

This file is used in conjunction with a header file designed for the specific chip being used. One of the addresses defined in the chip header file is the beginning address of each module in the chip. In this case, GPT_Register is the beginning address of the general-purpose timer control registers. All of the registers needed to run the timer are located at an offset from GPT_Register. These registers are all located in the top half of the top page of memory. In other words, the addresses of these registers are above the address 0xf8000. As such, access to the registers require a full 20-bit address. Therefore, when forcing the addresses to have the specific type needed at each memory location, the @far must be included in the cast operation. Also, note that the type Register is used as a type for several addresses. This type is defined in the header file for the chip, and in the case of the M68HC16, a Register is a collection of 16 bits in a single memory location. You will also notice that there are several instances where a memory location is given two names. When this happens, the memory location is made up of two M68HC11 type registers: one eight-bit register in the most significant bits and one eight-bit register in the least significant bits of the 16-bit register. When the bits are defined you will find them in the range 8 through 15 for one register and 0 through 7 for the other.

A header file hc16h.h must be included as the first line of code in any program. This file contains the basic register definitions along with all the offsets to the various peripheral control memory areas. For example, the beginning of the general-purpose timer control registers can be found at the address GPT_Register. This value, along with all of the beginning addresses of the other peripherals, are found in this file. Other peripherals included with this chip are the system integration module (sim.h), the analog-to-digital converter module (adc.h), the queued serial interface module (qsim.h), and the static ram module (sram.h). If the program is to make access to any of these modules, the appropriate header file must be included.

The compiler is a command line operation. The general command line interface to the compiler is as follows:

```
c [options] <filename.c>
```

*Motorola Manual GPTRM/AD.

```
#ifndef GPT_H
#define GPT_H

typedef struct
{
     unsigned Nul1gpt : 4;
     unsigned VBA     : 4;
     unsigned IRL     : 3;
     unsigned Nul2gpt : 1;
     unsigned PAB     : 4;
}ICRreg ;

typedef struct
{
      unsigned PWA : 8;
      unsigned PWB : 8;
} Bytes;

#define GPT_MCR (*(@far MCR_Register*)(GPT_Register+0))
#define ICR (*(@far ICRreg*)(GPT_Register+4))
#define PDDR (*(@far Register*)(GPT_Register+6))
#define OC1M (*(@far Register*)(GPT_Register+8))
#define OC1D OC1M
#define TCNT (*(@far unsigned volatile int*)(GPT_Register+0xa))
#define PACTL (*(@far Register*)(GPT_Register+0xc))
#define PACNT (*(@far unsigned volatile char*)(GPT_Register+0xd))
#define TIC1 (*(@far unsigned int*)(GPT_Register+0xe))
#define TIC2 (*(@far unsigned int*)(GPT_Register+0x10))
#define TIC3 (*(@far unsigned int*)(GPT_Register+0x12))
#define TOC1 (*(@far unsigned int*)(GPT_Register+0x14))
#define TOC2 (*(@far unsigned int*)(GPT_Register+0x16))
#define TOC3 (*(@far unsigned int*)(GPT_Register+0x18))
#define TOC4 (*(@far unsigned int*)(GPT_Register+0x1a))
#define TI4O5 (*(@far unsigned int*)(GPT_Register+0x1c))
#define TCTL1 (*(@far Register*)(GPT_Register+0x1e))
#define TCTL2 TCTL1
#define TMSK1 (*(@far Register*)(GPT_Register+0x20))
#define TMSK2 TMSK1
#define TFLG1 (*(@far volatile Register*)(GPT_Register+0x22))
#define TFLG2 TFLG1
#define CFORC (*(@far Register*)(GPT_Register+0x24))
#define PWMC CFORC
#define PWMA (*(@far Bytes*)(GPT_Register+0x26))
#define PWMA PWMB
```

Listing A.1 General-Purpose Timer Header File

```
#define PWMCNT (*(@far unsigned int*)(GPT_Register+0x28))
#define PWMABUF (*(@far Bytes*)(GPT_Register+0x2a))
#define PWMBBUF PWMABUF
#define PRESCALER (*(@far unsigned int*)(GPT_Register+0x2c))

/* MCR bit definitions 0x0 */

#define STOP bit15
#define FRZ1 bit14
#define FRZ0 bit13
#define STOPP bit12
#define INCP bit11
#define SUPV bit7

/* PDDR bit definitions 0x6 */

#define DDRI4O5 bit15
#define DDRO4 bit14
#define DDRO3 bit13
#define DDRO2 bit12
#define DDRO1 bit11
#define DDRI3 bit10
#define DDRI2 bit9
#define DDRI1 bit8
        .
        .
        .

#endif
```

Listing A.1 (continued)

There are many options that are needed to compile code for our purposes. A batch file that contains all the necessary options is quite useful here. The contents of this batch file are

```
c -dlistcs -dxdebug -dmodm +o %1.c
```

The option -dlistcs causes the compiler to create a listing file that contains the C program interleaved with the corresponding assembly code. It is planned to execute and debug the code on an evaluation board called the EVB16. The software for access to this board will permit limited source-level debugging. To create the files needed to do the debug operations, the -dxdebug option must be included in the command line. The -dmodm option causes the compiler to create code with the medium memory module. In this module, the program can contain up to 1 megabyte of code, but the directly accessible volatile RAM memory must be limited to 65 kilobytes. This arrangement is usually satisfactory for most applications. The +o option instructs the compiler to create a relocatable object module, and the %1.c entry is the file name entered on the command line when the batch file is executed.

The -dxdebug command causes the listing file to be increased greatly in size. If you are trying to get a clean compile and are not planning to debug the program, it is probably best to leave out the -dxdebug option.

The next phase of the compile procedure is the linking operation. It is in this phase that program and data modules are placed at specific memory locations. The linkng operation is probably best controlled by a command file. A typical command file needed to link the code is shown in Listing A.2. Note first that a special version of this file is needed for each program that you want to link. In this case, there are three lines, with the name timetest included. timetest is the name of the program being linked. Also, note that there is a file vectiot.o being linked into the program. This file must also be written specially for each program that you will link. Perhaps the startup routine crts.o will also have to be written as a unique program for your individual program.

In this linker, a # sign causes the remainder of the line to be a comment. Each line is commented to help explain the operation that takes place at that point in the link procedure. The first three lines are essentially bookkeeping operations. The +h option causes the program to be linked into multiple output segments. The second line notifies the linker of the maximum program size, and the third line causes memory banking options to be implemented. The next two lines control the outputs from the linker. A map file named timetest.ma will be generated and the output linked file will be named timetest.h16.

```
#
+h                      # multisegment output
-max 0xfffff            # maximum size
-ps16 -pc.              # set up banking options
+map=timetest.ma        # create a memory map file
-o timetest.h16         # output file name
+text -b 0              # reset vectors start address
vectors.o               # vectors
+text -b 0x400          # program start address
+data -b 0x20000        # data start address
crts.o                  # startup routine
timetest.o              # application program
ooplib.h16              # oop library
c:/cc16/lib/libi.h16    # C library (if needed)
c:/cc16/lib/libm.h16    # machine library
+def __memory=__bss__   # symbol used by library
```

Listing A.2. Linker Command File

This compiler system generates several different sections during its execution. These sections are linked into different modules at link time. An output code section is identified as a +text section, and an output data section is identified as +data. In the command file, the next operation is to load the vector table. This part of the program is covered in more detail later. The vector table is to be loaded at the address 0. The line text -b 0 sets up the linker to put this program at zero. There are no data contents to this portion of the program, so no +data command is needed yet. At the completion of the vector table, the startup routine followed by the main program followed by any library functions needed will be loaded. These portions of the program will be started at the address 0x400, and any data needed for these sections of the program will be loaded at 0x20000. These program modules will be loaded contiguously in their respective memories. After the program is loaded, three libraries will be searched for missing program modules. The first of these libraries is a special library generated for these test programs, and the next two, libi.h16 and libm.h16, are the standard integer and machine libraries for the M68HC16. The initialized data memory area is called the bss, and the internal representation of the end of this memory area is __bss__. This value is saved in the global memory location named __memory so that the executing program can find the end of the used RAM storage area.

This command file is redirected onto the linker command lnkh16 . The output from the linker is a file with an h16 extension. This output must be converted to an appropriate ASCII file to be loaded into the development system board. Also, the format of the h16 file must be converted to an appropriate debug level control file to aid in the source-level debug of the program. The command file shown in Listing A.3 will execute all these operations.

This file can be combined with the compile command file if the programmer wishes to compile in link with one command.

There are two more files that should be considered at this time. The first is the vector file. One such file is shown in Listing A.4. There are two lines at the head of the file that contain code that is not portable ANSI-compatible code. These lines of code are specifically needed to pass into the program addresses of functions needed in the vector table. The entries look like function prototypes that are marked as external with the extern key word. The first is the startup code, addressed as _stext in the file crts.s. The key word @far notifies the compiler that it should use a 20-bit address for this function and that it has the nature of an interrupt service routine. The modifier @port identifies _stext() as an interrupt service routine. The next line

```
lnkh16 < %1.lnk
hexh16 -s -o %1.s19 %1.h16
topne %1.h16
pause
```

Listing A.3 Link Phase Command File

of code is a function prototype for an interrupt service routine named _int(). The code for this function is found at the end of this file.

You can see that this file simply contains a single structure. The first four members of the structure are bookkeeping items that are needed to bring the chip on-line after reset. The first word is a combination of the several extension registers that will be loaded at reset. The next location contains the least significant 16 bits of the initial program counter value. The next entry is the initial stack pointer, and finally, the next memory location contains the least significant bits of the Z register at reset. These mandatory entries are followed by an array of 251 exception service routine addresses. The first 0x18 entries in this portion of the list are the preset exception vectors for the part and the initialization addresses. The address of a dummy service routine is placed in each of these vector addresses. This dummy routine called _int() merely returns control of the program to the background mode monitor. In debug, it is very important that _int() execute a bgnd command that will cause control of the program to be returned to the background mode monitor. This approach will let the programmer know that an unexpected exception has occurred. As the program is developed, it is expected that these vectors will be changed to proper locations within the program being developed. Also at the close of the program development, the bgnd command in _int() should be changed to a catch-all function that handles any accidental exception that might occur during normal operation.

Vectors 0x19 through 0x37 are reserved and not available for use at this time. Vectors 0x38 through 0xff are available for use by the program. We can see above how these vectors can be used. The program in this case needs an interrupt service routine for Output Compare 3. This routine is named OC3_Isr(). The programmer wants this interrupt service routine to be placed in the vector 0x46, which is at the address 0x8c. This externally linked routine is placed in vector 0x46 in the routine above. This routine is then compiled and linked with the main program at link time.

```
/* RESET AND INTERRUPT VECTORS
*/

extern @far @port void _stext(void);     /* startup routine */
extern @port void OC3_Isr(void);         /* OC3 isr address */

static @port void _int(void);

static   const struct reset {
         @far @port void (*rst)(void); /* reset+code extension */
         unsigned short isp;          /* initial stack pointer */
         unsigned short dpp;           /* direct page pointer */
         @port void (*vector[252])(void); /* interrupt vectors */
         } _reset = {
```

Listing A.4 Vector Table File

```
        _stext,         /* 1-start 20-bit address */
        0x03fe,         /* 2-stack pointer */
        0x0000,         /* 3-page pointer */
        _int,           /* 4-Breakpoint */
        _int,           /* 5-Bus Error */
        _int,           /* 6-Software Interrupt */
        _int,           /* 7-Illegal Instruction */
        _int,           /* 8-Divide by Zero */
        _int,           /* 9-Reserved */
        _int,           /* a-Reserved */
        _int,           /* b-Reserved */
        _int,           /* c-Reserved */
        _int,           /* d-Reserved */
        _int,           /* e-Reserved */
        _int,           /* f-Uninitialized Interrupt */
        _int,           /* 10-Reserved */
        _int,           /* 11-Level 1 Interrupt Autovector */
        _int,           /* 12-Level 2 Interrupt Autovector */
        _int,           /* 13-Level 3 Interrupt Autovector */
        _int,           /* 14-Level 4 Interrupt Autovector */
        _int,           /* 15-Level 5 Interrupt Autovector */
        _int,           /* 16-Level 6 Interrupt Autovector */
        _int,           /* 17-Level 7 Interrupt Autovector */
        _int,           /* 18-Spurious Interrupt */
        /* vectors 0x19-0x37 unassigned, reserved */
        0,0,0,0,0,0,0,
        0,0,0,0,0,0,0,0,0,0,0,0,0,0,0,0,
        0,0,0,0,0,0,0,0,0,0,0,0,0,0,0,0,
        /* put timer at vector 0x46 0x40 from ICR and 6 for OC3 */
        0,0,0,0,0,0,OC3_Isr    /* OC3_Isr vector at 0x46 address
                                  0x8c*/
        };

/* function to receive an undefined interrupt */
static @port void _int(void)
{
      _asm("bgnd\n");
}
```

Listing A.4 (continued)

We next have a small assembly language program that is used to initialize the part after reset. This routine is called crts.s (see Listing A.5). When a file has an extention .s it can be assembled by the compiler exactly as a C program. In this program, there are several things that must be handled properly. The first business in the program below is to set up the chip internal RAM to be located at the hex address 0x20000. The first seven instructions take care of this matter. The control registers for the internal RAM are found in the address range 0xffb00 through 0xffb04. One means of accessing this memory range is to use extended addressing with the EK register loaded with a 0xf. The first two instructions place an 0xf into EK. The next instruction places a 2 into the location 64260 (0xfb04). This action places the address at 0x20000. Next, some bits are set in the RAM module control register RAMMCR. The two instructions involving bits 2 and 3 place a value 2 in the RASP bit field, which causes the RAM to be placed in both program and data space. The next instruction clears the STOPR bit, which causes the RAM to operate in normal mode. Usually, these operations are easily done in the C portion of the program. There is one small problem, however. You will note that near the end of the program, a jsr (jump to subroutine) instruction is executed. If the stack is not placed in valid RAM when this program instruction is executed, the program will crash and burn. Therefore, we put the RAM setup into the assembly language initialization portion of the program.

```
; C STARTUP FOR 68HC16
;
    .external _main, __memory
    .external ._main, .__bss__
    .public _exit, __stext
    .psect _bss
sbss:
    .psect _text
__stext:
    ldk     #15          ; ram control registers are
    tbek                 ; in top memory page
    ldd     #2           ; put internal ram at 0x20000
    std     64260        ; 0xfb04
    bclr    64256,#3     ; ram for both program and
    bset    64256,#2     ; data
    bclr    64256,#128   ; ram in normal mode
    ldk     #.__bss__
    tbek                 ; initialize the extension
    tbxk                 ; registers to the msb of
    tbyk                 ; the bss
    tbzk
    tbsk
    ldx     #sbss        ; start of bss
    clrd                 ; to be zeroed
    bra     mtest        ; start loop
bcl:
    std     0,x          ; clear memory
    aix     #2           ; next word
```

Listing A.5. Initialization Program crts.s

```
mtest:
    cpx     #__memory      ; end of memory ?
    blo     bcl            ; no, continue
    lds     #1022          ; put stack at 203fe
    jsr     _main,#._main; call application
_exit:
    bgnd                   ; enter background mode here
                           ; in the event of unexpected
                           ; return from main
;
.end
```

Listing A.5 (continued)

APPENDIX B: M68HC16 HEADER FILES

This appendix contains listings of the important header files used to control the operation of the intermodule bus (IMB) peripherals. The IMB is an internal bus structure that Motorola employs on the larger of their microcontrollers, the M68HC16 and the M68300 families. Both of these chips comprise a core computer named either CPU16 or CPU32. The remainder of the components in the controllers are all IMB peripherals. In general, the programming language C takes care of essentially all aspects of the core computers. The only place where C fails its job here has to do with direct access to registers contained within the CPU components. These registers are not available to the language and it is necessary to work around the setup of the registers that control the system interrupts. These interrupts are a feature of the CPU and not the peripheral components. We will see how control within these registers can be handled in macros written in the appropriate chip header files.

The header files shown here establish access to the several registers and bit fields within these registers. Control of these registers control the several peripherals. There are many ways that these header files can be created. Two come to mind specifically: the technique used here, where each register is forced to a specific address in the computer memory map, and a scheme where all the registers are placed into a single structure, which is forced to the proper address. Both schemes work well. The approach used here has the disadvantage that it requires a little more typing when creating the file, but the structure approach has one serious drawback that makes it less attractive. If an offset error is made in the creation of the structure, all entries in the structure from the error on will be in error. Such an error can cause many errors in a program, and it is very difficult to find the error source. On the other hand, if each register is forced to its own address, and an error is made, the error will affect only the specific register, and any error diagnostic completed by the compiler will point to the exact location in memory where the error occurred.

In each module header file you will find a compiler control sequence of the following type:

```
#ifdef _PAGE0
#define _MEM @indir
#else
#ifdef _PAGEF
#define _MEM
#else
#define _MEM @far
#endif
#endif
```

This control sequence establishes a value for the constant _MEM that depends on certain command line options entered when the program is compiled. There are three possible situations. If the -dpage0 option is entered, the @indir modifier must be used with the address of each module control register. This definition causes all accesses to the I/O page to be done as direct negative addresses. As such, the value of the EK register must be zero. With the -dpagef option, all accesses to this page will be indirect through one of the index registers on the chip, and the @far modifier will be used otherwise. In this case, all accesses to the I/O page will be direct positive addresses, and the EK register must contain a value 0xf.

Also, the final header file defines.h is included in this section. This file, shown below, is not a chip-related header. It is very desirable to have a header file that defines all the constants that your programs might use. Inclusion of this file will eliminate many "magic" numbers that are found in many programs. These numbers make it very difficult to determine what is going on within any program.

```
#ifndef DEFINES_H
#define DEFINES_H


#ifndef NULL
     #define NULL (void *)0
#endif
#define EOM NULL
#define FOREVER while(TRUE)


typedef int Boolean;
typedef unsigned int WORD;
typedef unsigned char BYTE;
```

```
enum {FALSE,TRUE};
enum {OFF,ON};
enum {NO,YES};
enum {FAST,SLOW};
enum {OUTPUT, INPUT};


enum errors
{
     SEMAPHORE,
     SERIAL,
     TIMER,
     DELAY,
     PWM,
     PWMI
};


enum output_compares
{
     OC1=1,OC2,OC3,OC4
};


enum input_captures
{
     IC1=1,IC2,IC3
};


enum edges
{
     DISABLE,
     RISING,
     FALLING,
     ANY
};


enum output
{
     DISCONNECT,
     TOGGLE,
     CLEAR,
     SET
};

#endif
```

MC68HC16Y1 AND MC68HC16Z1 HEADER FILES

The following two header files are core CPU headers for different parts in the M68HC16 family. The first is for the MC68HC16Y1, which is used exclusively in this book and the second is for the MC68HC16Z1. The only difference you will notice between these two files is the peripheral addresses found near the middle of the file. The peripherals are somewhat different on these two parts.

```
#ifndef HC16Y1_H
#define HC16Y1_H


typedef struct
{
     unsigned bit0  : 1;
     unsigned bit1  : 1;
     unsigned bit2  : 1;
     unsigned bit3  : 1;
     unsigned bit4  : 1;
     unsigned bit5  : 1;
     unsigned bit6  : 1;
     unsigned bit7  : 1;
     unsigned bit8  : 1;
     unsigned bit9  : 1;
     unsigned bit10: 1;
     unsigned bit11: 1;
     unsigned bit12: 1;
     unsigned bit13: 1;
     unsigned bit14: 1;
     unsigned bit15: 1;
} Register;


typedef struct
{
     unsigned bit0  : 1;
     unsigned bit1  : 1;
     unsigned bit2  : 1;
     unsigned bit3  : 1;
     unsigned bit4  : 1;
     unsigned bit5  : 1;
     unsigned bit6  : 1;
     unsigned bit7  : 1;
} Char_Register;


typedef struct
{
```

```
    unsigned IARB : 4;
    unsigned bit4 : 1;
    unsigned bit5 : 1;
    unsigned bit6 : 1;
    unsigned bit7 : 1;
    unsigned bit8 : 1;
    unsigned bit9 : 1;
    unsigned bit10: 1;
    unsigned bit11: 1;
    unsigned bit12: 1;
    unsigned bit13: 1;
    unsigned bit14: 1;
    unsigned bit15: 1;
} MCR_Register;

#define ADC_Register 0xff700
#define MRM_Register 0xff820
#define GPT_Register 0xff900
#define SCIM_Register 0xffa00
#define TPURAM_Register 0xffb00
#define MCCI_Register 0xffc00
#define TPU_Register 0xffe00

/*   Macros and function to permit interrupt service
    routine programming from C.

    To use the vector call, do vector(isr, vector_address)
    where isr is a pointer to the interrupt service
    routine, and vector_address is the vector address where
    the isr pointer must be stored. The usual form for vector is
     #define vector(a,b)  (*(void**)(b)=(a)
    has been changed to that below to allow the calculated isr
    address to be sixteen bits rather than twenty for the HC16
*/

#define vector(isr,vector_address) (*(@far
int)vector_address)=(int)(isr))
#define cli() _asm("andp #0FF1FH\n") /* enable interrupts */
#define sei() _asm("orp #000E0H\n") /* disable maskable
                                                 interrupts */
#define wait() _asm("wai\n")
#endif
```

Following is the header file for the MC68HC16Z1.

```
#ifndef HC16
#define HC16
```

```
typedef struct
{
    unsigned bit0 : 1;
    unsigned bit1 : 1;
    unsigned bit2 : 1;
    unsigned bit3 : 1;
    unsigned bit4 : 1;
    unsigned bit5 : 1;
    unsigned bit6 : 1;
    unsigned bit7 : 1;
    unsigned bit8 : 1;
    unsigned bit9 : 1;
    unsigned bit10: 1;
    unsigned bit11: 1;
    unsigned bit12: 1;
    unsigned bit13: 1;
    unsigned bit14: 1;
    unsigned bit15: 1;
} Register;


typedef struct
{
    unsigned IARB : 4;
    unsigned bit4 : 1;
    unsigned bit5 : 1;
    unsigned bit6 : 1;
    unsigned bit7 : 1;
    unsigned bit8 : 1;
    unsigned bit9 : 1;
    unsigned bit10: 1;
    unsigned bit11: 1;
    unsigned bit12: 1;
    unsigned bit13: 1;
    unsigned bit14: 1;
    unsigned bit15: 1;
} MCR_Register;


#define ADC_Register 0xff700
#define GPT_Register 0xff900
#define SIM_Register 0xffa00
#define SRAM_Register 0xffb00
#define QSM_Register 0xffc00


/*  Macros and function to permit interrupt service
    routine programming from C.
```

```
    To use the vector call, do vector(isr, vector_address)
    where isr is a pointer to the interrupt service
    routine, and vector_address is the vector address where
    the isr pointer must be stored. The program must use
    the return_int() function for each return from an
    interrupt or exception. */

#define vector(isr,vector_address) (*(void *)(vector_address)=
(int)(isr))
#define cli() _asm("andp #0FF1FH\n") /* enable interrupts */
#define sei() _asm("orp #000e0H\n") /* disable maskable
                                                interrupts */
#endif
```

GENERAL-PURPOSE TIMER HEADER FILE

The general purpose timer is used on both of the varities of the M68HC16 discussed above. The header file for this peripheral system is shown below.

```
#ifndef GPT_H
#define GPT_H

#ifdef _PAGE0
#define _MEM @indir
#else
#ifdef _PAGEF
#define _MEM
#else
#define _MEM @far
#endif
#endif

typedef struct
{
      unsigned Null : 4;
        unsigned VBA  : 4;
        unsigned IRL  : 3;
        unsigned Nul  : 1;
        unsigned PAB  : 4;
}ICRreg ;

typedef struct
{
     unsigned EDGE1 : 2;
     unsigned EDGE2 : 2;
```

```
     unsigned EDGE3 : 2;
     unsigned EDGE4 : 2;
} Tctl2;

typedef struct
{
     unsigned GPT_NULL0 : 8;
     unsigned OML2      : 2;
     unsigned OML3      : 2;
     unsigned OML4      : 2;
     unsigned OML5      : 2;
}Tctl1;

typedef struct
{
     unsigned PWB : 8;
     unsigned PWA : 8;
} Bytes;

/* define the length of an interrupt vector */
#define VAL 2


#define GPT_MCR (*(_MEM MCR_Register*)(GPT_Register+0))
#define ICR (*(_MEM ICRreg*)(GPT_Register+4))
#define PDDR (*(_MEM Register*)(GPT_Register+6))
#define OC1M (*(_MEM Register*)(GPT_Register+8))
#define OC1D OC1M
#define TCNT (*(_MEM unsigned volatile int*)(GPT_Register+0xa))
#define PACTL (*(_MEM Register*)(GPT_Register+0xc))
#define PACNT (*(_MEM unsigned volatile char*)(GPT_Register+0xd))
#define TIC1 (*(_MEM unsigned int*)(GPT_Register+0xe))
#define TIC2 (*(_MEM unsigned int*)(GPT_Register+0x10))
#define TIC3 (*(_MEM unsigned int*)(GPT_Register+0x12))
#define TOC1 (*(_MEM unsigned int*)(GPT_Register+0x14))
#define TOC2 (*(_MEM unsigned int*)(GPT_Register+0x16))
#define TOC3 (*(_MEM unsigned int*)(GPT_Register+0x18))
#define TOC4 (*(_MEM unsigned int*)(GPT_Register+0x1a))
#define TI4O5 (*(_MEM unsigned int*)(GPT_Register+0x1c))
#define TCTL1 (*(_MEM Tctl1*)(GPT_Register+0x1e))
#define TCTL2 (*(_MEM Tctl2*)(GPT_Register+0x1e))
#define OMLREG TCTL1
#define TMSK1 (*(_MEM Register*)(GPT_Register+0x20))
#define TMSK2 TMSK1
#define TFLG1 (*(_MEM Register*)(GPT_Register+0x22))
#define TFLG2 TFLG1
#define CFORC (*(_MEM Register*)(GPT_Register+0x24))
#define PWMC CFORC
```

```
#define PWMA (*(_MEM Bytes*)(GPT_Register+0x26))
#define PWMB PWMA
#define PWMCNT (*(_MEM unsigned int*)(GPT_Register+0x28))
#define PWMABUF (*(_MEM Bytes*)(GPT_Register+0x2a))
#define PWMBBUF PWMABUF
#define PRESCALER (*(_MEM unsigned int*)(GPT_Register+0x2c))
/* MCR bit definitions 0x0 */

#define STOP bit15
#define FRZ1 bit14
#define FRZ0 bit13
#define STOPP bit12
#define INCP bit11
#define SUPV bit7

/* PDDR bit definitions 0x6 */

#define DDRI4O5 bit15
#define DDRO4 bit14
#define DDRO3 bit13
#define DDRO2 bit12
#define DDRO1 bit11
#define DDRI3 bit10
#define DDRI2 bit9
#define DDRI1 bit8

/* PDR bit definitions 0x6 */

#define IC4OC5 bit7
#define OC4 bit6
#define OC3 bit5
#define OC2 bit4
#define OC1 bit3
#define IC3 bit2
#define IC2 bit1
#define IC1 bit0

/* OC1M bit definitions 0x8*/

#define OC1M7 bit15
#define OC1M6 bit14
#define OC1M5 bit13
#define OC1M4 bit12
#define OC1M3 bit11

/* OC1D bit definitions 0x8*/
```

```
#define OC1D7 bit7
#define OC1D6 bit6
#define OC1D5 bit5
#define OC1D4 bit4
#define OC1D3 bit3

/* PACTL bit definitions 0x0c */

#define PAIS bit15
#define PAEN bit14
#define PAMOD bit13
#define PEDGE bit12
#define PCLKS bit11
#define I4O5 bit10
#define PACLK1 bit9
#define PACLK0 bit8

/* TCTL1 bit definition 0x1E*/

#define OL2 bit8
#define OM2 bit9
#define OL3 bit10
#define OM3 bit11
#define OL4 bit12
#define OM4 bit13
#define OL5 bit14
#define OM5 bit15

/* TCTL2 bit definitions 0x1E */

#define EDG4B bit7
#define EDG4A bit6
#define EDG1B bit5
#define EDG1A bit4
#define EDG2B bit3
#define EDG2A bit2
#define EDG3B bit1
#define EDG3A bit0

/* TMSK1 bit definitions 0x20 */

#define IC1I bit8
#define IC2I bit9
#define IC3I bit10
#define OC1I bit11
#define OC2I bit12
```

```
#define OC3I bit13
#define OC4I bit14
#define I4O5I bit15

/* TMSK2 bit definitions 0x20 */

#define TOI bit7
#define PAOVI bit5
#define PAII bit4
#define CPROUT bit3
#define CPR2 bit2
#define CPR1 bit1
#define CPR0 bit0

/* TFLG1 bit definitions 0x22 */

#define IC1F bit8
#define IC2F bit9
#define IC3F bit10
#define OC1F bit11
#define OC2F bit12
#define OC3F bit13
#define OC4F bit14
#define I4O5F bit15

/* TFLG2 bit definitions 0x22 */

#define TOF bit7
#define PAOVF bit5
#define PAIF bit4

/* CFORC bit definitions 0x24*/

#define FOC1 bit15
#define FOC2 bit14
#define FOC3 bit13
#define FOC4 bit12
#define FOC5 bit11
#define FPWMA bit9
#define FPWMB bit8

/* PWMC Bit definitions 0x24*/

#define PPROUT bit7
#define PPR2 bit6
#define PPR1 bit5
```

```
#define PPR0 bit4
#define SFA bit3
#define SFB bit2
#define F1A bit1
#define F1B bit0

#endif
```

MULTICHANNEL COMMUNICATIONS INTERFACE HEADER FILE

```
#ifndef MCCI_H
#define MCCI_H

#ifdef _PAGE0
#define _MEM @indir
#else
#ifdef _PAGEF
#define _MEM
#else
#define _MEM @far
#endif
#endif

typedef struct
{
     unsigned INTV :8;
     unsigned ILSCIA :3;
      unsigned ILSCIB :3;

}Ilsci;

typedef struct
{
      unsigned NU :11 ;
      unsigned ILSPI :3;
} Ilspi;

typedef struct
{
      unsigned BAUD :8;
      unsigned SIZE :1;
      unsigned LSBF :1;
      unsigned CPHA :1;
      unsigned CPOL :1;
```

```
        unsigned MSTR :1;
        unsigned WOMP :1;
        unsigned SPE  :1;
        unsigned SPIE :1;
}Spcr;

typedef struct
{
        unsigned LOWB :8;
        unsigned UPPB :8;
} Spdr;

typedef struct
{
unsigned BR :13;
} Sccr0;

typedef struct
{
unsigned DATA :8;
unsigned BIT8 :1;
} Scdr;

#define MCCI_MCR (*(_MEM MCR_Register*)(MCCI_Register+0x00))
#define ILSCI (*(_MEM Ilsci *)(MCCI_Register+0x04))
#define MIVR ILSCI
#define ILSPI (*(_MEM Ilspi *)(MCCI_Register+0x06))
#define MPAR (*(_MEM Char_Register*)(MCCI_Register+0x09))
#define MCCR (*(_MEM Char_Register*)(MCCI_Register+0x0b))
#define PORTMC (*(_MEM Char_Register*)(MCCI_Register+0x0c))
#define PORTMCP (*(_MEM Char_Register*)(MCCI_Register+0x0e))
#define SCCR0A (*(_MEM Sccr0 *)(MCCI_Register+0x18))
#define SCCR1A (*(_MEM Register *)(MCCI_Register+0x1a))
#define SCSRA (*(_MEM Register *)(MCCI_Register+0x1c))
#define SCDRA (*(_MEM Scdr *)(MCCI_Register+0x1e))
#define SCCR0B (*(_MEM Sccr0 *)(MCCI_Register+0x28))
#define SCCR1B (*(_MEM Register *)(MCCI_Register+0x2a))
#define SCSRB (*(_MEM Register *)(MCCI_Register+0x2c))
#define SCDRB (*(_MEM Scdr *)(MCCI_Register+0x2e))
#define SPCR (*(_MEM Spcr *)(MCCI_Register+0x38))
#define SPSR (*(_MEM Register*)(MCCI_Register+0x3c))
#define SPDR (*(_MEM Spdr *)(MCCI_Register+0x3e))

/* some useful values */

#define BAUD_4800 109 /* Baud rate codes for the HC16 */
#define BAUD_9600 55
#define BAUD_19K 27
```

```
/* PORTMCP bits */
#define MISO bit0
#define MOSI bit1
#define SCK bit2
#define SS bit3
#define RXDB bit4
#define TXDB bit5
#define RXDA bit6
#define TXDB bit7


/* SPSR bits */
#define MODF bit12
#define WCOL bit14
#define SPIF bit15


/* SCCR1 bits */
#define SBK bit0
#define RWU bit1
#define RE bit2
#define TE bit3
#define ILIE bit4
#define RIE bit5
#define TCIE bit6
#define TIE bit7
#define WAKE bit8
#define M bit9
#define PE bit10
#define PT bit11
#define ILT bit12
#define WOMC bit13
#define LOOPS bit14


/* SCSR bits */
#define PF bit0
#define FE bit1
#define NF bit2
#define OR bit3
#define IDLE bit4
#define RAF bit5
#define RDRF bit6
#define TC bit7
#define TDRE bit8


#endif
```

QUEUED SERIAL MODULE HEADER FILE

The QSM is used only with the MC68HC16Z1 component. This header file is included for reference only.

```
#ifndef QSM_H
#define QSM_H

#ifdef _PAGE0
#define _MEM @indir
#else
#ifdef _PAGEF
#define _MEM
#else
#define _MEM @far
#endif
#endif

typedef struct
{
    unsigned INTV   :8;
     unsigned ILSCI  :3;
     unsigned ILQSPI :3;
     unsigned NUL1   :2;
} Qilr;

typedef struct
{
     unsigned SP   :8;
     unsigned CPHA :1;
     unsigned CPOL :1;
     unsigned BITS :4;
     unsigned WOMQ :1;
     unsigned MSTR :1;
} Spcr0;

typedef struct
{
     unsigned DTL   :8;
     unsigned DSCLK :7;
     unsigned SPE   :1;
} Spcr1;

typedef struct
{
```

```
        unsigned NEWQP :4;
        unsigned NUL2  :4;
        unsigned ENDQP :4;
        unsigned NUL3  :1;
        unsigned WRTO  :1;
        unsigned WREN  :1;
        unsigned SPIFIE:1;
} Spcr2;

typedef struct
{
        unsigned char PCS   :4;
        unsigned char DSCK  :1;
        unsigned char DT    :1;
        unsigned char BITSE :1;
        unsigned char CONT  :1;
}Cr;

typedef struct
{
        unsigned SCBR :13;
        unsigned NUL4 :3;
} Sccr0;

#define QSMCR (*(_MEM MCR_Register*)(QSM_Register+0x00))
#define QILR (*(_MEM Qilr*)(QSM_Register + 0x04))
#define QIVR QILR
#define SCCR0 (*(_MEM Sccr0*)(QSM_Register+0x08))
#define SCCR1 (*(_MEM Register*)(QSM_Register+0x0a))
#define SCSR (*(_MEM volatile Register*)(QSM_Register+0x0c))
#define SCDR (*(_MEM volatile int*)(QSM_Register+0x0e))
#define PORTQS (*(_MEM volatile Register*)(QSM_Register +0x14))
#define PQSPAR (*(_MEM volatile Register*)(QSM_Register +0x16))
#define DDRQS PQSPAR
#define SPCR0 (*(_MEM Spcr0*)(QSM_Register + 0x18))
#define SPCR1 (*(_MEM Spcr1*)(QSM_Register +0x1a))
#define SPCR2 (*(_MEM SPCR2*)(QSM_Register +0x1c))
#define SPCR3 (*(_MEM MCR_Register)(QSM_Register+0x1e))
#define RR ((_MEM int*)(QSM_Register+0x100))
#define TR ((_MEM int*)(QSM_Register+0x120))
#define CR ((_MEM Cr*)(QSM_Register+0x140))

/*QSMCR bit definitions */

#define SUPV bit7
#define FRZ0 bit13
```

```
#define FRZ1 bit14
#define STOP bit15


/* SPCR3 bit definitions */
#define CPTQP iarb
#define HALTA bit5
#define MODF bit6
#define SPIF bit7
#define HALT bit8
#define HMIE bit9
#define LOOPQ bit10


#define SCCR2 SCCR1


/* SCCR1 bit definitions */
#define SBK bit0
#define RWU bit1
#define RE bit2
#define TE bit3
#define ILIE bit4
#define RIE bit5
#define TCIE bit6
#define TIE bit7
#define WAKE bit8
#define M bit9
#define PE bit10
#define PT bit11
#define ILT bit12
#define WOMS bit13
#define LOOPS bit14


/* SCSR bit definitions */
#define PF bit0
#define FE bit1
#define NF bit2
#define OR bit3
#define IDLE bit4
#define RAF bit5
#define RDRF bit6
#define TC bit7
#define TDRE bit8


#endif
```

SYSTEM INTEGRATION MODULE HEADER FILE

The SIM is used with the MC68HC16Z1 component. There are a few significant differences between the SIM and the SCIM (single chip integration module), which follows this one.

```
#ifndef SIM
#define SIM 1

#ifdef _PAGE0
#define _MEM @indir
#else
#ifdef _PAGEF
#define _MEM
#else
#define _MEM @far
#endif
#endif

typedef struct
{
     unsigned STEXT :1;
     unsigned STSIM :1;
     unsigned RSTEN :1;
     unsigned SLOCK :1;
     unsigned SLIMP :1;
     unsigned NO1   :2;
     unsigned EDIV  :1;
     unsigned Y     :6;
     unsigned X     :1;
     unsigned W     :1;
} Syncr;

typedef struct
{
     unsigned BMT :2;
     unsigned BME :1;
     unsigned HME :1;
     unsigned SWT :2;
     unsigned SWP :1;
     unsigned SWE :1;
}Sypcr;

typedef struct
{
     unsigned PIV :8;
```

```
        unsigned PIRQL :3;
        unsigned NO2   :5;
} Picr;

typedef struct
{
        unsigned PITM :8;
        unsigned PTP  :1;
        unsigned NO3  :7;
}Pitr;
typedef struct
{
        unsigned pr0 :2;
        unsigned pr1 :2;
        unsigned pr2 :2;
        unsigned pr3 :2;
        unsigned pr4 :2;
        unsigned pr5 :2;
        unsigned pr6 :2;
        unsigned pr7 :2;
} Cspar;

typedef struct
{
        unsigned BLKSZ   :3;
        unsigned HIADDR  :13;
} Csbar;

typedef struct
{
        unsigned AVEC  :1;
        unsigned IPL   :3;
        unsigned SPACE :2;
        unsigned DSACK :4;
        unsigned STRB  :1;
        unsigned RSW   :2;
        unsigned BYTE  :2;
        unsigned MODE  :1;
} Csor;

#define SIM_MCR (*(_MEM MCR_Register*)(SIM_Register))
#define SYNCR (*(_MEM Syncr*)(SIM_Register+0x4))
#define RSR (*(_MEM Register*)(SIM_Register+0x6))
#define SIMTRE (*(_MEM Register*)(SIM_Register+0x8))
#define PORTE0 (*(_MEM Register*)(SIM_Register+0x10))
#define PORTE1 (*(_MEM Register*)(SIM_Register+0x12))
#define DDRE (*(_MEM Register*)(SIM_Register+0x14))
```

```
#define PEPAR (*(_MEM Register*)(SIM_Register+0x16))
#define PORTF0 (*(_MEM Register*)(SIM_Register +0x18))
#define PORTF1 (*(_MEM Register*)(SIM_Register+0x1a))
#define DDRF (*(_MEM Register*)(SIM_Register+0x1c))
#define PFPAR (*(_MEM Register*)(SIM_Register+0x1e))
#define SYPCR (*(_MEM Sypcr*)(SIM_Register+0x20))
#define PICR (*(_MEM Picr*)(SIM_Register+0x22))
#define PITR (*(_MEM Pitr*)(SIM_Register+0x24))
#define SWSR (*(_MEM int*)(SIM_Register+0x26))
#define PORTC (*(_MEM Register*)(SIM_Register+0x40))
#define CSPAR0 (*(_MEM Cspar*)(SIM_Register+0x44))
#define CSPAR1 (*(_MEM Cspar*)(SIM_Register+0x46))
#define CSBARBT (*(_MEM Csbar*)(SIM_Register+0x48) )
#define CSORBT (*(_MEM Csor*)(SIM_Register+0x4a))
#define CSBAR0 (*(_MEM Csbar*)(SIM_Register+0x4c))
#define CSOR0 (*(_MEM Csor*)(SIM_Register+0x4e))
#define CSBAR1 (*(_MEM Csbar*)(SIM_Register+0x50))
#define CSOR1 (*(_MEM Csor*)(SIM_Register+0x52))
#define CSBAR2 (*(_MEM Csbar*)(SIM_Register+0x54))
#define CSOR2 (*(_MEM Csor*)(SIM_Register+0x56))
#define CSBAR3 (*(_MEM Csbar*)(SIM_Register+0x58))
#define CSOR3 (*(_MEM Csor*)(SIM_Register+0x5a))
#define CSBAR4 (*(_MEM Csbar*)(SIM_Register+0x5c))
#define CSOR4 (*(_MEM Csor*)(SIM_Register+0x5e))
#define CSBAR5 (*(_MEM Csbar*)(SIM_Register+0x60))
#define CSOR5 (*(_MEM Csor*)(SIM_Register+0x62))
#define CSBAR6 (*(_MEM Csbar*)(SIM_Register+0x64))
#define CSOR6 (*(_MEM Csor*)(SIM_Register+0x66))
#define CSBAR7 (*(_MEM Csbar*)(SIM_Register+0x68))
#define CSOR7 (*(_MEM Csor*)(SIM_Register+0x6a))
#define CSBAR8 (*(_MEM Csbar*)(SIM_Register+0x6c))
#define CSOR8 (*(_MEM Csor*)(SIM_Register+0x6e))
#define CSBAR9 (*(_MEM Csbar*)(SIM_Register+0x70))
#define CSOR9 (*(_MEM Csor*)(SIM_Register+0x72))
#define CSBAR10 (*(_MEM Csbar*)(SIM_Register+0x74))
#define CSOR10 (*(_MEM Csor*)(SIM_Register+0x76))


/* Bitfields in RSR */


#define TST bit0
#define SYS bit1
#define LOC bit2
#define HLT bit4
#define SW bit5
#define POW bit6
#define EXT bit7
```

```
/* Bitfields in PORTE0, PORTE1 and PEPAR*/

#define PE0 bit0
#define PE1 bit1
#define PE2 bit2
#define PE3 bit3
#define PE4 bit4
#define PE5 bit5
#define PE6 bit6
#define PE7 bit7

/* Bitfields in DDRE */

#define DDE0 bit0
#define DDE1 bit1
#define DDE2 bit2
#define DDE3 bit3
#define DDE4 bit4
#define DDE5 bit5
#define DDE6 bit6
#define DDE7 bit7

/* Bitfields in PORTF0, PORTF1 and PFPAR*/

#define PF0 bit0
#define PF1 bit1
#define PF2 bit2
#define PF3 bit3
#define PF4 bit4
#define PF5 bit5
#define PF6 bit6
#define PF7 bit7

/* Bitfields in DDRF */

#define DDF0 bit0
#define DDF1 bit1
#define DDF2 bit2
#define DDF3 bit3
#define DDF4 bit4
#define DDF5 bit5
#define DDF6 bit6
#define DDF7 bit7

/* Bitfields in CSPAR0 */
```

```
#define CSBOOT pr0
#define CSPA01 pr1
#define CSPA02 pr2
#define CSPA03 pr3
#define CSPA04 pr4
#define CSPA05 pr5
#define CSPA06 pr6

/* Bitfields in CSPAR1 */

#define CSPA10 pr0
#define CSPA11 pr1
#define CSPA12 pr2
#define CSPA13 pr3
#define CSPA14 pr4

#endif
```

SINGLE-CHIP INTEGRATION MODULE HEADER FILE

The SCIM is a peripheral component used with the MC68HC16Y1 component.

```
#ifndef SCIM_H
#define SCIM_H

#ifdef _PAGE0
#define _MEM @indir
#else
#ifdef _PAGEF
#define _MEM
#else
#define _MEM @far
#endif
#endif

typedef struct
{
    unsigned bit0 :1;
    unsigned bit1 :1;
    unsigned bit2 :1;
    unsigned bit3 :1;
    unsigned bit4 :1;
    unsigned bit5 :1;
    unsigned bit6 :1;
    unsigned bit7 :1;
} Port;
```

```
typedef struct
{
    unsigned STEXT  :1;
    unsigned STSCIM :1;
    unsigned RSTEN  :1;
    unsigned SLOCK  :1;
    unsigned SLIMP  :1;
    unsigned NULL1  :2;
    unsigned EDIV   :1;
    unsigned Y      :6;
    unsigned X      :1;
    unsigned W      :1;
} Syncr;

typedef struct
{
    unsigned BMT :2;
    unsigned BME :1;
    unsigned HME :1;
    unsigned SWT :2;
    unsigned SWP :1;
    unsigned SWE :1;
}Sypcr;

typedef struct
{
    unsigned PIV   :8;
    unsigned PIRQL :3;
    unsigned NULL2 :5;
} Picr;

typedef struct
{
    unsigned PITM  :8;
    unsigned PTP   :1;
    unsigned NULL3 :7;
}Pitr;

typedef struct
{
    unsigned pr0 :2;
    unsigned pr1 :2;
    unsigned pr2 :2;
    unsigned pr3 :2;
    unsigned pr4 :2;
    unsigned pr5 :2;
    unsigned pr6 :2;
    unsigned pr7 :2;
```

```
} Cspar;

typedef struct
{
    unsigned BLKSZ  :3;
    unsigned HIADDR :13;
} Csbar;

typedef struct
{
    unsigned AVEC  :1;
    unsigned IPL   :3;
    unsigned SPACE :2;
    unsigned DSACK :4;
    unsigned STRB  :1;
    unsigned RSW   :2;
    unsigned BYTE  :2;
    unsigned MODE  :1;
} Csor;

#define SCIM_MCR (*(_MEM MCR_Register*)(SCIM_Register))
#define SYNCR (*(_MEM Syncr*)(SCIM_Register+0x4))
#define RSR (*(_MEM Register*)(SCIM_Register+0x6))
#define SCIMTRE (*(_MEM Register*)(SCIM_Register+0x8))
#define PORTA (*(_MEM Port *)(SCIM_Register+0xa))
#define PORTB (*(_MEM Port *)(SCIM_Register+0xb))
#define PORTG (*(_MEM Port*)(SCIM_Register+0xc))
#define PORTH (*(_MEM Port *)(SCIM_Register+0xd))
#define DDRG (*(_MEM Port *)(SCIM_Register+0xe))
#define DDRH (*(_MEM Port *)(SCIM_Register+0xf))
#define PORTE0 (*(_MEM Port*)(SCIM_Register+0x11))
#define PORTE1 (*(_MEM Port*)(SCIM_Register+0x13))
#define DDRAB (*(_MEM Port*)(SCIM_Register+0x14))
#define DDRE (*(_MEM Register*)(SCIM_Register+0x15))
#define PEPAR (*(_MEM Register*)(SCIM_Register+0x16))
#define PORTF0 (*(_MEM Register*)(SCIM_Register +0x18))
#define PORTF1 (*(_MEM Register*)(SCIM_Register+0x1a))
#define DDRF (*(_MEM Register*)(SCIM_Register+0x1c))
#define PFPAR (*(_MEM Register*)(SCIM_Register+0x1e))
#define SYPCR (*(_MEM Sypcr*)(SCIM_Register+0x20))
#define PICR (*(_MEM Picr*)(SCIM_Register+0x22))
#define PITR (*(_MEM Pitr*)(SCIM_Register+0x24))
#define SWSR (*(_MEM int*)(SCIM_Register+0x26))
#define PORTFE (*(_MEM Register*)(SCIM_Register+0x28))
#define PFIVR (*(_MEM Register*)(SCIM_Register+0x2a))
#define PFLVR (*(_MEM Register*)(SCIM_Register+0x2c))
#define TSTMSRA (*(_MEM Register*)(SCIM_Register+0x30))
#define TSTMSRB (*(_MEM Register*)(SCIM_Register+0x32))
```

```
#define TSTSCA (*(_MEM char *)(SCIM_Register+0x34))
#define TSTMCB (*(_MEM char *)(SCIM_Register+0x35))
#define TSTRC (*(_MEM int *)(SCIM_Register+0x36))
#define CREG (*(_MEM int *)(SCIM_Register+0x38))
#define DREG (*(_MEM int *)(SCIM_Register+0x3a))
#define PORTC (*(_MEM Register*)(SCIM_Register+0x40))
#define CSPAR0 (*(_MEM Cspar*)(SCIM_Register+0x44))
#define CSPAR1 (*(_MEM Cspar*)(SCIM_Register+0x46))
#define CSBARBT (*(_MEM Csbar*)(SCIM_Register+0x48) )
#define CSORBT (*(_MEM Csor*)(SCIM_Register+0x4a))
#define CSBAR0 (*(_MEM Csbar*)(SCIM_Register+0x4c))
#define CSOR0 (*(_MEM Csor*)(SCIM_Register+0x4e))
#define CSBAR1 (*(_MEM Csbar*)(SCIM_Register+0x50))
#define CSOR1 (*(_MEM Csor*)(SCIM_Register+0x52))
#define CSBAR2 (*(_MEM Csbar*)(SCIM_Register+0x54))
#define CSOR2 (*(_MEM Csor*)(SCIM_Register+0x56))
#define CSBAR3 (*(_MEM Csbar*)(SCIM_Register+0x58))
#define CSOR3 (*(_MEM Csor*)(SCIM_Register+0x5a))
#define CSBAR4 (*(_MEM Csbar*)(SCIM_Register+0x5c))
#define CSOR4 (*(_MEM Csor*)(SCIM_Register+0x5e))
#define CSBAR5 (*(_MEM Csbar*)(SCIM_Register+0x60))
#define CSOR5 (*(_MEM Csor*)(SCIM_Register+0x62))
#define CSBAR6 (*(_MEM Csbar*)(SCIM_Register+0x64))
#define CSOR6 (*(_MEM Csor*)(SCIM_Register+0x66))
#define CSBAR7 (*(_MEM Csbar*)(SCIM_Register+0x68))
#define CSOR7 (*(_MEM Csor*)(SCIM_Register+0x6a))
#define CSBAR8 (*(_MEM Csbar*)(SCIM_Register+0x6c))
#define CSOR8 (*(_MEM Csor*)(SCIM_Register+0x6e))
#define CSBAR9 (*(_MEM Csbar*)(SCIM_Register+0x70))
#define CSOR9 (*(_MEM Csor*)(SCIM_Register+0x72))
#define CSBAR10 (*(_MEM Csbar*)(SCIM_Register+0x74))
#define CSOR10 (*(_MEM Csor*)(SCIM_Register+0x76))

/* Bitfields in RSR */

#define TST bit0
#define SYS bit1
#define LOC bit2
#define HLT bit4
#define SW bit5
#define POW bit6
#define EXT bit7

/* Bitfields in PORTE0, PORTE1, and PEPAR*/

#define PE0 bit0
#define PE1 bit1
#define PE2 bit2
```

```
#define PE3 bit3
#define PE4 bit4
#define PE5 bit5
#define PE6 bit6
#define PE7 bit7

/* Bitfields in DDRE */

#define DDE0 bit0
#define DDE1 bit1
#define DDE2 bit2
#define DDE3 bit3
#define DDE4 bit4
#define DDE5 bit5
#define DDE6 bit6
#define DDE7 bit7

/* Bitfields in PORTF0, PORTF1, and PFPAR*/

#define PF0 bit0
#define PF1 bit1
#define PF2 bit2
#define PF3 bit3
#define PF4 bit4
#define PF5 bit5
#define PF6 bit6
#define PF7 bit7

/* Bitfields in DDRF */

#define DDF0 bit0
#define DDF1 bit1
#define DDF2 bit2
#define DDF3 bit3
#define DDF4 bit4
#define DDF5 bit5
#define DDF6 bit6
#define DDF7 bit7

/* Bitfields in CSPAR0 */

#define CSBOOT pr0
#define CSPA01 pr1
#define CSPA02 pr2
#define CSPA03 pr3
#define CSPA04 pr4
```

```
#define CSPA05 pr5
#define CSPA06 pr6

/* Bitfields in CSPAR1 */

#define CSPA10 pr0
#define CSPA11 pr1
#define CSPA12 pr2
#define CSPA13 pr3
#define CSPA14 pr4
#endif
```

STATIC RAM MODULE HEADER FILE

This module is used only with the M68HC16Zx components. It is not associated with another peripheral component on the chip. There are 1K, 0x400, bytes of RAM in the SRAM module.

```
#ifndef SRAM_H
#define SRAM_H

#ifdef _PAGE0
#define _MEM @indir
#else
#ifdef _PAGEF
#define _MEM
#else
#define _MEM @far
#endif
#endif

typedef struct
{
    unsigned Nu    :8;
    unsigned RASP  :2;
    unsigned NULL1:1;
    unsigned RCLK  :1;
    unsigned NULL2:3;
    unsigned STOP  :1;
}Rammcr;

#define RAMMCR (*(_MEM Rammcr*)(SRAM_Register + 0x00))
#define RAMBAH (*(_MEM int*)(SRAM_Register + 0x04))
#define RAMBAL (*(_MEM int*)(SRAM_Register + 0x06))

#endif
```

TIMER PROCESSOR UNIT RAM HEADER FILE

The timer processor unit used in the MC68HC16Y1 and other parts contains a block of RAM. If not used for the TPU, this RAM is available to the processor for memory storage. This header file can be used to set up access to the TPURAM. There are 2K, 0x800, bytes of RAM in the TPURAM.

```
#ifndef TPURAM_H
#define TPURAM_H


#ifdef _PAGE0
#define _MEM @indir
#else
#ifdef _PAGEF
#define _MEM
#else
#define _MEM @far
#endif
#endif


typedef struct
{
    unsigned NULLTPU0 :8;
    unsigned RASP     :1;
    unsigned NULLTPU1 :6;
    unsigned STOPTPU  :1;
}Trammcr;


typedef struct
{
    unsigned RAMDS    :1;
    unsigned NULLTPU3 :2;
    unsigned AD11_23  :13;
} Trambar;


#define TRAMMCR (*(_MEM Trammcr*)(TPURAM_Register + 0x00))
#define TRAMBAR (*(_MEM int*)(TPURAM_Register + 0x04))
#endif
```

INDEX

LICENSE AGREEMENT AND LIMITED WARRANTY

READ THE FOLLOWING TERMS AND CONDITIONS CAREFULLY BEFORE OPENING THIS CD PACKAGE. THIS LEGAL DOCUMENT IS AN AGREEMENT BETWEEN YOU AND PRENTICE-HALL, INC. (THE "COMPANY"). BY OPENING THIS SEALED CD PACKAGE, YOU ARE AGREEING TO BE BOUND BY THESE TERMS AND CONDITIONS. IF YOU DO NOT AGREE WITH THESE TERMS AND CONDITIONS, DO NOT OPEN THE CD PACKAGE. PROMPTLY RETURN THE UNOPENED CD PACKAGE AND ALL ACCOMPANYING ITEMS TO THE PLACE YOU OBTAINED THEM FOR A FULL REFUND OF ANY SUMS YOU HAVE PAID.

1. **GRANT OF LICENSE:** In consideration of your purchase of this book, and your agreement to abide by the terms and conditions of this Agreement, the Company grants to you a nonexclusive right to use and display the copy of the enclosed software program (hereinafter the "SOFTWARE") on a single computer (i.e., with a single CPU) at a single location so long as you comply with the terms of this Agreement. The Company reserves all rights not expressly granted to you under this Agreement.

2. **OWNERSHIP OF SOFTWARE:** You own only the magnetic or physical media (the enclosed CD) on which the SOFTWARE is recorded or fixed, but the Company and the software developers retain all the rights, title, and ownership to the SOFTWARE recorded on the original CD copy(ies) and all subsequent copies of the SOFTWARE, regardless of the form or media on which the original or other copies may exist. This license is not a sale of the original SOFTWARE or any copy to you.

3. **COPY RESTRICTIONS:** This SOFTWARE and the accompanying printed materials and user manual (the "Documentation") are the subject of copyright. The individual programs on the CD are copyrighted by the authors of each program. Some of the programs on the CD include separate licensing agreements. If you intend to use one of these programs, you must read and follow its accompanying license agreement. If you intend to use the trial version of Internet Chameleon, you must read and agree to the terms of the notice regarding fees on the back cover of this book. You may not copy the Documentation or the SOFTWARE, except that you may make a single copy of the SOFTWARE for backup or archival purposes only. You may be held legally responsible for any copying or copyright infringement which is caused or encouraged by your failure to abide by the terms of this restriction.

4. **USE RESTRICTIONS:** You may not network the SOFTWARE or otherwise use it on more than one computer or computer terminal at the same time. You may physically transfer the SOFTWARE from one computer to another provided that the SOFTWARE is used on only one computer at a time. You may not distribute copies of the SOFTWARE or Documentation to others. You may not reverse engineer, disassemble, decompile, modify, adapt, translate, or create derivative works based on the SOFTWARE or the Documentation without the prior written consent of the Company.

5. **TRANSFER RESTRICTIONS:** The enclosed SOFTWARE is licensed only to you and may not be transferred to any one else without the prior written consent of the Company. Any unauthorized transfer of the SOFTWARE shall result in the immediate termination of this Agreement.

6. **TERMINATION:** This license is effective until terminated. This license will terminate automatically without notice from the Company and become null and void if you fail to comply with any provisions or limitations of this license. Upon termination, you shall destroy the Documentation and all copies of the SOFTWARE. All provisions of this Agreement as to warranties, limitation of liability, remedies or damages, and our ownership rights shall survive termination.

7. **MISCELLANEOUS:** This Agreement shall be construed in accordance with the laws of the United States of America and the State of New York and shall benefit the Company, its affiliates, and assignees.

8. **LIMITED WARRANTY AND DISCLAIMER OF WARRANTY:** The Company warrants that the SOFTWARE, when properly used in accordance with the Documentation, will operate in substantial conformity with the description of the SOFTWARE

set forth in the Documentation. The Company does not warrant that the SOFTWARE will meet your requirements or that the operation of the SOFTWARE will be uninterrupted or error-free. The Company warrants that the media on which the SOFTWARE is delivered shall be free from defects in materials and workmanship under normal use for a period of thirty (30) days from the date of your purchase. Your only remedy and the Company's only obligation under these limited warranties is, at the Company's option, return of the warranted item for a refund of any amounts paid by you or replacement of the item. Any replacement of SOFTWARE or media under the warranties shall not extend the original warranty period. The limited warranty set forth above shall not apply to any SOFTWARE which the Company determines in good faith has been subject to misuse, neglect, improper installation, repair, alteration, or damage by you. EXCEPT FOR THE EXPRESSED WARRANTIES SET FORTH ABOVE, THE COMPANY DISCLAIMS ALL WARRANTIES, EXPRESS OR IMPLIED, INCLUDING WITHOUT LIMITATION, THE IMPLIED WARRANTIES OF MERCHANTABILITY AND FITNESS FOR A PARTICULAR PURPOSE. EXCEPT FOR THE EXPRESS WARRANTY SET FORTH ABOVE, THE COMPANY DOES NOT WARRANT, GUARANTEE, OR MAKE ANY REPRESENTATION REGARDING THE USE OR THE RESULTS OF THE USE OF THE SOFTWARE IN TERMS OF ITS CORRECTNESS, ACCURACY, RELIABILITY, CURRENTNESS, OR OTHERWISE.

IN NO EVENT, SHALL THE COMPANY OR ITS EMPLOYEES, AGENTS, SUPPLIERS, OR CONTRACTORS BE LIABLE FOR ANY INCIDENTAL, INDIRECT, SPECIAL, OR CONSEQUENTIAL DAMAGES ARISING OUT OF OR IN CONNECTION WITH THE LICENSE GRANTED UNDER THIS AGREEMENT, OR FOR LOSS OF USE, LOSS OF DATA, LOSS OF INCOME OR PROFIT, OR OTHER LOSSES, SUSTAINED AS A RESULT OF INJURY TO ANY PERSON, OR LOSS OF OR DAMAGE TO PROPERTY, OR CLAIMS OF THIRD PARTIES, EVEN IF THE COMPANY OR AN AUTHORIZED REPRESENTATIVE OF THE COMPANY HAS BEEN ADVISED OF THE POSSIBILITY OF SUCH DAMAGES. IN NO EVENT SHALL LIABILITY OF THE COMPANY FOR DAMAGES WITH RESPECT TO THE SOFTWARE EXCEED THE AMOUNTS ACTUALLY PAID BY YOU, IF ANY, FOR THE SOFTWARE.

SOME JURISDICTIONS DO NOT ALLOW THE LIMITATION OF IMPLIED WARRANTIES OR LIABILITY FOR INCIDENTAL, INDIRECT, SPECIAL, OR CONSEQUENTIAL DAMAGES, SO THE ABOVE LIMITATIONS MAY NOT ALWAYS APPLY. THE WARRANTIES IN THIS AGREEMENT GIVE YOU SPECIFIC LEGAL RIGHTS AND YOU MAY ALSO HAVE OTHER RIGHTS WHICH VARY IN ACCORDANCE WITH LOCAL LAW.

ACKNOWLEDGMENT

YOU ACKNOWLEDGE THAT YOU HAVE READ THIS AGREEMENT, UNDERSTAND IT, AND AGREE TO BE BOUND BY ITS TERMS AND CONDITIONS. YOU ALSO AGREE THAT THIS AGREEMENT IS THE COMPLETE AND EXCLUSIVE STATEMENT OF THE AGREEMENT BETWEEN YOU AND THE COMPANY AND SUPERSEDES ALL PROPOSALS OR PRIOR AGREEMENTS, ORAL, OR WRITTEN, AND ANY OTHER COMMUNICATIONS BETWEEN YOU AND THE COMPANY OR ANY REPRESENTATIVE OF THE COMPANY RELATING TO THE SUBJECT MATTER OF THIS AGREEMENT.

Should you have any questions concerning this Agreement or if you wish to contact the Company for any reason, please contact in writing at the address below.

Robin Short
Prentice Hall PTR
One Lake Street
Upper Saddle River, New Jersey 07458